Lyric Resonance
Glosses on Some Poems of Yeats, Frost, Crane, Cummings and Others

David Ridgley Clark

This collection of essays demonstrates how much can be added to the existing material on well-known poems (e.g., Frost's "Directive"), and how much there is yet to be said about certain neglected poems (e.g., Frost's "The Thatch"). Explicating Hart Crane's "Repose of Rivers," Professor Clark cuts through long-standing critical confusion: "The speaker of the poem is *not* Crane but a *river*." In these essays in "evaluative explication," Clark tries never to lose sight of the total effect of a poem while examining its parts.

Presented first are essays on Irish writers: Yeats, Wilde, Gogarty, O'Sullivan, Campbell, and Kinsella. Professor Clark then comes "home from Ireland to America" to approach Frost, Crane and Cummings. Always provocative and lucid in his discussions, the author journeys through works lengthy and brief, patiently allowing the poems to expand in meaning to a full gloss.

Also included is a valuable record of the composition of some of Professor Clark's own poems, which brings the reader closer to the poetic process itself. The book concludes with a transcript of correspondence between Robert Tucker and Cummings concerning Cummings' participation in a series of taped radio programs on freedom, and the alleged censorship of his contribution. The piece, delightful and yet frightening, is a reminder that censorship takes many ironic forms.

David Ridgley Clark has just celebrated his twentieth year of teaching English at the University of Massachusetts, Amherst. He was collaborating editor on *Druid Craft: The Writing of the Shadowy Waters* (1971), Volume I of a new series, *Manuscripts of W.B. Yeats* (University of Massachusetts Press: Amherst), for which he serves as General Editor.

Professor Clark is also the author of *W.B. Yeats and the Theatre of Desolate Reality* (1965); co-editor of *Irish Renaissance, A Gathering of Essays, Memoirs and Letters from The Massachusetts Review* (1965); co-author of a book of poems, *A Curious Quire* (1962, 1967); author of *Dry Tree: Poems* (1967); co-author of the textbook *Reading Poetry* (1968); editor of John Millington Synge *"Riders to the Sea"* (1970), *Studies in The Bridge* (1970), *Twentieth Century Interpretations of Murder in the Cathedral* (1971); and co-editor of *A Touch of Polished Black Stones: Early Versions of The Shadowy Waters* (1971).

Lyric Resonance

Lyric Resonance

Glosses on Some Poems of Yeats, Frost, Crane,
Cummings & Others by David Ridgley Clark
Including 'Freedom, Joy, and Indignation: Letters
from E.E. Cummings' edited by Robert G. Tucker
and David R. Clark

The University of Massachusetts Press Amherst
1972

FOR MY MOTHER

IDELLA MAY HILL CLARK

ON HER EIGHTIETH BIRTHDAY

APRIL 19, 1972

CONTENTS

Balance the miniscal soul where full sight spills
All timbres on a filmy music,
Where wind as bow to the bough
Pianoed waters answer,

And bird-songs bud in all the feathering trees!
Over and over the sun this water
Practised the runs of love.
Now swings out of twisted staves
The golden nest of God.

Introduction

INTRODUCTION

The Riddling Sphinx & the Limping Critic

"The critic will certainly be an interpreter, but he will not treat Art as a riddling Sphinx, whose shallow secret may be guessed and revealed by one whose feet are wounded and who knows not his name " (Wilde, *Artist,* p. 373). So wrote Oscar Wilde in 1890, insisting that the critic must see the work not only from the top of his own consummate scholarship but also through the lens of his own intensified individual personality. Moreover, interpretation is not the highest form of criticism. "Yes; the critic will be an interpreter, if he chooses. He can pass from his synthetic impression of the work as a whole, to an analysis or exposition of the work itself, and in this lower sphere, as I hold it to be, there are many delightful things to be said and done" (Wilde, *Artist,* p. 372).

In most of the essays on poems by Yeats, Frost, Crane, Cummings and others gathered here I have attempted analysis rather than "synthesis" in Wilde's sense, and I confess that I have often treated the poem analyzed as a "riddling Sphinx." I try to demonstrate the resonant wedding of theme and technique in these poets, and the book is unified insofar as it needs to be by its technique of what I hope is sensitive and percipient glossing. Not all of the poems are presented as free of historical and literary context, but in most of my essays attention to these matters is minimal. The poem is here regarded as an artifact to be turned over and over before the mind's eye. It is a subject of meditation. The reader and critic, too, are creators of a poem as well as the artist, and a poem does not exist until it is read. The reading is a creative process. The reader, like the poet, has to give himself to the poem, letting the full richness of implication speak to him of itself without his trying to force it. The form is not to be willed, by reader or by poet.

I do not know what Wilde may have meant by a critic's

wounded feet, but Wilde would think that to know his own
name a critic must have culture and individualism, must know
how his own age stands in relation to past ages and must know
who he is in his own age. Here again Wilde's ideal is an em-
barrassment to me, as it would be to many critics. Yet unlike
Oedipus I do know who my antecedents are. They are T. S. Eliot,
I. A. Richards, R. P. Blackmur, John Crowe Ransom, Allen
Tate, Cleanth Brooks, Robert Penn Warren, William Empson
and others. And my siblings are legion.[1]

My antecedents would stand up well against the high critical
ideal which Wilde expresses. Yet they would disagree with him
in at least one regard. For Wilde the "synthetic impression of
the work as a whole" meant the impression as made on the
critic's fascinating Wildean personality. Modern criticism tries
to see the work as a whole, yes, but uncolored by the personality
of the critic. Is "Coleridge's *Hamlet*," Eliot asks, "an honest
inquiry as far as the data permit, or is it an attempt to present
Coleridge in an attractive costume?" (Eliot, *Essays*, pp. 21–22).
" 'Interpretation' is only legitimate when it is not interpretation
at all, but merely putting the reader in possession of facts which
he would otherwise have missed" (Eliot, *Essays*, p. 20). Far
from asserting with Wilde that "the primary aim of the critic is
to see the object as in itself it really is not" (Wilde, *Artist*, p.
369), Eliot believed that the test of interpretation was "to apply
it again and again to the original, with your view of the original
to guide you" (Eliot, *Essays*, p. 20). Even when Eliot took "the
extreme position that the *only* critics worth reading were the
critics who practised, and practised well, the art of which they
wrote" (Eliot, *Essays*, p. 20), this was not an instance of
Wilde's "personality" getting into criticism by the back door,
for "The progress of an artist is a continual self-sacrifice, a
continual extinction of personality" (Eliot, *Essays*, p. 7).

The aseptic surgery which removes the personality of the
critic, however, may go too far and destroy the life of his criticism. This almost never happens in Eliot's own criticism. W. K.
Wimsatt has pointed out that no matter how hard Eliot insists
here and there in his work that the production of facts, not of

judgment or appreciation, is the critic's job, his own critical prose is "bristly . . . with evaluative terms," and Wimsatt would justify such "evaluative explication" as opposed to "neutral explication" (Wimsatt, pp. 19–20). Certainly it may be said of the distinguished critics whom I have mentioned that their criticism is never neutral explication. I think that this is because they always hold before the reader a vivid realization of the total effect of the whole poem.

Unfortunately I have often seen in my own students, and therefore have feared in myself, a cold, mechanical way of explicating poetry. For example I have been astonished, when I have interrupted a student's well-played intellectual game to remark "What a great poem!" to have him sometimes reply, "Oh, really? I didn't care for it!" and then proceed with his admirably rational analysis. It is a mistake to trace the relation of part to part without implying that synthetic view of the whole which Wilde said was of a higher order than interpretation. I think that view is *part* of interpretation, and I like Wimsatt's phrase "evaluative explication." The value of a part must be judged in relation to the other parts and to the whole. It seems to me that this is the truth which lurks behind Wilde's apparent attack on rationality. "There are two ways of disliking art. . . . One is to dislike it. The other, to like it rationally" (Wilde, *Artist,* p. 392). "As art springs from personality, so it is only to personality that it can be revealed . . . " (Wilde, *Artist,* p. 374).

Another way of stating the issue is to say that in a critical essay the tone is of greater importance than is often realized. As in other writing the tone should communicate the writer's attitude. In the analysis of a poem, however, the writer's attitude should only be a desire to communicate the reality of the work before him. He does not need to seek any individual tone or vision of his own. Wilde was wrong here. The critic will have the individual vision without seeking. Of course, his whole life is a preparation, and the reading a full man gives will be richer than that of an empty man. But among full men either a Pater or an Eliot may at times—by their different methods—effectively communicate to the reader a new sense of the reality of a work. That originality in criticism is best which is least conscious, least intended.

How my own essays live up to my principles is not for me to judge. Do as I say, not as I do, is a good admonition. But in case I have failed in any of my analyses to keep before the reader's mind's eye a total realization of the poem as I point out part after part, I should at least like him to know that my intentions were good. It may be that I assume falsely that the reader and I, in the intensity of our shared meditation, are looking at the same total object and that I need but place my finger on a part for him, too, to see its relation to the totality. If I have made this mistake, it is a failure of achievement not of intent. I know that one's most successful criticism—not simply one's most skillful writing but that criticism in which one is truest to the work analyzed—will inevitably be that in which one has never forgotten the total effect of the work. One may write very clever criticism in which the poem being analyzed becomes merely an occasion, a pretext, for the demonstration of the critic's brilliance. This type of writing may have an interest and value of its own, but it disserves the cause of literary criticism. To keep the poem, the tone of each phrase, the total effect, always real to the critic as he writes and the reader as he reads is obligatory.

This book begins with three essays on poems by Yeats. The first concerns Yeats's life-long desire to write "out of a people to a people" like the Young Ireland nationalists and finds some of Yeats's very latest poems echoing verse which Yeats gathered in his 1895 *A Book of Irish Verse.* These late poems repeatedly dramatize moments of crisis in which a powerful personality goes beyond individual intellect and speaks with the archetypal voice of a people. Yeats's "He bids his Beloved be at Peace," though full of a deliberate personal symbolism known only to the poet is shown to be full also of an unconscious symbolism, evident to the reader, but probably not to the poet, who must have been unaware how much he had revealed himself. From this early poem we move in the third essay to one of Yeats's very last poems where the intellectual and emotional symbols are masterfully fused. Yeats's use of a painting by Poussin as a model for lines from "News for the Delphic Oracle" gives an opportunity to isolate exactly what he took from the painting and what he forebore to use and thus reveals the particular force of these symbols.

In the group of analyses of Irish poems which follows next the choice is determined by what I have been pleased to lecture on rather than by any evaluative principle of selection. Thus Oscar Wilde's "Requiescat," delicately beautiful at first glance, is revealed by analysis to be an example of Wilde's fatal gift of imitation. Oliver Gogarty's poems, with the exception of "Ringsend," are seen on close reading not to come all the way up to Yeats's high estimation of them, the heroic personality he felt in them being much more evident in Yeats's own work. The poems of Seumas O'Sullivan, too, are minor, but they have genuine craftsmanship and a unique charm. Somehow Joseph Campbell's "The Dancer" stands out supreme over the other poems in his *Irishry* and in his other volumes, being one of those poems which the anthologists rightly skim from a total work to immortalize in isolation. All of these poets are treated here as very much in the shadow of Yeats. The final essay of this group, on Kinsella's "Downstream," was written freely for love of the poem.

In the next section of the book I come home from Ireland to America to relate two of Robert Frost's poems about decay and enduring values, "Directive" and "The Thatch," the first perhaps Frost's most admired poem, at least by the critics, the second a much neglected earlier poem which I defend as one of Frost's highest achievements, although it lacks the philosophical calm of Frost's post-tempest guide in "Directive."

The section on Hart Crane starts off with a general essay showing both the extraordinary advantages and disadvantages of Crane's technique and follows with interpretations of four poems. A new reading of "Repose of Rivers" demonstrates that many critics and readers have missed the meaning of the poem by failing to identify its speaking voice. My approach to "At

Melville's Tomb" shows how a saturation in the context from which Crane draws his allusions simplifies interpretation. Probably there is little new in my analysis of "For the Marriage of Faustus and Helen," Crane's earliest major poem, except for an individual approach and a hitherto unnoted allusion. I have not seen before an analysis of "The Dance" which treats as I have the fusion in that poem of the imagery of the wilderness with the imagery of modern industry.

Two essays on E. E. Cummings follow, with a third placed in an appendix. The essay on "anyone lived in a pretty how town" shows how Cummings balances, against the loveless loneliness of the individual in contemporary society, the values of uniqueness and integrity—"noone loved him more by more." My brief comparison of two versions of Cummings' "Poem" is the first example I have seen of an analysis of Cummings' manuscript versions and shows how much, in Cummings' case in particular because of his typographical experiments, can be learned from a comparison of the drafts with the finished poems.

"The *Dry Tree* When Green," a record of the composition of some of my own poems, seems to me, from one point of view, as useful as any essay in the book. My poems are few and minor, but surely I am the best authority on the history and psychology of their composition. I am not necessarily, I suppose, the best analyst of the poems themselves as poems. But the essay has value as an account by a poet of the way in which the particles of a poem accrete in the currents and eddies of his meditation. What I have to say of these poems may have more genuine value as criticism than what I am able to produce about Yeats, Frost, Crane or Cummings.

I have long wanted to reprint the fascinating correspondence between E. E. Cummings and Robert Tucker concerning Cummings' participation in "New England Anthology," a series of taped radio programs on freedom, made by New England poets in 1953 at the University of Massachusetts for the National Association of Educational Broadcasters. That was in the McCarthy era and academics were up-tight about potential investigations by legislative committees. One or two of the poems

Cummings read onto his tape frightened some people and raised the question of whether or not the Cummings program should be released. Robert Tucker as the unlucky chairman of a divided committee tried heroically and futilely to reconcile his duty to the committee as its chairman with his personal commitment as a writer to Cummings' artistic freedom. Up until a year or more ago, the whole affair might have seemed a tempest in a teapot. Readers and hearers used to present-day license may still be puzzled to know what the fuss was all about. But perhaps with the again-rising spirit of McCarthyism and pressures in various forms on universities, this piece may warn the reader of the sort of pettiness to which university professors are liable to sink in their anxiety over the danger of outside pressure and interference. But whatever the relevance of the piece today, Cummings' letters are witty gems which the reader will enjoy. Because "Freedom, Joy & Indignation" is not an example of "pure" poetry explication like the other essays, it has been sectioned off in an appendix.

For several reasons I have taken a very personal pleasure in putting this book together, more so than other books I have done. Most of these essays are on poets of whom I am especially fond, and the relatively few poems treated include several that I greatly admire. I have marked the book my own by including two of my poems, one at the beginning and one at the end. They come from my section of *A Curious Quire* (1962), poems by three colleagues and myself. Although Yeats, with the right of eminence and age, used his own verse in this way when he chose, most twentieth-century poets do not mix their own poetry and their criticism. With even more temerity I have kept in the essay by myself on my own poems.

The volume is published by the University of Massachusetts Press, with which I have had a happy association. It is completed in my twentieth year as a faculty member at the University of Massachusetts. Nobody meant it that way, but the book does mark the end of a period in my teaching at the University. Many of the ideas expressed in the essays have emerged in discussions with students and colleagues. The episodes described in "Freedom, Joy & Indignation" are now bathed for me in a glow of nostalgia for my first years at the University. I am grateful for my long association with the University of Massachusetts and glad to mark it with this book.

Finally the book is a birthday present for my mother, who, in the face of obstacles, helped me to get, not only an education, but the particular education out of which this book has come.

W. B. Yeats

W. B. YEATS

Out of a People to a People

When in his 1937 "A General Introduction for my Work," Yeats paid tribute to Thomas Davis and the mid-nineteenth century Young Ireland poets of whom Davis was the leader, he laid a ghost with which he had struggled during his entire career: "I . . . hated that dry eighteenth-century rhetoric; but they had one quality I admired and admire: they were not separated individual men; they spoke or tried to speak out of a people to a people: behind them stretched the generations" (Yeats, *Essays,* p. 510). The "Young Ireland Party" came into existence with the founding of the *Nation* newspaper in 1842. It differed with the moderate aims and methods of the Great Liberator, Daniel O'Connell, and favored policies of separation from England to be achieved by force. Davis, James Clarence Mangan and others filled the *Nation* with ballads and poems based on Irish history and legend going back to early times. Many of these works were free translations from the Irish. Most were written in stirring popular rhythms and had a great effect upon the people.

Yeats found his theme, he said, when the old Fenian leader John O'Leary gave him the poems of Davis. He did not find his form in these poems, however. Even O'Leary whose life they had changed said that "they were not good poetry" (Yeats, *Essays,* p. 510). Like Yeats, the Young Ireland poets "wanted to cry as all men cried, to laugh as all men laughed, . . . but they did not know that the common and its befitting language is the research of a lifetime and when found may lack popular recognition" (Yeats, *Essays,* p. 511). Obviously Yeats felt in 1937, his seventy-second year, that he had learned at last to put the thoughts of a wise man into the words of the common people. He therefore had assimilated what the Young Ireland poets had to offer and could forgive them for being popular, though he was not.

Earlier he had been less kind. He had remembered in his autobiographical "The Trembling of the Veil" (1922) how when organizing the National Literary Society he had been compared to Thomas Davis and to Michael Davitt (the leader of the Land League, whose reforms effected the change from absentee landlordism to peasant ownership). He had thought, he says, "to succeed as they did, and as rapidly. . . . It was many years before I understood that I had surrendered myself to the chief temptation of the artist, creation without toil" (Yeats, *Autobiography*, p. 122). In "Reveries over Childhood and Youth" (1915) he implies that it took oratory such as that of eloquent barrister John F. Taylor to bring Davis's verse to life. "When Taylor spoke, it was a great event, and his delivery in the course of a speech or lecture of some political verse by Thomas Davis gave me a conviction of how great might be the effect of verse, spoken by a man almost rhythm-drunk, at some moment of intensity, the apex of long mounting thought. Verses that seemed when one saw them upon the page flat and empty caught from that voice, whose beauty was half in its harsh strangeness, nobility and style" (Yeats, *Autobiography*, pp. 60–61).

Yeats's interest here seems to be in verse-speaking. Yet no doubt he is even more interested in the poet's opportunity for combining powerful syntax and insistent rhythm, for writing poems in which a powerful personality is brought to some moment of crisis in which the voice of "individual intellect" suddenly becomes the voice of "what the Upanishads call 'that ancient Self' " (Yeats, *Essays*, p. 525). Such is the effect of much of Yeats's greatest poetry, of poems like "The Tower" (1927),

> Now shall I make my soul,
> Compelling it to study
> In a learned school
> Till the wreck of body,
> Slow decay of blood,
> Testy delirium
> Or dull decrepitude,
> Or what worse evil come—

The death of friends, or death
Of every brilliant eye
That made a catch in the breath—
Seem but the clouds of the sky
When the horizon fades,
Or a bird's sleepy cry
Among the deepening shades.

(Yeats, *Variorum Poems,* p. 416)

Or of "All Souls' Night" (1921), in which Yeats cries

... I have a marvellous thing to say,
A certain marvellous thing
None but the living mock

(Yeats, *Variorum Poems,* p. 471)

where Yeats has built into the poem a speaker of great dramatic presence. Such was the effect of hearing Taylor read Davis, but Davis's poems by themselves, which did not have a speaker of great dramatic presence built into them, often seemed "flat and empty."

Yeats dated the "Preface" to "Reveries over Childhood and Youth," where these remarks appear, as "Christmas Day, 1914" (Yeats, *Autobiography,* p. 2). On November 20 of the same year he himself had had an opportunity to declaim Davis's verse at the Thomas Davis centenary meeting.[1] It seems likely that Yeats had Taylor's declamation of Davis in mind when he found himself in the same situation. Apparently he well knew how to provide the context which would give the verses their strongest effect. At least a somewhat wry account of the incident by Austin Clarke, now the dean of living Irish poets, makes one suspect that Yeats was trying to capture the "rhythm-drunk" intensity of Taylor. As a young man Clarke was present at the Davis centenary and gives this account,

When Yeats rose to speak, I wondered how he would deal with the poetic problem of the Young Ireland school of the 'Forties, for I knew that in his early years he had denounced, because of their rhetorical style, the political and historical ballads of Davis, T. D'Arcy McGee, Gavan Duffy and others. The double rhymes of those hasty ballads were noisy and "Ireland" was constantly rhymed with "Sireland." But the poet had been wily enough to choose the one ballad of Davis which suited his own method of chanting: "The Lament for the Death of Owen Roe O'Neill."[2] After a few preliminary remarks, he rose to his full height, swayed and, with waving hands, intoned the poem. I seemed to see once more the dim romantic figure on the Abbey stage as the words spread on his voice in rhythmic movement throughout the hushed hall:

Did they dare—did they dare, to slay Owen Roe O'Neill?
Yes, they slew with poison him they feared to meet with steel.
May God wither up their hearts! May their blood cease to flow!
May they walk in living death who poisoned Owen Roe!

There was a tremendous outburst of applause when the poem came to an end. So thrilling were those few minutes that I forget the rest of the speech and remember only that it was carefully phrased. The poet did not commit himself to any political views. Had he not—wrongly as I now believe—helped to break the long tradition of poetry in this country as an influence in public affairs? (Clarke, "A Centenary Celebration," pp. 91–92)

That Clarke could see in the forty-nine-year-old public man the "dim romantic figure on the Abbey stage" of a decade earlier shows that Yeats had succeeded in dramatizing not only the poem but the speaker of the poem and the moment in which it was spoken. He had produced an effect parallel to that which J. F. Taylor had made on him and which he himself often elicits in his own middle and late verse.

The words of Yeats's talk have been preserved. In his *Tribute to Thomas Davis* he admits that he need not, as a young man, have been "so anxious to show what was lacking in the gift of Davis." He explains, however, that "It seemed then as if our new generation could not do its work unless we overcame the habit of making every Irish book, or poem, shoulder some political idea; it seemed to us that we had to escape by some great effort from the obsession of public life, and I had come to feel that our first work must be to close, not knowing how great the need of it still was, the rhymed lesson book of Davis. I might have remembered Goethe's phrase that great care is taken that the trees shall not grow up into the sky" (Yeats, *Tribute*, pp. 18–19).

Most of the talk, echoing Section XXIII of "The Death of Synge" (Yeats, *Autobiography*, p. 314) isolates in Davis, in his public role, "a moral quality akin to that quality of style which can alone make permanent a picture and a book." This quality is "magnanimity" (Yeats, *Tribute*, pp. 18, 16), a quality lacking, according to Yeats, in O'Connell, who chose to quarrel with Davis, or in his successor as editor of the *Nation*, John Mitchel. One of the several moments of beauty and power in this address is directed against Mitchel's influence and echoes the later "A Prayer for my Daughter." "Mitchel played upon international suspicion and exalted the hate of England above the love of Ireland that Davis would have taught us, and his gaping harpies are on our roof-tree now. How could we learn from the harsh Ulster nature, made harsher still by the tragedy of the famine, and the rhetoric of Carlyle, a light that is the discovery of truth, or a sweetness that is obedience to its will?" (Yeats, *Tribute*, p. 18). In "A Prayer for my Daughter" (1919) Yeats is again concerned with magnanimity. He prays that all his daughter's thoughts

> ... may like the linnet be,
> And have no business but dispensing round
> Their magnanimities of sound. ...

For he knows that,

> ... all hatred driven hence,
> The soul recovers radical innocence
> And learns at last that it is self-delighting,
> Self-appeasing, self-affrighting,
> And that its own sweet will is Heaven's will. ...
>
> (Yeats, *Variorum Poems*, p. 404–05)

Thus most of Yeats's address celebrates Davis's moral quality, his magnanimity, rather than any poetic talent or genius. "He had poetical feeling, but he saw that he had a work to do which would not set him in that road, and he made himself the foremost moral influence of our politics" (Yeats, *Tribute,* pp. 12–13). Even Davis's peculiar poignancy in "The Lament for Owen Roe," Yeats credits to Davis the man, not Davis the poet. "Davis is mourning, not as poet, but as man over the sorrows of Ireland." By what seems a trick of words, but may actually be a deeply held conviction, Yeats makes it the language's fault, not Davis's, that he was a limited poet.

> Had he been born in the time of Elizabeth, he would, I believe, have been a great poet, for while the common language was still so little spoilt that deep emotion created its own speech, a man visibly moved could not but speak nobly. Men of the camp and of the council board, like Raleigh and like Sydney, could be great poets, but when the language is worn down to mere abstraction by perpetual mechanical use, nobody can write tolerably, unless by some momentary accident without exhausting continuous sedentary labour. He may have soldier or statesman in his blood, but all must be put away, for his work is to make a laborious personal language that the heart may still speak." (Yeats, *Tribute,* pp. 14–15)

In spite of Yeats, noble speech is not necessarily poetry or verse, and it seems hard on Raleigh and Sydney to give the language all the credit for their achievements. But if his argument is weak, Yeats's concept is a powerful one. He pictures, once again, a man of "deep emotion" speaking "out of a people to a people" in the noble language they share. The poem is the utterance in a dramatic context of a dramatic speaker at that moment of crisis when the "visibly moved" individual begins to speak with the deeper voice of all, when he ceases to be himself and becomes some great type or pattern, when he speaks with the voice of "that ancient Self."

Certainly the poem which Yeats brings in at this point to praise, and tacitly to contrast with Davis's, shows a richly individual speaker in the process of becoming, through the depth and universality of his emotion, the type of the Exile. Yeats refers to "The County of Mayo," adapted from the Irish of Thomas Lavelle, by George Fox, a contemporary of Davis. The poem is one which Yeats himself imitates, or at least echoes, as we shall see, in a late poem. He brings it in here to demonstrate the necessity to great verse of a vigorous and beautiful common speech which will seem but the spontaneous thoughts of an active man speaking. "I know, indeed, one Irish poem that seems to be the emotion of a gallant unsedentary man and has yet an altogether living style. It begins 'On the deck of Patrick Lynch's boat,' and it had two men for its making—one an exile who gave all his thought to life itself, and a bookish man who turned it from Gaelic into English. Nobody, no not Sir Walter Raleigh, could have beaten that. It seems as much alive, body and soul, as a mountain hare" (Yeats, *Tribute*, p. 15). The poem begins:

On the deck of Patrick Lynch's boat I sat in woful plight,
Through my sighing all the weary day, and weeping all the
    night;
Were it not that full of sorrow from my people forth I go,
By the blessed sun! 'tis royally I'd sing thy praise, Mayo!
                    (*A Book of Irish Verse*, pp. 115–16)

Three pages before referring to this poem Yeats has asked: "Was it possible to be a good Irishman and not remember the curse of Cromwell and churches the Danes had burnt?" (Yeats, *Tribute*, p. 12). Yeats's poem "The Curse of Cromwell" (1937) employs a variation of the meter of "The County of Mayo" and echoes some of its phrases. Instead of being an exile *from* Ireland, the speaker is an exile *in* Ireland.

You ask what I have found, and far and wide I go:
Nothing but Cromwell's house and Cromwell's murderous crew,
The lovers and the dancers are beaten into the clay,
And the tall men and the swordsmen and the horsemen, where
    are they?
And there is an old beggar wandering in his pride—
His fathers served their fathers before Christ was crucified.

O what of that, O what of that,
What is there left to say?

All neighbourly content and easy talk are gone,
But there's no good complaining, for money's rant is on.
He that's mounting up must on his neighbour mount,
And we and all the Muses are things of no account.
They have schooling of their own, but I pass their schooling by,
What can they know that we know that know the time to die?
O what of that, O what of that,
What is there left to say?

The Swiftean persona here is a far more grim voice than that of "The County of Mayo." Like Gulliver in the fourth book of the *Travels* he is misanthropic and prefers the stable to the house.

And when I pay attention I must out and walk
Among the dogs and horses that understand my talk.
(Yeats, *Varorium Poems,* pp. 580–81)[3]

This terrible voice is not the voice of "The County of Mayo," in whose charming irritability one hears only the disappointed lover of the land that must be left.

When I dwelt at home in plenty, and my gold did much
abound,
In the company of fair young maids the Spanish ale went
round—
'Tis a bitter change from those gay days that now I'm forced
to go,
And must leave my bones in Santa Cruz, far from my own
Mayo.

They are altered girls in Irrul now; 'tis proud they're grown
and high,
With their hair-bags and their top-knots, for I pass their buckles
by—
But it's little now I heed their airs, for God will have it so,
That I must depart for foreign lands, and leave my sweet Mayo.
(*A Book of Irish Verse,* p. 116)

Sir Walter Raleigh would indeed have been hard pressed to equal the marvelous "With their hair-bags and their top-knots, for I pass their buckles by—", and Yeats did not surpass it with his bitter "They have schooling of their own, but I pass their schooling by." The endings of the poems also differ, Fox (or Lavelle) not breaking the theme of melancholy farewell, and Yeats introducing his supernaturalism— though in as near to folk fashion as he could manage:

> I came on a great house in the middle of the night,
> Its open lighted doorway and its windows all alight,
> And all my friends were there and made me welcome too;
> But I woke in an old ruin that the winds howled through.
>   (Yeats, *Variorum Poems,* p. 581)

In spite of the differences, the specific echoes suggest that in seeking to speak "out of people to a people" Yeats deliberately cultivated as a model this poem of Davis's generation which he singled out for special praise and which has, in the original, "one of the most popular songs of the peasantry of the West of Ireland, and was . . . combined with one of the sweetest of Irish melodies—the very soul of plaintive Irish music" (*Irish Literature,* III, 1224).

In "J. M. Synge and the Ireland of His Time" (1911), Yeats had singled out another poem as rising above the "rhetorical, conventional, sentimental" Young Ireland verse. "At rare moments," he wrote, "some *Memory of the Dead* can take its strength from one . . ." (Yeats, *Essays,* p. 313). He refers to the poem of that title by the political economist and Trinity professor of classics John Kells Ingram, nine years Davis's junior, who wrote the poem in his student days.

> Who fears to speak of Ninety-eight?
> Who blushes at the name?
> When cowards mock the patriot's fate,
> Who hangs his head for shame?
> He's all a knave or half a slave
> Who slights his country thus;

> But a true man, like you, man,
> Will fill your glass with us,
> (*A Book of Irish Verse*, p. 148)

This patriotic drinking song was clearly the model for "Come Gather Round Me Parnellites" (1937), one of Yeats's poems celebrating Ireland's great late nineteenth-century political leader whose disgrace (for loving a married woman) and sudden death in 1891 struck Ireland so deeply.

> Come gather round me, Parnellites,
> And praise our chosen man;
> Stand upright on your legs awhile,
> Stand upright while you can,
> For soon we lie where he is laid,
> And he is underground;
> Come fill up all those glasses
> And pass the bottle round.
> (Yeats, *Variorum Poems*, p. 586)

Ingram's eight-line stanza is metrically the same as Yeats's, except for the seventh line in which both poets break the established rhythm in dissimilar manners. Ingram's rhyme scheme is tighter, but the similarities both in theme and form are notable. On the other hand, it may be doubted that Yeats's poem speaks "out of a people to a people." He is entirely too true in it to "Nature, who never does the same thing twice, or makes one man like another . . ." (Yeats, *Essays*, p. 313). The attitudes expressed in Yeats's poem are calculated not to join people but to divide them. Yeats has added to the dignified original Burnsian concepts of drunkenness and illicit love—

> And here's another reason,
> That Parnell love a lass

—which make it unlikely that his poem will ever gain the currency among patriotic people which "The Memory of the Dead" has had. On a deeper level Yeats's poem is undergirded by the marvelous—but uniquely individual—observation, also found in "A Drunken Man's Praise of Sobriety" (1938), that "all dead men are drunk" (Yeats, *Variorum Poems,* p. 592). This concept is especially confortingly touched on in the third and fourth lines of "Come Gather Round Me Parnellites": "Stand upright on your legs awhile,/Stand upright while you can." The idea that " a proud man's a lovely man" also seems the point of view of a unique individual, rather than a great commonplace which will strike a chord in all men. According to Yeats, "Thomas Davis . . . had understood that a country which has no national institutions must show its young men images for the affections, although they be but diagrams of what should be or may be. He and his school imagined the Soldier, the Orator, the Patriot, the Poet, the Chieftain, and above all the Peasant. . . ." Such a diagram, the true man, the Patriot, is both the subject and the speaker of Ingram's poem. The result is that the poem is ineffective for an unsympathetic but not unsophisticated reader, say an American undergraduate in a class in modern Irish literature, who may find the swinging refrain "But a true man, like you, man" a ridiculous blemish. Momentarily renouncing his hope of speaking "to a people," Yeats asserted that "ideas and images which have to be understood and loved by large numbers of people must appeal to no rich personal experience, no patience of study, no delicacy of sense . . ." (Yeats, *Essays,* pp. 312–13). But in "Come Gather Round Me Parnellites" he obviously tried to make both speaker and subject individual as well as archetypal.

His approach is once again dramatic. He wishes to create an individual character, who, grown excited with wine, speaks eloquently what is in all hearts. By contrast, there is no conscious self-dramatization in the Ingram poem. The speaker exists: he is not acting a role in a play. Yeats's "active man speaking" (Yeats, *Autobiography,* p. 263) speaks in "Come Gather Round Me Parnellites" more with the individual than the group voice. Yeats has avoided the fault of the Young Ireland verse, a language which, "because it is carried beyond life perpetually, will be worn and cold like the thought, with unmeaning pedantries and silences, and a dread of all that has salt and savour" (Yeats, *Essays,* p. 313). Yeats has here an overabundance of salt and savour, but only in the last verse does he reach that archetypal anger and grief of the lament for a dead leader which, for example, Joyce evokes so successfully in "Ivy Day in the Committee Room." Here is the last stanza of Yeats's poem:

> The Bishops and the Party
> That tragic story made,
> A husband that had sold his wife
> And after that betrayed;
> But stories that live longest
> Are sung above the glass,
> And Parnell loved his country,
> And Parnell loved his lass.
>
> (Yeats, *Variorum Poems,* p. 587)

Yeats distinguished the rage which here spurs him and his speaker into song, from the hatred felt by a fanatical patriot. "Hate is a kind of 'passive suffering' but indignation is a kind of joy. . . . Joy is the salvation of the soul. You say we must love, yes but love is not pity. It does not desire to change its object. It is a form of the eternal contemplation of what is. . . . It is not our business to reply to this & that, but to set up our love and indignation against their pity & hate . . ." (Yeats, *Letters on Poetry,* pp. 126–27). Those remarks were made in response to Dorothy Wellesley's adverse criticism of Yeats's "The Ghost of Roger Casement" (1938) a poem much in the mood and style of "Come Gather Round Me, Parnellites." In writing to Yeats she had called the poem "your ballad of hate" (Yeats, *Letters on Poetry,* p. 123).

In his expression of love and indignation Yeats felt himself to be on the side of life with the magnanimous Davis, whereas minds filled with hate and abstraction were on the side of death —a generation like "an hysterical woman who will make unmeasured accusations and believe impossible things, because of some logical deduction from a solitary thought which has turned a portion of her mind to stone" (Yeats, *Essays,* p. 314). This hysterical patriotic figure appears in such poems as "A Prayer for My Daughter" (1919), "On a Political Prisoner" (1920), and "Lapis Lazuli" (1938), and the mind turned to stone is "in the midst of all" and troubling "the living stream" in "Easter 1916" (1920) (Yeats, *Variorum Poems,* p. 393). Power, we know from section four of "Blood and the Moon" (1928), is "a property of the living"; wisdom is "the property of the dead" (Yeats, *Varorium Poems,* p. 482). Great verse keeps a balance between the dead and the living, between the ghostly voice of the meter and the vigorous syntax of an "active man speaking." It keeps a balance too between the archetype and the individual. If the archetype is totally dissociated from a living figure, it becomes a mere dead diagram, an abstraction. On the other hand, the living figure without archetypal qualities becomes irrelevant and accidental. Poetry must speak out of a people to a people, but in living accents, to a living people. The dead stone is merely a stone, the living stream merely changeable, but in the music made by the two there is a terrible beauty.

Even though Davis's moral quality of magnanimity was on the side of life, Yeats set James Clarence Mangan and Sir Samuel Ferguson far above him as poets because his verse was often "flat and empty," on the side of death (Yeats, *Essays,* p. 256). In *A Book of Irish Verse* (1895) Yeats attributes Mangan's "many powerful lyrics" to his having been "kept out of public life by a passion for opium and rum" (*A Book of Irish Verse,* p. xvi),[4] a daring idea also found in "The Secret Rose" (1896) where Yeats speaks of those who sought the rose "in the Holy Sepulchre,/Or in the wine-vat" (Yeats, *Variorum Poems,* p. 169). By contrast the active Davis "is often a little insincere and mechanical in his verse" although "No man was more sincere, no man had a less mechanical mind" (*A Book of Irish Verse,* p. xv). While paying this tribute to Davis, the anthology in its rigid selection turns, as Yeats noted in the "Preface" which he added in 1900, to "the traditions of good literature, which are the morality of the man of letters" and he separates "what has literary value from what has only a patriotic and political value, no matter how sacred it has become to us" (*A Book of Irish Verse,* 1900, pp. xiv–xv). This and other attacks "on verse which owed its position to its moral or political worth, roused a resentment . . . that showed what large numbers could not call up certain high feelings without accustomed verses, or believe we had not wronged the feelings when we did but attack the verses" (Yeats, *Essays*, pp. 256–57). Yeats respects emotion, but deplores abstract rhetoric.

Little has been said here about Yeats's well-known indebtedness to James Clarence Mangan and Samuel Ferguson. My interest was rather in the influence on Yeats of his struggle against Young Ireland rhetorical verse, a lovers' quarrel, although a bitter one, in which he envied the ability of the Young Ireland poets to speak "out of a people to a people" of their emotion for Ireland. It is common knowledge that Yeats's choice of the rose as a symbol in his early poems was based not solely on Rosicrucianism but in large part on the "Dark Rosaleen" cult of the Irish patriots which inspired Mangan's famous poem, of which Yeats admired the passionate abandonment in its latter stanzas. Less well known are echoes such as those of Mangan's "Lament for the Princes of Tyrone and Tyrconnell":

> The youths whose relics moulder here
> Were sprung from Hugh, high Prince and Lord
> Of Aileach's lands;
> Thy noble brothers, justly dear,
> Thy nephew, long to be deplored
> By Ulster's bands.
> Theirs were not souls wherein dull Time
> Could domicile Decay or house
> Decrepitude!
> They passed from Earth ere Manhood's prime,
> Ere years had power to dim their brows
> Or chill their blood.
> (*A Book of Irish Verse*, pp. 33–34)

Surely the thought "What made us dream that he could comb grey hair?" in Yeats's famous elegy for "Our Sidney and our perfect man," "In Memory of Major Robert Gregory" (1919) (Yeats, *Variorum Poems*, pp. 327, 325), may have its origin here. The rhyme of "decay of blood" with "dull decrepitude" in a passage quoted above from "The Tower" (1927) (Yeats, *Variorum Poems*, p. 416) at the beginning of this essay, as well as the phrase "Bodily decrepitude" in "After Long Silence" (1932), probably also has its origin in Mangan's poem.

> Speech after long silence; it is right,
> All other lovers being estranged or dead,
> Unfriendly lamplight hid under its shade,
> The curtains drawn upon unfriendly night,
> That we descant and yet again descant
> Upon the supreme theme of Art and Song:
> Bodily decrepitude is wisdom; young
> We loved each other and were ignorant.
>
> (Yeats, *Variorum Poems*, p. 523)

Yeats felt, however, as he says in an 1887 essay, that Mangan "can never be popular like Davis, for he did not embody in clear verse the thoughts of normal mankind. He never startles us by saying beautifully things we have long felt. He does not say look at yourself in this mirror; but, rather, 'Look at me— I am so strange, so exotic, so different.' "[5] Thus Mangan did not have the note of one who wrote out of a people to a people. "This scrivener's clerk brought one thing into the world that was not there before, one new thing into letters—his misery—a misery peculiar in quality" (Yeats, *Uncollected Prose*, pp. 118–19).

The influence of Samuel Ferguson is pervasive in Yeats. Yeats's first two prose pieces were on Ferguson, the author of *Lays of the Western Gael,* in the year of his death, 1886. Ferguson was:

> the greatest poet Ireland has produced, because the most central and most Celtic. Whatever the future may bring forth in the way of a truly great and national literature . . . will finds its morning in these . . . volumes of one who was made by the purifying flame of National sentiment the one man of his time who wrote heroic poetry—one who, among the somewhat sybaritic singers of his day, was like some aged sea-king sitting among the inland wheat and poppies—the savour of the sea about him, and its strength.
>
> (Yeats, *Uncollected Prose*, pp. 103–104)

But Ferguson's influence on Yeats, as for example the influence of Ferguson's "Deirdre" on Yeats's, was more in the over-all poetic conception than in the language. (Ferguson was endowed with that power of forming great conceptions valued by Longinus). In any case the influence of Ferguson is a subject for a separate treatise. A study, in relation to Yeats's poetry, of the poems included or mentioned in *A Book of Irish Verse* is a fruitful and surprisingly unexplored subject. The "Introduction," revised in 1900 as "Modern Irish Poetry," shows that Yeats knew exactly what he admired and what he did not in the verse of Thomas Moore, Callanan, Walsh, Doheny, William Allington and Aubrey de Vere. It shows him condemning mechanical rhythms and preferring the hesitating rhythms in which what he would later call "the ghostly voice" (Yeats, *Essays,* p. 524) of the meter does not mechanically obscure the living Irish speech. Perhaps the reason that the relation of these poems to Yeats's own has not been much studied is that critics have tended to look to Yeats's early poems for their influence, as Austin Clarke finds the rhythm of Thomas Moore's "At the Mid Hour of Night" in "The Lake Isle of Innisfree" (Clarke, *Nineties,* p. 34). Here I have tried to show that in such late poems as "The Curse of Cromwell" and "Come Gather Round me Parnellites" Yeats used as models some of these favorite poems of his young manhood.

In concluding, another such relationship may be mentioned. The much admired and anthologized "John Kinsella's Lament for Mrs. Mary Moore" (1938) has an even sharper bite if one realizes that it is a travesty of the anonymous romantic ballad "Lament of Morian Shehone for Miss Mary Rourke," based on an Irish keen.

There's darkness in thy dwelling-place, and silence reigns above,
And Mary's voice is heard no more, like the soft voice of love.
Yes! thou art gone, my Mary dear! and Morian Shehone
Is left to sing his song of woe, and wail for thee alone.
O! snow-white were thy virtues—the beautiful, the young,
The old with pleasure bent to hear the music of thy tongue:

The young with rapture gazed on thee, and their hearts in love
    were bound,
For thou wast brighter than the sun that sheds its light around.
                  (*A Book of Irish Verse,* pp. 242–43)[6]

How brutal is the descent from this ethereal (read "bloodless")
emotion to:

> A bloody and a sudden end,
>   Gunshot or a noose,
> For Death who takes what man would keep,
>   Leaves what man would lose.
> He might have had my sister,
>   My cousins by the score,
> But nothing satisfied the fool
>   But my dear Mary Moore,
> None other knows what pleasures man
>   At table or in bed.
> *What shall I do for pretty girls*
>   *Now my old bawd is dead?*
>   (Yeats, *Variorum Poems,* p. 620)

The older poem even ends with something like the Edenic
vision at the end of Yeats's poem:

For thee thy friends lament and mourn, and never cease to
    weep—
O! that their lamentations could awake thee from thy sleep!
O! that thy fearless form again could meet my loving clasp!
O! that the cold damp hand of Death could loose his iron grasp!
Yet, when the valley's daughters meet beneath the tall elm
    tree,
And talk of Mary as a dream that never more shall be,
Then may thy spirit float around, like music in the air,
And pour upon their virgin souls a blessing and a prayer.
                (*A Book of Irish Verse,* p. 245)

Yeats's poem has a superabundance of "salt and savour" and
individual character. But the violence and vulgarity of the first

two stanzas prepare for the dramatic shift of tone in stanza three, and it is there, in John Kinsella's vision of Eden, that the voice shifts from that of an individual, in this case idiosyncratic, "active man speaking" to the archetypal voice speaking not so much "out of a people to a people" as out of the race to the race:

> The priests have got a book that says
> But for Adam's sin
> Eden's Garden would be there
> And I there within.
> No expectation fails there,
> No pleasing habit ends,
> No man grows old, no girl grows cold,
> But friends walk by friends.
> Who quarrels over halfpennies
> That plucks the trees for bread?
> *What shall I do for pretty girls*
> *Now my old bawd is dead?*
>
> (Yeats, *Variorum Poems,* p. 621)

W. B. YEATS

'He bids his Beloved be at Peace'

I hear the Shadowy Horses, their long manes a-shake,
Their hoofs heavy with tumult, their eyes glimmering white;
The North unfolds above them clinging, creeping night,
The East her hidden joy before the morning break,
The West weeps in pale dew and sighs passing away,
The South is pouring down roses of crimson fire:
O vanity of Sleep, Hope, Dream, endless Desire,
The Horses of Disaster plunge in the heavy clay:
Beloved, let your eyes half close, and your heart beat
Over my heart, and your hair fall over my breast,
Drowning love's lonely hour in deep twilight of rest,
And hiding their tossing manes and their tumultuous feet.

(Yeats, *Variorum Poems,* p. 154)

On the face of it, although the poem is somewhat mysterious, there are no strange words or allusions to look up. But Yeats's note reveals that he had more than the ordinary meanings in mind for horses and for the points of the compass:

> November, the old beginning of winter, or of the victory of the Fomor, or powers of death, and dismay, and cold, and darkness, is associated by the Irish people with the horse-shaped Púcas, who are now mischievous spirits, but were once Fomorian divinities. I think that they may have some connection with the horses of Mannannan, who reigned over the country of the dead, where the Fomorian Tethra reigned also; and the horses of Mannannan, though they could cross the land as easily as the sea, are constantly associated with the waves. Some neo-platonist, I forget who, describes the sea as a symbol of the drifting indefinite bitterness of life, and I believe there is like symbolism intended in the many Irish voyages to the islands of en-

chantment, or that there was, at any rate, in the mythology out of which these stories have been shaped. I follow much Irish and other mythology, and the magical tradition, in associating the North with night and sleep, and the East, the place of sunrise, with hope, and the South, the place of the sun when at its height with passion and desire, and the West, the place of sunset, with fading and dreaming things. (Yeats, *Variorum Poems,* p. 808)

So Yeats associates the "Shadowy Horses" with the Púcas (Pookas), with the horses of Manannan king of the dead, with the waves of the sea, and with the drifting indefinite bitterness of life.

Actually, if one had found this poem in a floating bottle and did not know who wrote it there is nothing in it to connect it with the Púcas or Manannan or anything Irish. They are called "Horses of Disaster" in the poem, so that we know without being told by the note that they have to do with misery and death. Whether or not one would get the point that the horses have something to do with the waves without reading the notes I do not know. Once this association has been made, the first two lines seem very appropriate:

> I hear the Shadowy Horses, their long manes a-shake,
> Their hoofs heavy with tumult, their eyes glimmering white.

The glimmering white of the eyes perhaps suggests the foam of the sea. Yeats uses the same image for the sea later in his verse as in the chorus from *Oedipus at Colonus* where he speaks "Of horses and horses of the sea, white horses" (Yeats, *Variorum Poems,* p. 447). But I do not think I should have thought of the sea at all in "He bids his Beloved be at Peace" unless Yeats's note had told me to. And when I got to the line:

> The Horses of Disaster plunge in the heavy clay

I should wonder why the sea plunges in clay rather than sand. Of course real horses are more likely to plunge in clay, and clay is symbolic of mortality, and these are horses of disaster.

It is only through Yeats's notes, then, that we learn that "the

Shadowy Horses" are meant as a specific allusion rather than as simply a suggestive image. And we have to read around in Yeats to find out more about these horses. Yeats has written about the Pooka in "The Solitary Fairies" section of *Fairy and Folk Tales of the Irish Peasantry,* first published in 1888. He says the Pooka "seems essentially an animal spirit. . . ." He is "of the race of the nightmare," which seems relevant to the poem. Douglas Hyde had told Yeats of a story in which "out of a certain hill in Leinster, there used to emerge as far as his middle, a plump, sleek, terrible steed, and speak in human voice to each person about November-day, and he was accustomed to give intelligent and proper answers to such as consulted him concerning all that would befall them until the November of next year." This steed may have been a Pooka or may have been a water-horse, says Yeats. These water horses "were common once, and used to come out of the water to gallop on the sands and in the fields, and people would often go between them and the marge and bridle them, and they would make the finest of horses if only you could keep them away from sight of the water; but if once they saw a glimpse of the water, they would plunge in with their rider, and tear him to pieces at the bottom." The steed in the story was more probably a Pooka, Yeats decided, "for November-day is sacred to the Pooka," and he continues, "It is hard to realize that wild, staring phantom grown sleek and civil." The phrase "wild, staring phantom" may show what Yeats had in mind when speaking of "their eyes glimmering white" in the poem. The Pooka is "shadowy" enough. "He has many shapes—is now a horse, now an ass, now a bull, now a goat, now an eagle. Like all spirits he is only half in the world of form" (Yeats, *Fairy and Folk Tales,* p. 100). These horses of the sea may be found as well in the poem "Cuchulain Fights with the Sea." Cuchulain has slain a young warrior who challenged him, only to find out later that it was his own, and only, son. King Conchubar fears that Cuchulain will go mad and slay them all.

> Then Conchubar, the subtlest of all men,
> Ranking his Druids round him ten by ten,

Spake thus: 'Cuchulain will dwell there and brood
For three days more in dreadful quietude,
And then arise, and raving slay us all.
Chaunt in his ear delusions magical,
That he may fight the horses of the sea.'
The Druids took them to their mystery,
And chanted for three days.
       Cuchulain stirred,
Stared on the horses of the sea, and heard
The cars of battle and his own name cried;
And fought with the invulnerable tide.
     (Yeats, *Variorum Poems,* pp. 110–11)

This poem was published first in 1892, but I am afraid that
the image of the horses of the sea was added in 1924 long
after *The Wind Among the Reeds* had been written. By that
time Yeats had also written the play *The Only Jealousy of
Emer* in which Cuchulain, drowned, is saved from death, that
is from a woman of the Sidhe who serves Manannan, god
of the sea and of death. Yeats had to revise the early poem so
that he does not actually kill Cuchulain off in it. This woman
of the Sidhe and Bricriu, god of discord, ride the bridleless
horses of the sea in that play.

  Old Manannan's unbridled horses come
  Out of the sea, and on their backs his horsemen.
     (Yeats, *Varorium Plays,* p. 539)

They have put a changeling in the place of Cuchulain, and
Cuchulain's wife Emer has to win back his life. She says:

        It may be
 An image has been put into his place,
 A sea-borne log bewitched into his likeness,
 Or some stark horseman grown too old to ride
 Among the troops of Manannan, Son of the Sea,
 Now that his joints are stiff.
     (Yeats, *Variorum Plays,* p. 537)

The play too, first published in 1919, is much later than *The
Wind Among the Reeds.*

We do not really then, even have the context of other works, considering the dates, to give us the meaning of the shadowy horses. When *The Wind Among the Reeds* was published Yeats's note and Yeats's note alone—and that only indirectly—could tell us that he associated the horses with the sea.

In terms of the volume itself it would make much more sense to associate the horses with the hosting of the Sidhe, the ordinary Sidhe, not the special Sidhe of the sea. But this would make the first eight lines hard to interpret.

If the horses are meant to suggest the sea, and the sea, as Yeats says, the drifting indefinite bitterness of life, then the first eight lines make more sense to me as a symbolic landscape. We have the sea, the perpetual flux of life (and thus the death, the end of all) spread out in its unchanging mutability, but over it we have the sky and the motions of the sun and the seasons to which all man's aims relate. North, East, West, or South—all is sky, and night for sleep, morning for hope, sunset for dream, and noon, I suppose for endless desire. All these are vain. The sky is a vanity over the perpetual disaster of the sea. I do not know whether in line seven,

> O vanity of Sleep, Hope, Dream, endless Desire

the poet is calling on vanity, addressing vanity, or whether vanity is the object of the word "plunge." It doesn't really matter, I suppose. Life is in vain in either case and the poet wishes to escape from the threat of the disaster that will eventually overwhelm him. Therefore, since there is all this threat of disaster:

> Beloved, let your eyes half close, and your heart beat
> Over my heart, and your hair fall over my breast,
> Drowning love's lonely hour in deep twilight of rest,
> And hiding their tossing manes and their tumultuous feet.

There is a strange echo here of Matthew Arnold's "Dover Beach."

> Ah, love, let us be true
> To one another! for the world, which seems

To lie before us like a land of dreams,
So various, so beautiful, so new,
Hath really neither joy, nor love, nor light,
Nor certitude, nor peace, nor help for pain;
And we are here as on a darkling plain
Swept with confused alarm of struggle and flight,
Where ignorant armies clash by night.

(Arnold, *Selected Poetry,* p. 90)

However, to be quite accurate, Yeats's poem does not say let us be *true* to one another, but let us rest together and hide away all that threat of disaster. One meets the threatening fact of the vanity of sleep not by looking it straight in the eye, but by half closing the eyes. One meets the threat of the horses of the sea—if that's what they are—by *drowning* in deep twilight of rest.

There seems to be a strange parallel between the positions of sky and sea (if the sea is meant) and the positions of beloved and lover. The sky is above the sea and the beloved is asked to let "your heart beat/Over my heart." Just as the beloved is asked to let "your hair fall over my breast," so the North unfolds night above the shadowy horses, the East unfolds her hidden joy to them or over them before the morning breaks, and the South pours down roses, presumably upon them. One may say parenthetically that North, East, West, and South seem to have other suggestions of the lady: the night as the dark hair, a certain coyness in the clinging and creeping, and the hidden joy, the weeping and sighing, and the pouring down of the symbolic roses which have meant love for the past two volumes of Yeats's poetry. The efforts of the compass points are without avail, however, as the horses continue to plunge. The beloved's efforts are much more efficacious, the horses being hidden away by her hair. By this simple expedient she is able to accomplish what all the world, North, East, South, West, has never been able to do before. Or perhaps it is twilight which has been able to accomplish what night, morning sunset, and noon could not, being too definite.

Yeats calls the Pooka a "wild staring phantom," and it is interesting, as I have said, to reflect that the eyes of the horses are glimmering white while the beloved is to let her eyes half close, perhaps in an attempt to see no evil—again an easy way to solve the problem.

It is interesting that at the same time as the lady lets her hair fall over the lover's breast she hides the tossing manes and tumultuous feet of the horses. What are the horses in relation to the hair—outside it or beneath it? The poet does not say that she hides him from the horses but that she hides them—hiding their tossing manes. Yet she is lying above *him* and her hair is covering his breast. The drowning of love's lonely hour and the hiding of the horses is the same act, done with the gesture of the hair. Therefore the cosmic import of the horses is not as impressive as the sexual import, and they simply begin to stand for the lover's sexual excitement or unrest which the lady allays by letting her heart beat over his heart and her hair fall over his breast.

Now we can understand how the two images of hair—the lady's hair and the manes of the horses—can be resolved. The lady's hair suggests her power to soothe and comfort the lover sexually and to hide him from the awkward realities of life. The manes of the horses identified with the sexual excitement of the male, are hidden away by the lady's hair. Her love is dignified, deliberate, formal; his, excited and unhappy, and therefore like wild horses. The natures of the man and of the woman are thus portrayed by the two images of hair, and the relation between them is also projected by this means.

Yeats's title, "He bids his Beloved be at Peace," seems to me a misnaming. This langorous lady seems nearly at peace already. *He* is the one who needs pacification.

Thematically the cosmic imagery and the sexual imagery coalesce. The perception of the vanity of life, the way the four quarters of the sky and all man's rhythm of sleep, hope, dream, and desire are perpetually frustrated by death, makes the poet take shelter under the tent of his mistress' hair and shut out the thought. But taking shelter in love is not merely escape, it is the counterforce, the perpetual war of the life force against death. Thus these horses of disaster can stand for the erotic excitement of the lover, because it is this perpetual fear of death which arouses his desire for life and stirs his specifically erotic unrest. And this is why the deep twilight of rest in love both allays *his* unrest and hides away the horses of disaster. Love's lonely hour is identified both with the feelings of the lovers and with the horses of disaster. It is what they mean. Thus love emerges as both the escape from disaster and the disaster itself—for without love no procreation—and without procreation no human "Sleep, Hope, Dream, endless Desire." As Yeats put it much later

> How could passion run so deep
> Had I never thought
> That the crime of being born
> Blackens all our lot?
> But where the crime's committed
> The crime can be forgot.
>
> (Yeats, *Variorum Poems,* p. 534)

Poussin & 'News for the Delphic Oracle'

T. R. Henn has demonstrated that "The Marriage of Peleus and Thetis" by Nicolas Poussin (National Gallery of Ireland, No. 814, Lane bequest 1918) "offers such startlingly exact correspondence" to W.B. Yeats's poem "News for the Delphic Oracle" (first printed in March 1939),

> that there can be no doubt as to the source. The picture has an interesting history. . . . [It] originally had the title of 'Acis and Galatea.' Then it became 'The Marriage . . .', and was thus known when Yeats knew it. After the first edition was published the picture reverted to its original title, this being a result of the *Colloque Poussin* in 1958. It is, perhaps, the classical instance of a word-for-word transposition." (Henn, *Lonely Tower*, p. 249)

As we shall see, the transposition is not quite that faithful, and the differences between the painting and the poem are instructive. I have found no detailed analysis of the painting as "The Marriage of Peleus and Thetis." Thomas MacGreevy's sensitive analysis of it as "Acis and Galatea" is useful in making us more fully aware of the detail of the painting, even though Yeats related that detail to a different story. Polyphemus, the gigantic cyclops (the figure sitting on a rock playing the pipes in the upper background of the painting), loved the sea nymph Galatea. She, however, was not attracted by his rugged physique, or even by the unique eye in the middle of his forehead, but loved young Acis (with whom we see her very much involved in the left foreground). Thomas MacGreevy remarks that "the care-free lovers in their draperies of deep gold and luminous blue against a shimmer of white, are as beautiful as the ideal of young love has ever been imagined in art. . . ." This was not the reaction of Polyphemus, who rose from his melancholy

piping, and from a love song which takes up innumerable pages of Ovid's *Metamorphoses*, to catch sight of the lovers. In his anger he hurled a huge rock which crushed Acis, though Galatea escaped into the sea. In MacGreevy's description:

> One of [the gambolling creatures of the sea] on his fantastic horse, which has a ram's head and horns and a fish tail, throws his head back to blow on a conch trumpet—perhaps in warning to the *amorini* in the air above him of the looming danger to the devotees of young love. . . . [There is a] second figure of Galatea, in *contraposto*, on the right—safe in the arms of her father, Neptune. . . . (MacGreevy, *Nicolas Poussin,* pp. 14–15)

One might add that the two draperies, the ominously red one held up by the *amorini* behind the seated couple on the left, and the blue drapery which the Galatea on the right holds floating over her, seem intended to shield her from the sight of the giant in the background. Mount Aetna looms in the distance.

Yeats, however, knew the picture as "The Marriage of Thetis and Peleus." Let us review the familiar story. It was foretold that Thetis' son would be greater than his father. Zeus, though he admired and desired Thetis himself, thus decreed for reasons of state that the beautiful sea-goddess should marry Peleus, a mortal. Since Thetis would object to the insult to her divinity involved in such a marriage, the affair had to be managed by stealth and force. Proteus, the old man of the sea (who is the same God as Nereus, Thetis' father), arranged the whole thing. He told Peleus of a cave where the naked goddess slept and told him to overpower her there. Like Proteus, she could turn into many shapes, including that of a spotted tigress—which she did. But eventually Peleus gained the mastery and of that union was born Achilles. We should not forget that it was at their wedding that the "apple of discord" started the chain of events that led to the Trojan war.

To relate the painting to this story in close detail is more difficult than to relate it to the story of "Acis and Galatea." Clearly Yeats did not bother to do so. Moreover, he may not have noticed, as did the art critic, that the lady on the right is the same nymph as the one on the left, in *contraposto*. And whereas MacGreevy saw fatherly solicitude in the attitude of the mature male figure carrying her, Yeats probably saw lust. An analysis of the painting, elaborating on MacGreevy's perception of the detail but relating it to the Peleus and Thetis story, might go as follows: At the bidding of Zeus, the little loves, who are connected by their similarity in color and by various lines with Zeus's authority in the sky, threaten Thetis with the barbs of love. One of the little fellows carries a bow, the other a long arrow or short spear. These weapons are clearly aimed toward the nymph who is being carried in a man's arms on the right. If she is Thetis, the male figure may be that of her father, the Old Man of the Sea, visually indicating his role in the story by carrying Thetis toward, not away from, shore, where according to the plan Peleus is to take her by force. The nymph's downward glance and a marvelous chain of interlocked limbs lead us first to a couple in active love play or struggle on the very edge of the shore and then on to the serenely poised couple embracing at the left. The former couple may represent the next stage of the action, the actual rape of Thetis by Peleus. He seems to be holding on with some difficulty; his muscles stand out because of his exertions. The figure blowing the conch shell trumpet is one of the old sea-god's right hand men who feels that he ought at this moment to do something official. The couple at the far left are the now happily united lovers. Their figures form a stable triangle which contrasts with the violent activity on the other side of the painting. This Peleus' muscles are smooth and relaxed. An imaginary line extended from Thetis' right leg up to the *amorini* in the sky would form another triangle with the line which we have already described from the arrow to Thetis' heart—thus linking the beginning and the end of the story. Who the figure looming in the background is, I cannot explain. I do not think Polyphemus was invited to the marriage of Peleus and Thetis. Perhaps it is Paris the shepherd, though greatly out of scale, who will soon be asked to decide—on Mount Ida which is in the background—whether Hera, Athena, or Aphrodite is the fairest.

Now this is *not* the way Yeats saw the painting, and his account is really much simpler than my own. He sees not a series of actions but one moment full of tension. Let us look closely at stanza three of the poem:

> Slim adolescence that a nymph has stripped,
> Peleus on Thetis stares.
> Her limbs are delicate as an eyelid,
> Love has blinded him with tears;
> But Thetis' belly listens.
> Down the mountain walls
> From where Pan's cavern is
> Intolerable music falls.
> Foul goat-head, brutal arm appear,
> Belly, shoulder, bum,
> Flash fishlike; nymphs and satyrs
> Copulate in the foam.
>
> (Yeats, *Variorum Poems,* pp. 612)

"Slim adolescence" refers, grammatically speaking, to Peleus, but both, in the painting, are slim adolescents. Is Thetis the nymph in the first line of the stanza? If so, has she stripped herself, or Peleus, or both? In the myth the emphasis is on Thetis' sleeping naked in the cave. If it is Peleus whose slim adolescence gets stripped, Thetis' taking the initiative is in strange contrast to the original story. But Yeats is looking at the painting, in which we can see Thetis' hands on Peleus' orange garment at the neck and at the leg. Peleus' arms embrace her and his hands cannot be seen. That Yeats makes the lady the aggressor lines her up with "Man-picker Niamh" in stanza one, who insisted on running off with Oisin to the Land of Youth. Richard Ellmann in *The Identity of Yeats* notes that in the painting Peleus is too close to Thetis to stare at her. Yeats has separated them to get, by means of the stare, the stasis which Poussin gets through the triangle which the lovers' bodies make. As Ellmann says, "The result is to throw into even stronger relief the pagan sensuality of the last four lines of the poem" (Ellmann, *Identity,* pp. 284–85). Yeats does retain in this stanza the contrast between serene repose and violent activity which we find in the painting: the left side of the painting corresponds to the first half of the stanza, in which Peleus stares and Thetis listens; the right side of the painting corresponds to the last half, about the nymphs and satyrs.

The line "Her limbs are delicate as an eyelid" is an appropriate comment on the extraordinarily beautiful form the painter has moulded. Moreover, the simile might have been suggested by the way Thetis' eyes are painted. The lids call attention to themselves. The mask-like face conceals thoughts from Peleus as well as from us. Peleus' eyes are indistinct, perhaps closed. If open they look past Thetis toward the other side of the painting where there is so much going on. But he doesn't really look as if he sees it. Perhaps Yeats is right that "Love has blinded him with tears."

> But Thetis' belly listens.
> Down the mountain walls
> From where Pan's cavern is
> Intolerable music falls.

This is the thought which Thetis' mask-like face has concealed. The baser part of her being throbs to the intolerable music of lustful Pan. But her face is abstracted, still. It is her belly that listens, and it is, as yet, just listening, not participating. (Her belly, by the way, does not appear in the painting, although her body, in its attitude, may appear to "listen".) The figure of Peleus is more tense, with one knee drawn up and the foot braced, than is the figure of Thetis. Her hands—fingers rather —are on him with the very lightest touch. Her body is balanced, at rest, and connects with the seated figure piping above her in the background. If one looks at Thetis' face for a while with Yeats's line "Thetis' belly listens" in mind, the effect is extraordinary. She seems a contemplative, but a contemplative who meditates or anticipates in stillness on a sensuous experience which is so complete, so perfect, that any movement, even any thought, would diminish it, would be loss rather than gain. The time for motion is not yet, but it will come.

Probably Yeats identifies the seated figure in the center of the painting with Pan. This figure is neither goat-footed nor horned, and, to substantiate MacGreevy's conviction that the subject is "Acis and Galatea," he does have something in the center of his forehead which could be the one eye of the cyclops Polphemus. His size too suggests the giant. It is true, however, that the goat-head of one of the sea-beasts is partly juxtaposed on the foot of the figure playing the pan-pipes, connecting him visually at least with goatishness. The "mountain walls" are there in the painting and there is a straight line from the pipes to the figures in the water ("Intolerable music falls"), a line formed by the shepherd's staff which the piper holds.

> Foul goat-head, brutal arm appear,
> Belly, shoulder, bum,
> Flash fishlike; nymphs and satyrs
> Copulate in the foam.

In these lines Pan is seen emerging from his cavern, or else the satyrs are seen gathering. But in the painting the only goat-head is on the sea-beast which the trumpeter rides. There are several quite muscular arms, but no nonhuman bum. There are no horned and goat-footed satyrs in the painting. No one is misbehaving to anywhere near the degree that Yeats's last line suggests, though he may have misinterpreted some of the figures. In the second stanza of the poem the souls are seen riding "brute dolphins" which "plunge" about in the sea. "Flash fishlike" and "brutal arm" echo this second stanza. "Flash fishlike" describes the central action which most of the figures on the right side of the painting seem engaged in—the sea-beasts, the plunging forms of the man riding a sea-beast, the struggling man and woman, and the little fellow on the large sea-shell. In fact, if the eye follows the *amorini,* beginning with the two sprawling in the water and coming to shore lower right, then moving to the two with arched backs holding up the red robe, then following the line of the arched back of the nearest one up into the sky where there are a third pair, one erect, back arched, the other plunging down, one has the whole movement of the painting. These are probably the same two *amorini* at three separate moments. I think that visually these little figures take the eye from right to left and from low to high, although the movement is admittedly circular. The arm of the trumpeter takes the eye right up into the sky where the two *amorini* are flying about. The movement in Yeat's poem, however, is downward, towards the copulation in the foam.

Having examined stanza three in relation to Poussin's painting, we may now be in a better position to grasp the poem as a whole:

NEWS FOR THE DELPHIC ORACLE

I

There all the golden codgers lay,
There the silver dew,
And the great water sighed for love,
And the wind sighed too.
Man-picker Niamh leant and sighed
By Oisin on the grass;
There sighed amid his choir of love
Tall Pythagoras.
Plotinus came and looked about,
The salt-flakes on his breast,
And having stretched and yawned awhile
Lay sighing like the rest.

II

Straddling each a dolphin's back
And steadied by a fin,
Those Innocents re-live their death,
Their wounds open again.
The ecstatic waters laugh because
Their cries are sweet and strange,
Through their ancestral patterns dance,
And the brute dolphins plunge
Until, in some cliff-sheltered bay
Where wades the choir of love
Proffering its sacred laurel crowns,
They pitch their burdens off.

III

Slim adolescence that a nymph has stripped,
Peleus on Thetis stares.
Her limbs are delicate as an eyelid,
Love has blinded him with tears;
But Thetis' belly listens.
Down the mountain walls
From where Pan's cavern is
Intolerable music falls.
Foul goat-head, brutal arm appear,
Belly, shoulder, bum,
Flash fishlike; nymphs and satyrs
Copulate in the foam.

(Yeats, *Variorum Poems,* pp. 611–12)

The first word is "There." If we ask where "There" is, we can
turn to another poem of Yeats for the explanation. "There" is
the title of one of the poems in "Supernatural Songs."

There all the barrel-hoops are knit,
There all the serpent-tails are bit,
There all the gyres converge in one,
There all the planets drop in the Sun.

(Yeats, *Variorum Poems,* p. 557)

The serpent is an old symbol for time; the serpent with his tail
in his mouth makes a circle, symbol of eternity. I do not quite
understand the barrel hoops, but the poem obviously refers to
the end of time; things have run their full course, the gyres converge in one, the planets drop in the sun in a death by fire. But
the planets originally came from the sun, and the serpent with
tail in mouth makes end and beginning meet. "There" is that
state which is the end—the ultimate goal, completion and purpose—of life. And yet that state contains within it the beginning, the potentiality for the entire cycle.

"There all the golden codgers lay." Yeats has taken our
phrase "old codgers" and made it "golden codgers" to suggest
the heroes, including golden-thighed Pythagoras, of various
golden ages—Classical, Christian, and Celtic. Yeats calls them

"codgers" to warn us that he is going to treat these heroes irreverently. All of them have arrived at whatever consummation the athletic and aspiring soul reaches beyond death. Oisin's wanderings are over; he has arrived at the end of his last journey (and his author, W. B. Yeats, has been two months dead when the poem is first printed). Pythagoras and Plotinus too have reached their goals.

Plotinus, great mystic and Neoplatonic philosopher, is the archetypal aspiring soul. The Cumaean Sylbil described his fate in the after-life as follows:

> Celestial! Man at first, but nearing now the lot of the divine! The bonds of human fate are loosed for you, and, strong of heart, you beat your eager way from out the roaring tumult of this fleshly life to the shores of that wave-washed coast free from the thronging of the guilty, thence to take the grateful path of the sinless soul. Where glows the splendor of God, where Right is throned in the stainless place, far from the wrong that mocks at law, where all is unison and winning tenderness and guileless joy. Where dwell the just Aeacus, and Plato, consecrated power, and fair Pythagoras and all else that form the choir of Immortal Love; there where the heart is ever lifted in joyous festival. O Blessed One, you have fought your many fights; now, crowned with unfading life, your days are with the Ever-Holy! (*Plotinus,* p. 10)

Yeats had used this passage in the final poem of the Crazy Jane series, *Words for Music Perhaps,* giving the impersonal voice of the oracle the last word on the struggles of soul and body.

THE DELPHIC ORACLE UPON PLOTINUS
Behold that great Plotinus swim,
Buffeted by such seas;
Bland Rhadamanthus beckons him,
But the Golden Race looks dim,
Salt blood blocks his eyes.

Scattered on the level grass
Or winding through the grove
Plato there and Minos pass,
There stately Pythagoras
And all the choir of Love.
(Yeats, *Variorum Poems*, pp. 530–531)

"The Delphic Oracle upon Plotinus" and "News for the Delphic Oracle" must be read together for dramatic reasons as well as thematic ones. "Behold that great Plotinus swim,/ Buffeted by such seas." Plotinus is making a great spiritual fight to win through to immortality. The first stanza is full of the violence of the struggle; the second full of the serenity and fulfillment of the goal—if he can reach it. In "News for the Delphic Oracle" he has at last reached the shores of eternity. What does he do about it? "Plotinus came and looked about,/ The salt-flakes on his breast,/And having stretched and yawned awhile/Lay sighing like the rest." Everyone and everything was sighing in this place. ". . . The great water sighed for love,/ And the wind sighed too." They were sighing *for* love; not sighing contentedly *with* love attained, in a land "where all is unison and winning tenderness and guileless joy," but sighing restlessly with desire.

Here I part company with F.A.C. Wilson, who writes:

> All the inhabitants of Yeats's island paradise are sighing 'for love', and here he is probably bringing Dante into his argument; for, in the circle of limbo to which Dante consigns the Platonists, their only punishment is to sigh, in their frustrated desire for closer contact with God.
>
> > *Non avea pianto, ma' che di sospiri*
> > *Che l'aura eterna facevan tremare.*
>
> 'Here was no plaint that could be heard, except of sighs, which caused the eternal air to tremble.'

Yeats, I think, designedly inverts Dante's argument, for the sighs of his Platonists come less from frustration than from content. (Wilson, *Tradition*, pp. 218–19).

I cannot see the necessity for bringing in Dante (particularly since Dante mentions none of the figures Yeats does), and I feel that Yeats's figures are not sighing with contentment but with desire, though not the "frustrated desire for closer contact with God." I part company also with Richard Ellmann who writes that Yeats's "too pure lovers [Oisin and Niamh], caught up in mutual contemplation when they might have embraced, are fitting companions for the thoughtful philosophers and fitting denizens of a heaven of such rarefied love." (Ellmann, *Identity,* pp. 284–85).

In my view, Plotinus, having heroically reached his goal and having stretched and yawned awhile, was already bored with resting on his laurels, and "Lay sighing like the rest." That they are all sighing with desire—that the sighing is prelude to the act of love—is indicated partly by echoes in these lines of Enobarbus' description of Cleopatra (as Ellmann and Thomas Whitaker have pointed out) (Ellmann, *Identity,* pp. 284–85; Whitaker, *Swan and Shadow,* p. 128). In Shakespeare's famous lines, the purple sails of Cleopatra's barge were "so perfumed that/The winds were lovesick with them; the oars were silver,/ Which to the tune of flutes kept stroke, and made/The water which they beat to follow faster,/As amorous of their strokes." And Cleopatra's entourage—"pretty dimpled boys, like smiling Cupids" and "gentlewomen like the Nereides,/So many mermaids"—makes us look forward to the last stanza in which Yeats describes the scene of Poussin's picture. The whole passage (II, ii, 196–251) is relevant. Perhaps most relevant, thematically, is the idea that Cleopatra "makes hungry/Where most she satisfies," for that is what has happened here. Plotinus has reached the final goal, eternity, only to find, with Blake, that eternity is in love with the productions of time. He lies sighing with animal desire, sighing to start the whole process of spiritual evolution all over again from its basest beginning. The vulgar phrase "man-picker" for Niamh and the salt-flakes on Plotinus' breast help establish the tone of earthly rather than heavenly love.

To Richard Ellmann the three stanzas "represent heaven in three aspects, with decreasing propriety, the first being devoted to heavenly love, the second to innocence, and the third to carnal love." According to this interpretation the sighs of stanza one are fulsome and rather silly sighs of satisfaction. I find a different three-part division into maturity, childhood, and youth. In the first stanza, with Niamh and Oisin, Pythagoras and Plotinus, we have figures who have been through the whole human experience. Niamh and Oisin, as lovers, are perpetually youthful, I suppose, yet *The Wanderings of Oisin* took them through centuries of adventures. The souls who come over the sea of time to eternity in the second stanza are all under two years old. They are the Holy Innocents slaughtered by King Herod. Appropriately for children, they are having rides on the backs of dolphins. They are being carried. They have not had to struggle through the water like Plotinus, because they are innocent and, I think, because they are part of a Christian frame of reference whereas the others are Pagan. Their martyrdom in innocence is their salvation. They ride dolphins, Ellmann tells us, because "under the Roman empire, 'The dolphins . . . form a mystic escort of the dead to the Island of the Blest' " as Yeats "had read in Eugenie Strong's *Apotheosis and After Life. . . .*" These innocents relive their deaths—the wounds open again—as they cross this sea, because in Yeats's theory of the after-life the shade must dream "back through events in the order of their intensity" and again, as Spiritual Being, live "back through events in the order of their occurrence" (Yeats, *Variorum Plays,* p. 777).

> Straddling each a dolphin's back
> And steadied by a fin,
> Those Innocents re-live their death,
> Their wounds open again.
> The ecstatic waters laugh because
> Their cries are sweet and strange,
> Through their ancestral patterns dance,
> And the brute dolphins plunge
> Until, in some cliff-sheltered bay
> Where wades the choir of love
> Proffering its sacred laurel crowns,
> They pitch their burdens off.

Ellmann says that Yeats's "waters laugh at the babies' cries, as if the unhappy events which the Innocents relive are now far off, and their suffering only a part of the purifying ritual." I feel that this is at best only half the truth. It does not take much probing to bring to the surface a vivid realization of the suffering of the babies. To have one's wounds open again (especially in salt water) is not a particularly pleasant experience. I think the lines "The ecstatic waters laugh because/Their cries are sweet and strange" are absolutely blood-curdling! These sweet strange cries, after all, are the cries of babies being murdered. There is no reason that we should share the amusement of the waters or the brutishness of the dolphins. I think that Yeats has here for once used his theory of the after-life as metaphor for real life—that he is not so much interested in the Holy innocents' reliving their death in a Yeatsian purgatory as he is in the repetition of birth, suffering and death for countless innocents throughout history. The intolerable idea of the same tragedies happening over and over again, countless births that lead to countless cruel deaths, was, I think, uppermost in his mind. These are the waters of generation in time which ecstatically produce and destroy. They dance through "ancestral patterns," patterns, that is, of generation after generation. In them the brute dolphins plunge. The dolphin is a love-beast, F. A. C. Wilson reminds us: "and when Yeats says that 'the brute dolphins plunge' into the sea, his adjective is probably applied to stress the carnal aspect of love. . . ." (Wilson, *Tradition,* p. 221). Thus the plunging of the dolphins carrying the babies has a sexual significance. What we have here is the grotesque cheerfulness with which the waters of all time bring on wave on wave of children whether we are ready for them or not, and with no feeling for or against what will happen to them, but only an ecstatic, but otherwise aimless, enthusiasm in production. The sudden shrug with which the dolphins pitch off their burdens is nature's carelessness about the end of life, being preoccupied with the beginning of it. The choir of love may be waiting with arms outstretched holding crowns of immortality, but the brute dolphins have no more interest in that ceremony than would a busy ferryman.

The first stanza then looks backward from the goal and shows the desire for repeating the whole everlasting process of life. The second stanza looks forward from the beginning toward the horror and ridiculousness of the process. The third stanza shows once again that "where the crime's committed/The crime can be forgot" and shows us nymphs and satyrs copulating in the foam which marks the border between the sea of time and the eternal Isle of the Blest. We are led to believe that Thetis, a sea-goddess, and Peleus, her mortal husband—figures who rank with the golden codgers of stanza one—will soon follow the example of the nymphs and satyrs. And we reflect that a shudder in these loins may, with the birth of Achilles and his ruinous wrath, engender all the troubles of the Trojan War which were not already programmed by Leda and her swan. Perhaps Achilles has already been conceived and "Thetis' belly listens" to the fated child in her womb. (The images of cavern and of forms simultaneously human, bestial, and fishlike are appropriate to the theme of birth and perhaps can be said to suggest, however latently, the pregnant womb.) The music is intolerable because it symbolizes the desire—and Thetis is full of desire—which will start the tragic human drama all over again —with her son as tragic victim.

The phrase "intolerable music" is the only suggestion that the conjunction of Peleus and Thetis was, to begin with, a rape that Yeats has retained from the myth. But her horror is a fascinated horror, and she desires what happens. It is not Yeats's intention, as it was in "Leda and the Swan," to dramatize the violation, for it is the possession of the human by the divine that he is interested in and here the male aggressor is a mere mortal. Yeats therefore has been careful to make the goddess if anything the more aggressive of the two. He has made sure that it is she whose thought is directed downwards into the flesh, while Peleus is full of idealized love. So although the sexes are reversed, the figurative positions of divine and human are the same as those in "Leda and the Swan." That is, the divine desires fleshly experience, the human desires ideal knowledge.

For these reasons Yeats, in interpreting Poussin's painting, or at least in using it as a model for his poem, would not wish to associate Peleus and Thetis with the violent activity going on in the right half of the picture, but only with the serene equipoise of the couple at the left. He would not see the girl who is being lifted in a man's arms as Thetis *in contraposto*. He would not see the active love play or struggle of the couple at the edge of the shore as the forcing of Thetis. What happens at the right of the canvas is seen as the externalization of Thetis' unspoken desires.

While what motivates suffering man is his "longing for the tomb," for the end of life, for the isle beyond the sea, what motivates the abundantly happy immortals is the desire to put us through it all again, to make us "live it all again" as Yeats himself said he was content to do. (He may have thought he lacked the choice, which the "golden codgers" had, of escaping rebirth.)

> I am content to live it all again
> And yet again, if it be life to pitch
> Into the frog-spawn of a blind man's ditch,
> A blind man battering blind men. . . .
>
> (Yeats, *Variorum Poems,* p. 479)

Poor Peleus is also blinded, though with tears of love, not anger, as salt blood blocks the eyes of the swimming sage in "The Delphic Oracle upon Plotinus." It is the mortal condition to be blind. The imagery of bellies, shoulders, and bums flashing fish-like is amphibious enough to parallel "the frog-spawn of a blind man's ditch," so that it is instructive to regard these lines from "A Dialogue of Self and Soul" (1929) as an unheroic, a non-Poussian-like, version of human life, the life which starts another weary round when "nymphs and satyrs/Copulate in the foam."

Some Irish Poems

OSCAR WILDE

'Requiescat'

Tread lightly, she is near
   Under the snow,
Speak gently, she can hear
   The daisies grow.

All her bright golden hair
   Tarnished with rust,
She that was young and fair
   Fallen to dust.

Lily-like, white as snow,
   She hardly knew
She was a woman, so
   Sweetly she grew.

Coffin-board, heavy stone,
   Lie on her breast,
I vex my heart alone,
   She is at rest.

Peace, Peace, she cannot hear
   Lyre or sonnet,
All my life's buried here,
   Heap earth upon it.

(Wilde, *Poems,* p. 57)

When W. B. Yeats asked Wilde for permission to publish "Requiescat" in *A Book of Irish Verse* (1895), Wilde suggested another poem as more characteristic (Yeats, *Autobiography,* p. 171.), but Yeats chose it anyway. It is a delicate little poem about a girl's death, reminiscent of many a similar poem. The question is whether Wilde has really made a poem or merely assembled some traditional elements of this *sort* of poem.

The meter, beautifully chosen, nevertheless echoes familiar poems: about an unfortunate girl who was a suicide, "The Bridge of Sighs" by Thomas Hood.

> One more Unfortunate,
> Weary of breath,
> Rashly importunate,
> Gone to her death!
>
> (Hood, *Works,* IX, 204)

and about a lover's separation, "When We Two Parted" by Byron,

> Pale grew thy cheek and cold,
> Colder thy kiss;
> Truly that hour foretold
> Sorrow to this.
>
> (Byron, *Selected Poetry,* p. 1)

The concept that

> She hardly knew
> She was a woman, so
> Sweetly she grew

owes something to the "Lucy" poems of Wordsworth:

> Grace that shall mould the Maiden's form
> By silent sympathy.
>
> .   .   .   .   .   .
>
> And vital feelings of delight
> Shall rear her form to stately height
> Her virgin bosom swell. . . .
>
> (Wordsworth, *Selected Poems,* p. 48)

The lily (she is "Lily-like") is no doubt the pre-Raphaelite lily. The theme

> I vex my heart alone,
> She is at rest

is the same as that of Matthew Arnold's "Requiescat,"

Strew on her roses, roses,
And never a spray of yew!
In quiet she reposes;
Ah, would that I did too!

          (Arnold, *Selected Poetry*, p. 66)

There is nothing wrong with having such echoes, especially in such a traditional form as the lament, so long as the poem is a poem in its own right, and it certainly is a lovely thing which one would hate to lose. But there are other seeming loose ends in the poem. In stanza one she can hear the daisies grow; in stanza five she cannot hear lyre or sonnet. In stanza one we have both snow and daisies. What time of year is it? Not only the time but the situation is unclear. Has the lady been buried or is she being buried? She is under the snow in stanza one yet the command to the gravediggers to "Heap earth" does not occur until the last line.

I suppose these images can be reconciled. Perhaps she has been buried long enough for snow to be over her grave, but perhaps under the snow the flowers are getting ready to appear. The last lines then would refer not to the command to the gravediggers to fill in the girl's grave, but to the poet's own death wish: Heap earth upon my life, since hers is over.

But is not the line "Tarnished with rust" in the second stanza a bad line?

All her bright golden hair
Tarnished with rust.

Gold does not rust, nor is it easily tarnished. Hair does not decay quickly, witness Donne's "bracelet of bright hair about the bone." What does he mean, "tarnished with rust"? If the lady has not been dead, even buried, long, her hair would be unaffected. The reddish-brown rust color evokes a macabre picture. Did the lady die a violent death, and is this dried blood? An unpleasant thought. Nor does it speak well for the care of those who prepared the body for burial. Surely they would have washed away such traces. How long has she been buried? She has already "fallen to dust" according to the last line of the second stanza. The line "All my life's buried here," on the other hand, suggests an ejaculation one would make within a year or two of a death, or immediately after it, not what one would say after many years when one had come to accept bereavement. If that is the case she must have fallen to dust in a great hurry, if Hamlet's gravedigger can be trusted for estimates: "Faith, if 'a be not rotten before 'a die (as we have many pocky corses now-a-days, that will scarce hold the laying in), 'a will last you some eight year or nine year" (V, i, 180–84). I do not mean to be shocking, I just wonder whether Wilde was really looking at what he was writing.

> All her bright golden hair
> Tarnished with rust
> She that was young and fair
> Fallen to dust.

Those last two lines weren't hard to write, especially if Hood's lines were ringing in one's ears:

> Take her up tenderly,
> Lift her with care;
> Fashion'd so slenderly,
> Young, and so fair!
> Hood, *Works,* IX, 204)

Or Thomas Nashe's earlier lines:

> Brightness falls from the air
> Queens have died young and fair
> Dust hath closed Helen's eye
> (*Elizabethan Verse,* p. 91)

"Tarnished with rust" is the only line which calls attention to itself as original expression, and when we give it that attention we feel that we are giving it something that Wilde did not. Gold suggested metal, metal suggested tarnish and rust, and rust rhymed beautifully with dust as well as expressing the same idea of decay. The lines work only if we think about the idea to which they refer—the body of a beautiful young girl now dead and decayed, an affecting idea no matter how expressed—and if we avoid looking too closely at Wilde's words. It is a poem on which one has to tread lightly.

Well, let us tread the poem once again, this time more lightly, excusing clichés such as "tread lightly," "bright golden hair," "young and fair," "fallen to dust," "white as snow," "she is at rest," as ritual utterances.

The structure of the poem follows the psychological progress of the mourner's mood. Stanza one expresses the speaker's unwillingness to accept the girl's death. The death is hinted at, implied, not stated, certainly not accepted. Rather the opposite, the livingness of the girl, her fineness of sensibility, are stressed. Only the terms in which these assertions are made qualify her vividness and make her a sort of wraith. "She is near," but "under the snow." "She can hear/The daisies grow" (a feat usually reserved to heroes in Celtic mythology) only because her ears are filled with the dirt in which the daisies root.

"She is at rest," and therefore one must "tread lightly" and "speak gently" for fear of waking her, and it is easy to wake someone so near and of such fine sensibility. Actually what the speaker fears to wake is his own agonized awareness of her death. To wake *her,* is to wake the reality, the vivid life of what she was, into being before his mind's eye and thus increase his pain. "Tread lightly" and "Speak gently": In other words, do not shout out that she is dead so that I have to face it. Thus the wraith of the girl's presence, really buried in his mind, becomes something almost to fear. Tread lightly, she is around here someplace. Speak gently or she will hear us, and we do not want her to know what we are saying.

There is also the sense of fear of harm to the loved one, and this is the sense which provides transition to the next stanza. Speak gently, her ears are inordinately sensitive and you will cause her pain if you speak loudly. Tread lightly, you may *step* on her.

Of course you may, the grave is right there. But the speaker isn't facing up to this fact yet. She is only *near,* at some indeterminate place, under the snow.

Whereas stanza one presented the vivid life of his memory

of the girl, even the lightness and gentleness of the way one must tread and speak evoking the light, gentle, extremely sensitive and alive nature of the creature who is gone, stanza two plunges into stark awareness of her death: the bright golden hair soiled with the grave, the body disintegrated.

Stanzas three and four repeat this pattern, stanza three presenting her innocence in terms of the lightness and gentleness and the image of snow of stanza one, stanza four again concentrating on the grave with images of heavy weight. She was chaste and innocent, the lily and snow of stanza three tell us. "She hardly knew/She was a woman, so/Sweetly she grew." She grew to be a woman without excessive sex-consciousness, I suppose that means. (I gather that he *did* know she was a woman!) These are perhaps the best lines in the poem, prepared for as they are by "tread lightly," "speak gently." She was a girl to whom one would speak gently in life, especially about love and desire, since she hardly knew she was a woman. You'd want to break it to her gently!

The idea of sweet growth is delicately suggested by the relation of syntax to verse form. Line one provides a firm stasis as a starting point. Snow is arranged horizontally and suggests the inhibition of growth in winter and is also the familiar image of chastity. There is some tension here with stanza one. The snow of a clear complexion and of chastity in stanza three reminds one of the snow of death in stanza one. And after all the process of growth is a process of increasing fullness of life, moving from nonbeing to full being. And on the other hand stanza one, where the girl is under the snow, delicately suggests her beauty and innocence while it tells us that she is dead.

The lily too is an image of innocence and chastity, but whereas the snow suggests the inhibition of growth in winter the lily suggests spring and new life; its flowering is its biological prime, the equivalent of womanhood. The snow is level, the lily erect. Thus the line combines, against a background of death, images of innocence and retarding of growth with images of biological maturity and live beauty. "Lily" (a noun), the flowering aimed at, begins the stanza. "Grew" (a verb), indicating the completion of the growth process, ends the stanza.

From the pause at the end of line one, the next three lines rise without a pause at the line ends to stop only at "grew." Every other stanza has a strong pause at the end of the second line:

> All her bright golden hair
> Tarnished with rust,
> She that was young and fair
> Fallen to dust.

But this stanza grows gently, lightly sweetly:

> She hardly knew
> She was a woman, so
> Sweetly she grew.

To know she was a woman is a gentle and sweet way of putting the idea of sexual maturity. I think also the rhyme word "so," which quickly directs one on into the next line, modestly attracting no attention to itself, helps achieve the extraordinary delicacy of this stanza.

In the next stanza we return to images of the grave: heaviness as opposed to lightness, stones versus lilies. I cannot feel that this is a successful stanza. The lady sounds decidely uncomfortable when "Coffin-board, heavy stone / Lie on her breast," yet he says in the next lines that "She is at rest," while *he* is the uncomfortable one, vexing his heart alone. That *alone* is beautifully put. Does it mean that he wants to vex hers too, that he is the only one who misses her, or just that he feels all alone?

Also there's an unassimilated sexual metaphor running through the poem. In stanza three she is so lily-like, innocent and chaste she hardly knew she was a woman, yet in stanza four all sorts of heavy things "Lie on her breast." Is Wilde awaking the old metaphor of the ravages of time: *ravage, ravish, rapid, rape?* I hope not. Yet he says that she is at rest, that something lies on her breast, that he is alone. The structure of the stanza, contrasting himself with her, seems to imply that she is not alone and that he wishes something were lying on *his* breast!

It *does* work this way, because in the next stanza he *asks* for something heavy to be dumped on his own breast.

> All my life's buried here,
> Heap earth upon it.

I am afraid that Wilde, without the courage of his convictions, or perhaps unconsciously, is considering death as a rape or as a bed of love, and not making up his mind which it is.

"Then worms shall try that long preserved virginity" as Marvell put it in "To his Coy Mistress."

Or as Romeo to Juliet:

> Shall I believe
> That unsubstantial Death is amorous
> And that the lean abhorred monster keeps
> Thee here in dark to be his paramour?
>
> (V, iii, 102–05)

Or Charmian of Cleopatra:

> Now boast thee death in thy possession lies
> A lass unparalleled.
>
> (V, ii, 319–20)

Actually of course it is both. In stanza one we were to tread lightly for fear of treading on one who is near, under the snow. But in stanza two we realize that the harm has been done. The girl is "tarnished," "fallen." In stanza three we establish her former innocence, in stanza four we see the guilty assaulter: "Coffin-board, heavy stone/Lie on her breast." But since she is dead, death becomes a desirable thing to the speaker. "She is at rest," "I vex my heart alone," therefore let me be at rest too. Heap earth on my life as well. Let me not remain alone but have heavy stone lying on my breast too.

Unfortunately this metaphor is neither dead nor alive in the poem. It does not rise to the beautiful clarity of the seventeenth-century poems quoted. Yet the fact that something is lying on her breast while he vexes his heart alone will not let the sexual metaphor sleep. It is a bad stanza. It has to contain crudity to represent the crudity of death. But it does not have to *be* crude.

"Peace, Peace" in the last stanza, parallels "tread lightly" and "speak softly" in stanza one. But now instead of being an admonition relevant to the lady's intense hearing ("she can hear/The daisies grow") it is a statement of futility ("she cannot hear/Lyre or sonnet"). Her death is bitterly accepted. There is no point in writing poems about her. The two statements are not contradictory. She can hear the daisies grow in the sense that she is pushing up daisies now, not just dead but united with nature in Wordsworthian fashion: "Rolled round in earth's diurnal course." The only trouble is that Wilde is not Wordsworth. The idea is chucked in, it is not part of the man and the body of his poetry. That she cannot hear lyre or sonnet is the bitter personal way of saying the same thing: that she is dead. The accent is on *him* now, rather than her. His life is buried with her burial. Heap earth upon it. End it.

OLIVER GOGARTY

'The Crab Tree'

The course of modern Irish verse as Yeats saw it, or at least one course of modern Irish verse, was, first, a return to the folk tradition, but with perhaps too strong a reaction against rhetoric occasionally forcing on such writers as Joseph Campbell, Padraic Colum, and the early Yeats "a facile charm, a too soft simplicity." Then "Synge brought back masculinity . . . with his harsh disillusionment, and later, when the folk movement seemed to support vague political mass excitement, certain poets began to create passionate masterful personality." Oliver St. John Gogarty's poetry, "a gay, stoical . . . heroic song" is instanced as an expression of such personality, and Gogarty is one of the "great lyric poets of our age" (*Oxford Book of Modern Verse,* pp. xiii–xv).

Not all the poems of Gogarty which Yeats anthologizes, still less those chosen by Donagh MacDonagh and Lennox Robinson for the *Oxford Book of Irish Verse,* support either this claim to greatness or the claim of having created passionate masterful personality. "Non Dolet" appears in both anthologies.

> Our friends go with us as we go
> Down the long path where Beauty wends,
> Where all we love foregathers, so
> Why should we fear to join our friends?
>
> Who would survive them to outlast
> His children; to outwear his fame—
> Left when the Triumph has gone past—
> To win from Age, not Time, a name?
>
> Then do not shudder at the knife
> That Death's indifferent hand drives home,
> But with the Strivers leave the Strife,
> Nor, after Caesar, skulk in Rome.
>
> (Gogarty, *Collected Poems,* p. 192)

In this poem a powerful image, the assassination of Caesar, stands for the death of friends which makes life no longer worth bothering with. The poem is certainly written in a dated manner with its personified Beauty, Triumph, Age, Time, and Death and its tired rhymes: fame, name; life, strife. Perhaps these words are typical of what Yeats called the dull, numb words of "an active man speaking." Yeats says that he changed exotic phrases like "the curd-pale moon" to the "brilliant moon" in revising his own early poems in order to get this effect of genuine speech (Yeats, *Autobiography,* p. 263). The sort of personality which Yeats felt to be behind Gogarty's poems would perhaps use succinct terms like Beauty, Triumph, Age, without elaboration.

But I do not feel that the reality of the personality speaking this poem has really been created. The friends, too, are left completely unrealized. We must accept them on faith. One needs only mention Yeats's "The Municipal Gallery Revisited," in which he recalls Synge, Lady Gregory, and others, and ends "And say my glory was I had such friends" (Yeats, *Variorum Poems,* p. 604), to realize that Gogarty has left the faces and personalities of the speaker and his friends quite blank.

The handling of the verse too is unexceptional. Look at line three where occurs the same "so" rhyme which we found in Wilde's "Requiescat": "so/sweetly she grew." The effect here is colloquial, and it intensifies and speeds up the last line, but that is all it does. The poem is saved only by its great last line, which *does* have the energy of personality, being very lordly and scornful about death and making a magnificent gesture:

> Nor, after Caesar, skulk in Rome.

The classical reference is a key to what Gogarty tries to do, echoing Latin poetry of the classical period, echoing also Walter Savage Landor, the foremost practitioner of this sort of thing in recent times, and in past times some of the Cavalier poets, the shorter poems of Ben Jonson, even some of Dryden. But except for the last line the poem seems merely competent verse with nothing memorable about it either in conception or technique.[1]

The classical echoes persist in *"Per Iter Tenebricosum."*

> Enough! Why should a man bemoan
> A Fate that leads the natural way?
> Or think himself a worthier one
> Than those who braved it in their day?
> If only gladiators died,
> Or Heroes, Death would be his pride;
> But have not little maidens gone,
> And Lesbia's sparrow—all alone?
>
> (Gogarty, *Collected Poems,* p. 191)

The idea of the poem is certainly a fine one: Why should a man fear to face death since little maidens and Lesbia's sparrow have done the same. And the contrast between men, gladiators, heroes, on the one hand, and sparrows on the other, is effective. The simplicity of the last two lines is very tender and beautiful. The idea is universal and thus moves one. Yet I cannot believe in Gogarty's gladiators. I have never seen a gladiator. The poem doesn't come close to home until "little maidens"; I do know some of *them.* "Little maidens" prepares us to accept the reality of Lesbia (even though she was no maiden), who died nearly 2,000 years ago, and thus to accept the reality of Lesbia's sparrow, who died a little while before that. "All alone" is a poignant twist—after all, gladiators die amidst a great deal of company—and the off-rhyme, though a familiar enough one, is effective in the context because it contains the idea: "gone . . . all alone."

"Golden Stockings" is a lovely poem, successful because of its remarkable fineness of observation and of sentiment and the discovery of an apt comparison.

> Golden stockings you had on
> In the meadow where you ran;
> And your little knees together
> Bobbed like pippins in the weather,
> When the breezes rush and fight
> For those dimples of delight,
> And they dance from the pursuit,
> And the leaf looks like the fruit.

> I have many a sight in mind
> That would last if I were blind;
> Many verses I could write
> That would bring me many a sight.
> Now I only see but one,
> See you running in the sun,
> And the gold-dust coming up
> From the trampled butter-cup.
>
> (Gogarty, *Collected Poems,* p. 160)

The "dimples of delight," something of an embarrassing phrase, does not refer to the knees, but to the apples which are like the knees. As the poet's daughter (Jeffares, "Gogarty, Irishman," p. 167) runs through the grass, the light hits her moving knees, in the same way that the light hits apples when the wind is blowing the branches so that one keeps mistaking leaf for fruit. The apples regularly bob back into the light just as the knees do. Those "dimples of delight" that dance are the apples. Thus the knees are like apples which are dimpled like knees and dance like knees! The tree image associated with childhood all the movement and warmth of summer.

Beginning with "Golden stockings," the poem ends with a linking image:

> And the gold-dust coming up
> From the trampled butter-cup.

The observation here is fine, almost a symbol—golden stockings trampling the gold dust out of buttercups. It catches the static picture, but it also conveys the rapid, destructive movement of running—careless, joyous, thoughtless of passing time and trampled buttercups. In addition it catches the ephemeral dust of beauty which arises for a moment from this trampling process and then dissipates. The fact that the picture is seen from the distance of many years, as stanza two tells us, gives especial emphasis to this theme of the passing of time, this running in the sun.

In "The Crab Tree" there is an attempt to explore the meaning of another symbol:

Here is the crab tree,
Firm and erect,
In spite of the thin soil,
In spite of neglect.
The twisted root grapples
For sap with the rock,
And draws the hard juice
To the succulent top:
Here are wild apples,
Here's a tart crop!

No outlandish grafting
That ever grew soft
In a sweet air of Persia,
Or safe Roman croft;
Unsheltered by steading,
Rock-rooted and grown,
A great tree of Erin,
It stands up alone,
A forest tree spreading
Where forests are gone.

Of all who pass by it
How few in it see
A westering remnant
Of days when Lough Neagh
Flowed up the long dingles
Its blossom had lit,
Old days of glory
Time cannot repeat;
And therefore it mingles
The bitter and sweet.

It takes from the West Wind
The thrust of the main;
It makes from the tension
Of sky and of plain,
Of what clay enacted,
Of living alarm,

A vitalised symbol
Of earth and of storm,
Of Chaos contracted
To intricate form.

Unbreakable wrestler!
What sapling or herb
Has core of such sweetness
And fruit so acerb?
So grim a transmitter
Of life through mishap,
That one wonders whether
If that in the sap,
Is sweet or is bitter
Which makes it stand up.

(Gogarty, *Collected Poems,* pp. 48–49)

The poem is full of qualities which the writer associates with Ireland, with a certain spirit that may be found there, with glories that have been and gone. The tree stands "Firm and erect,/In spite of the thin soil,/In spite of neglect." It is a great tree of Erin. The lone tree is a relic of the great forests once found in the North near Lough Neagh. As is Ireland in some ways, it is a unique survival of an earlier time, and thus representative of earlier values and customs:

A great tree of Erin,
It stands up alone,
A forest tree spreading
Where forests are gone.

It is a relic of the great forests which once grew near Lough Neagh. One may imagine thousands of trees, many of them crab trees, in bloom in the valleys around the Lough.

A westering remnant
Of days when Lough Neagh

Flowed up the long dingles
Its blossom had lit,

> Old days of glory
> Time cannot repeat.

The tree is thus a link between the past and the present, the formed, forming and formless, the substantial and the turbulent, sea, sky and plain.

> It takes from the West Wind
> The thrust of the main;
> It makes from the tension
> Of sky and of plain,
> Of what clay enacted,
> Of living alarm,
> A vitalised symbol
> Of earth and of storm,
> Of Chaos contracted
> To intricate form.

"What clay enacted" is I suppose what earth, and man who was formed of clay, have achieved or perpetrated in the past. One perpetration would be the clearing of those forests. "Living alarm" would be all the moving elements of the present, not only winds but also I suppose all the human tempests. The tree is a "vitalised symbol . . . Of Chaos contracted/To intricate form." Earth and sky and sea, past and present and future, all tossed about together. With its roots in the ground, and its branches in the air, and in another sense, its roots in the past, its branches in the present, and its leaves exploring towards the future, it seems an epitome of the principle of survival and of creating intricate form out of life's chaotic forces.

It wrestles and has always wrestled with these forces. Its core is sweet, its fruit bitter. There is great sweetness there, deep down, at the core. But a grim life has made its fruit bitter. You taste it at your peril. The fruit is that through which a tree communicates with the nontree world of birds and humans, and the crab tree's message is a bitter one.

> So grim a transmitter
> Of life through mishap,

> That one wonders whether
> If that in the sap,
> Is sweet or is bitter
> Which makes it stand up.

Is it the sweet virtues, mercy, pity, love, which make for survival, or is it bitter stubbornness, one's unregenerate "bitchiness," which enables one to hang on? That tree would know. It is sweet in the core, bitter in the fruit. The sap which keeps its life flowering may be either.

The verse form is very appropriate to the content of most of the stanzas; the idea of lean strength is conveyed by the short lines with two stresses, the irregular meter, iambic, trochaic, and anapestic by turns, the ten-line stanza, and an intricate rhyme scheme which nevertheless contains a number of nonrhymes and off rhymes. Look for a moment at the rhyme scheme. In stanza one "Erect" rhymes with "neglect," "rock" (believe it or not) rhymes with "top" and "up" (as one can tell from the other stanzas—"grown," "alone" and "gone," for instance, in stanza two), and "grapples," line five, rhymes with "apples," line nine. This odd pattern is maintained throughout. I think it is meant to express, in its odd combination of irregularity and uniformity, the ideas of "Chaos contracted/To intricate form" of stanza four. I think it is a clever and successful technical device. The play of feminine versus masculine endings in the poem is also worth looking at. There is no regularity among the unrhymed lines in this regard, but all the rhyme words have masculine endings except the rhyme words of lines five and nine in each stanza: grapples-apples, steading-spreading, dingles-mingles, enacted-contracted, transmitter-bitter. So the form really is fairly "intricate," though there's also plenty of "thrust" and "storm" in the rhythm and sound of the poem.

On first reading the poem, however, I fear one gets the idea of a tall thin tree, not a "great tree of Erin," a "forest tree spreading," and I think that this is because the meter expresses tallness and thinness. If one wants to suggest spreading limbs one has to use a wider line

> O chestnut-tree, great-rooted blossomer,
> Are you the leaf, the blossom, or the bole?
>
> (Yeats, *Variorum Poems*, p. 446)

or even

Under the spreading chestnut tree the village smithy stands.

The content of stanza two then wars a bit with the meter, but the meter is perfect for the content of stanza one where

> The twisted root grapples
> For sap with the rock.

None of the poems I have treated above is particularly effective in conveying the sense of a powerful personality speaking. But in "Ringsend," the poem of Gogarty's which I like best, that personality is in and behind the poem. By including this poem among those from Gogarty in *The Oxford Book of Modern Verse* Yeats ensured that his selection would be superior to any, like that in *The Oxford Book of Irish Verse*, which excluded it.[2] I shall not analyze it, but I must quote it.

RINGSEND
(After reading Tolstoi)

I will live in Ringsend
With a red-headed whore,
And the fan-light gone in
Where it lights the hall-door;
And listen each night
For her querulous shout,
As at last she streels in
And the pubs empty out.

To soothe that wild beast
With my old-fangled songs,
Till she feels it redressed
From inordinate wrongs,
Imagined, outrageous,
Preposterous wrongs,
Till peace at last comes,

Shall be all I will do,
Where the little lamp blooms
Like a rose in the stew;
And up the back-garden
The sound comes to me
Of the lapsing, unsoilable,
Whispering sea.

(Gogarty, *Collected Poems,* p. 102)

This is a very beautiful poem indeed and, for once, worthy of "one of the great lyric poets of our age."

SEUMAS O'SULLIVAN

Some Poems

Oliver Gogarty was given twelve pages of Yeats's *Oxford Book of Modern Verse,* a slice equal to T. S. Eliot's. Louis MacNeice got eight pages, W. H. Auden four, Thomas Hardy three and one-third, Gerard Manley Hopkins seven. Seumas O'Sullivan has the distinction of having been left out entirely. He may have been rejected as one of those "fleas" which that "wild dog," Yeats, refused to praise.[1] O'Sullivan is of course the pen name of James Sullivan Starkey, founder of *The Dublin Magazine* and its editor for thirty-five years. His first published poems appeared in 1904 in *New Songs,* a collection by poets in Æ's circle. In 1922 Ernest Boyd thought O'Sullivan's *Poems* (1912) "one of the finest books of contemporary Anglo-Irish verse" (Boyd, *Ireland's Literary Renaissance,* p. 259). Today his poetry is usually neglected, although he was a fine technician and a person of rarely sensitive and delicate perceptions. One can see from "The Others," which is too long to quote in full, how O'Sullivan would have been overshadowed by Yeats, who had done this same sort of thing very early.

> From our hidden places
> By a secret path,
> We troop in the moonlight
> To the edge of the green rath.
>
> There the night through
> We take our pleasure,
> Dancing to such a measure
> As earth never knew.
> (O'Sullivan, *Collected Poems,* p. 126)

Yeats's fairy poems (such as "The Host of the Air"), while more vivid and energetic, are not more sensitive and delicate than, in their melancholy way, are Seumas O'Sullivan's. Here is a stanza which seems un-Yeatsean, yet which shows an excellent ear for speech and excellent technical skill in adapting speech to the requirements of stanza and meter.

> Music so forest wild
> And piercing sweet, would bring
> Silence on blackbirds singing
> Their best in the ear of Spring.
> (O'Sullivan, *Collected Poems*, p. 127)

The early poems were about *The Twilight People* (1905). Later poems were about city life, a subject which Yeats and most other poets of the Irish Renaissance avoided. "Nelson Street," with great control and lack of overemphasis, gives a realistic report of a Monday morning scene and mood. One can see that Yeats would have disliked O'Sullivan's early poems because they seemed to trespass on the ground which he had staked out himself and then abandoned for "passionate masterful personality" (*Oxford Book of Modern Verse*, p. xiv). One can see that he would not have liked "Nelson Street" either. It is too honest and unheroic. The speaker has no Yeatsean mask. If he had a mask once, he has no doubt lost it over the weekend. He is facing life as late as possible in the morning with no mask at all to protect him from the perception that it is Monday again.

> There is hardly a mouthful of air
> In the room where the breakfast is set,
> For the blind is still down tho' it's late,
> And the curtains are redolent yet
> Of tobacco smoke, stale from last night.
> There's the little bronze teapot, and there
> The rashers and eggs on the plate,
> And the sleepy canary, a hen,
> Starts faintly her chirruping tweet,
> And I know could she speak she would say:
> "Hullo there—what's wrong with the light?
> Draw the blind up, let's look at the day."
> I see that it's Monday again,

For the man with the organ is there;
Every Monday he comes to the street
(Lest I, or the bird there, should miss
Our count of monotonous days)
With his reed-organ, wheezy and sweet,
And stands by the window and plays
"There's a Land that is Fairer than This."

(O'Sullivan, *Collected Poems*, p. 83)

The poem actually reminds one very much of Eliot's "Preludes," except that the latter is much more experimental in form and more violent in its aversion to the scene:

The morning comes to consciousness
Of faint stale smells of beer
From the sawdust-trampled street
With all its muddy feet that press
To early coffee-stands.
With the other masquerades
That time resumes,
One thinks of all the hands
That are raising dingy shades
In a thousand furnished rooms.

(Eliot, *Complete Poems*, p. 12)

Cutting out the two lines about the "masquerades . . . That time resumes," Yeats commented on this passage as representative of Eliot's first book: "No romantic word or sound. . . . Poetry must resemble prose, and both must accept the vocabulary of their time; nor must there be any special subject-matter. Tristram and Isoult were not a more suitable theme than Paddington Railway Station. The past had deceived us: let us accept the worthless present. . . . We older writers disliked this new poetry, but were forced to admit its satiric intensity" (Yeats, *Essays,* p. 499).

There is no satiric intensity in "Nelson Street," and there is a romantic lift (complicated by melancholy humor) at the end when the man with the organ plays "There's a Land that is Fairer than This." But one could not expect Yeats to include beside the heroic Senator Gogarty—who when captured tricked his enemies, "plunged under a shower of revolver bullets and . . . swam the ice-cold December" Liffey to escape them (*Oxford Book of Modern Verse*, p. xv)—this unheroic figure who cannot really face even Monday morning.

In "Nelson Street" there is a remarkable balance between pleasant and unpleasant images.

> There is hardly a mouthful of air
> In the room. . . .

Yet there's a nice breakfast waiting:

> . . . the little bronze teapot, and there
> The rashers and eggs on a plate.

There's stale tobacco smoke in the atmosphere, yet the word used is a pleasant one: "redolent." He and perhaps his friends had a good time making that smoke. The reed-organ is "wheezy and sweet." The speaker's remark about "monotonous days" and his insistence that there must be "a Land that is Fairer than This" are melancholy enough, yet it is the bird's attitude, indulged, not shared, by the speaker, which is given a voice:

> 'Hullo there—what's wrong with the light?
> Draw the blind up, let's look at the day.'

There is a double perspective in the poem. The little room is obviously very dear to the speaker, yet he yearns for something that a man, and not a canary, can desire. "Passive suffering is not a theme for poetry," said Yeats, after Matthew Arnold (*Oxford Book of Modern Verse*, p. xxxiv), yet passive suffering, relieved by comic self-criticism, furnishes both the tone and theme of "Nelson Street" and of enough of the rest of O'Sullivan to have persuaded Yeats to keep him out of his anthology. Yet "Nelson Street" is a good poem, rather a unique poem, unpretentious yet deep in its expression of love and of melancholy unrest.

> BIRDS
> Truly these women are like birds; they take
> Their pleasures delicately; now they stand

Upon the pavement with a foot upraised,
Nestling an ankled softness. Now launch out
Across the crowded street, scarce touching it,
Like water-hens across the sedgy lake,
Or stand in sunlight preening, like a bird
Above still water, or, when rain looms dark,
Crowd into some tall doorway wing by wing,
Like peacocks under yew trees in the Park,
Delicate and delightful and absurd,
Then venture forth again. Upgathering
Feather-like frills, they step demure as nuns,
Nor heed the menacing eyes on every side,
Dead set unceasingly like levelled guns,
Truly I think each women is a bird.

(O'Sullivan, *Collected Poems,* pp. 188–89)

The subject of "Birds," how women look to men, is perpetually interesting to men as well as women—and the bird imagery captures the fact that women seem to men "Delicate and delightful and absurd"!

. . . they take
Their pleasures delicately; now they stand
Upon the pavement with a foot upraised,
Nestling an ankled softness.

A wonderful line, that last one, though I don't completely get the picture. I get it as far as the bird is concerned—a water bird, a heron say, often stands with one foot up. But is the woman holding her ankle for a moment, or just nesting one ankle against the other?

The men are in the poem too, a perpetual source of attention leveled at the women, who demurely carry on regardless.

Nor heed the menacing eyes on every side,
Dead set unceasingly like levelled guns. . . .

The hunters!
The aspect of woman presented here is no doubt woman in that quintessential pursuit, the shopping expedition. They are taking

their "pleasures," so I gather that their activity has nothing to do with men, who are for women in a male dominated society a *duty* for the most part, and thus an inhibition on full enjoyment! These women are free, for the afternoon at least, taking their pleasures delicately . . . standing, nestling, launching, standing again, crowding, upgathering, nor heeding the menacing eyes. The words work well for both women and birds. One can almost hear the momentary flutter of wings in that

> Upgathering
> Feather-like frills.

The poem makes no strong assertion; the poet notes the way women appear, and obviously loves them, but does not like Yeats rather egotistically, and naively, chant

> May God be praised for woman
> That gives up all her mind.
> (Yeats, *Variorum Poems,* p. 345)

Yeats had obviously never accompanied a woman on a shopping expedition if he thought she gave up all her mind to him! O'Sullivan tries to see what women are like in themselves, not in relation to his own driving ego. The refusal to involve that ego perhaps limits the poem. The protagonist, or antiprotagonist, is again the consciousness which was too polite and unassertive to tell Monday morning, in the poem "Nelson Street," what he really thought of it—and anyway did not completely think. We cannot therefore have the involvement which could create both the objective picture and the subjective history and then go on to assimilate these to a total understanding of life as is done in W. B. Yeats's "In Memory of Eva Gore-Booth and Con Markiewicz."

> Two girls in silk kimonos, both
> Beautiful, one a gazelle.
> But a raving autumn shears
> Blossom from the summer's wreath. . . .
> Dear shadows, now you know it all,
> All the folly of a fight
> With a common wrong or right.

> The innocent and the beautiful
> Have no enemy but time. . . .
>
> (Yeats, *Variorum Poems,* pp. 475–76)

Generalizations of this level soar high above

> Truly I think each woman is a bird,

showing O'Sullivan in his limitations. But the deliberate acceptance of these limitations creates a personality of a sort, a negative personality, not heroic, but one which is hauntingly attractive.

"Birds" reminds me of a passage in *The Odyssey.* It is the simile used when Telemachus, at Odysseus' command, hangs all the girls who had slept with the suitors during Odysseus' absence. Homer allows us to feel all the beauty and soft delicacy of these unfortunate and helpless offenders. They are, he says, like birds caught in the fowler's snare. As they are drawn up by the ropes, they struggle, but not for long. There's a certain amount of very refined sexual pleasure, I think, in this contemplation of the death of beautiful creatures in the Homeric passage—it is a very affecting passage. The same elements are here in O'Sullivan's poem. Though the women pay no attention at the moment, the threatening, desiring eyes are leveled at them. Love and death are closely related themes. "For each man kills the thing he loves," as Wilde wrote.

It is interesting that the poem begins in the plural and ends in the singular, begins with analogy and ends with identity: from "Truly these women are like birds" to "Truly I think *each* woman *is* a bird." The leveled guns of the male eyes are singling the women out, getting ready to shoot.

The tone is gently humorous but the content of the last lines has under the surface humor a certain amount of melancholy and even of the sinister.

> THE SHEEP
> Slowly they pass
> In the grey of the evening
> Over the wet road,
> A flock of sheep.

Slowly they wend
In the grey of the gloaming
Over the wet road
That winds through the town.
Slowly they pass,
And gleaming whitely
Vanish away
In the grey of the evening.
Ah, what memories
Loom for a moment,
Gleam for a moment,
And vanish away,
Of the white days
When we two together
Went in the evening
Where the sheep lay,
We two together,
Went with slow feet
In the grey of the evening,
Where the sheep lay.

Whitely they gleam
For a moment, and vanish
Away in the dimness
Of sorrowful years,
Gleam for a moment,
All white, and go fading
Away in the greyness
Of sundering years.
(O'Sullivan, *Collected Poems,* pp. 18–19)

O'Sullivan's "The Sheep," again, is a poem which is perfectly beautiful within the limitations of its range. The sheep passing along the wet road at evening become an emblem of events passing along the road of life and disappearing in time. The repetitions lull the mind to accepting this one wistful melancholy mood. This is O'Sullivan's equivalent of W. B. Yeats's "The Wild Swans at Coole." The dumb acceptance of sorrow is beautifully expressed by O'Sullivan's image of the sheep. But

sheep are a pretty tame lot. When Yeats treats the same subject
of the passing of time, the swiftly passing years become like
wild swans flying away before one can count them:

> I saw, before I had well finished,
> All suddenly mount
> And scatter wheeling in great broken rings
> Upon their clamorous wings.

The swans which remind Yeats of his youth are wild, "brilliant
creatures"; "Passion or conquest wander where they will,/At-
tend upon them still." Moreover the poem is not finally melancholy about the future, even though the poet's own death is
anticipated:

> Among what rushes will they build,
> By what lake's edge or pool
> Delight men's eyes when I awake some day
> To find they have flown away?
>
> (Yeats, *Variorum Poems,* pp. 322–23)

Passive suffering is not a theme for Yeats's poetry, though it is
for O'Sullivan's. Passion and conquest do not attend upon sheep.
Sheep have no control over the road they take, as winged creatures do. Even the varying rhythms of Yeats's poem, contrasting
with the deliberate monotony of O'Sullivan's, show the difference of range. But not all of us are world-beaters, though we
would not want to wallow in self-pity all the time, and when
the melancholy fit shall fall, O'Sullivan's expression of it here
is perfectly beautiful.

JOSEPH CAMPBELL

'The Dancer'

In discussing "Anglo-Irish Ballads" in the introduction to a
series of *Broadsides* issued in 1935, F. R. Higgins and W. B.
Yeats tell how, whatever their source, "these ballads, generally
in the towns, always in the country cottages, are sung to Irish
music, their rhythm modified, sometimes enriched, by the new
notes. . . ." Some of the ballads may have been danced, for
(Yeats and Higgins note) "one of the present writers saw at
Rosses Point, county Sligo, a man dance a ballad called 'The
Rocky Road to Dublin.' . . . The dancer at Rosses Point used
his whole body; he went by steamer, swayed his body as the
steamer tossed on the waves, came at last to the rocky road,
wherever that is, moved his feet as if climbing over great rocks."
But, they write, this dance was in contrast to "the Gaelic dance,
no expression, no movement above the waist, the Gaelic dance
as we know it. . . ." And they quote from Joseph Campbell's
"The Dancer" for illustration (Yeats, *Broadsides*, pp. ix–xii).
Campbell saw his dancer in Clare (Campbell, *Irishry*, p. vii).

THE DANCER
The tall dancer dances
With slowly taken breath:
In his feet music,
And on his face death.

His face is a mask,
It is so still and white:
His withered eyes shut,
Unmindful of light.

The old fiddler fiddles
The merry *'Silver Tip'*
With softly beating foot
And laughing eye and lip.

And round the dark walls
The people sit and stand,
Praising the art
Of the dancer of the land.

But he dances there
As if his kin were dead:
Clay in his thoughts,
And lightning in his tread!

(Campbell, *Irishry,* p. 10)

The poem is a description, but is it the description of a particular dance and dancer or of a type of dance? The poem has been
quoted to illustrate the traditional Gaelic dance, "no expression,
no movement above the waist," but we cannot, at the same
time, avoid seeing individual tragedy in the figure of the dancer.

I think the strength of this poem, and it is very effective indeed, comes not only from the marvelous handling of the
rhythm, but also from the way in which the individual and the
type are fused. This fusion would be impossible if the dance
were one which demanded animation of the dancer's face and of
his entire body. Consider the happily foolish grimaces of the
popular tap dancers in the motion pictures. The dance in the
poem is different. The music is merry. "The old fiddler fiddles"
with "laughing eye and lip," but the dancer must dance with no
expression and no movement above the waist. The proper effect
of such a dance is that all the dancer's vitality of mind as well
as of body seems to be poured into his legs and feet. He ceases
to live, so to speak, except in his feet. And his surroundings
seem to cease to exist for him. He is the center of attention yet
looks completely oblivious, eyes closed, face still. Any individual dancer would have to dance this type of dance in this way.
The supreme dancer, "the dancer of the land," would most successfully express the contrast which is the essence of the dance.
His face and torso would be the most corpse-like, and clay-like,
of all the dancers, while his feet would reach a vitality of existence seemingly beyond possibility for mere flesh and bone—
there would be "lightning in his tread!"

The tall dancer is "the dancer of the land." This means not

only that he is the best dancer but that his is a traditional dance which expresses aspects of the life of this people, or of all life—suffering and death on the one hand and passionate vitality on the other. But the on-lookers are not consciously thinking of the wider implications of their favorite art form. It is technical accomplishment which they are there to admire and take pride in, in their dancer: "Praising the art/Of the dancer of the land." It is not that they don't understand the dance. They do. But really great accomplishment in art takes the expression beyond what the group as a group can admire. The dance becomes an individual experience rising out of group experience. The exciting contrast of motionlessness above the waist with swift and intricate and expert motion below rises, in a supreme performance, into the expression of individual tragedy.

I don't use the word tragedy carelessly. A necessary element of tragedy is that the protagonist to whom the catastrophe happens should put up a great battle. The poem would be pathetic, rather than tragic, if it presented a dancer who seemed like a man unable to dance because of his great sufferings. This poem presents a dancer who seems to dance supremely in the midst of sufferings—in spite of suffering, even because of suffering.

> . . . He dances there
> As if his kin were dead

works for both the upper part of his body and the lower:

> Clay in his thoughts
> And lightning in his tread!

It works for the upper part of his body in that his face looks utterly lifeless as if from the shock of bereavement, "As if his kin were dead." It works for the lower part of his body in that his feet, in their violent motion, express the agony of grief. He dances wildly and desperately, "As if his kin were dead." This poise of action and passion is of the essence of tragedy. The great dancer's art rises to tragic expression.

The greatest art is always a bit beyond the audience. The listeners in Wallace Stevens' poem "The Man with the Blue Guitar" (also a poem about the artist) ask the player of the guitar for "A tune beyond us, yet ourselves" (Stevens, *Collected Poems*, p. 165). The tall dancer seems oblivious of the approval or nonapproval of the audience. He dances beyond the audience for the dance alone, and seems to lose all thought, of suffering and of everything else, in the movements of his feet. He dances as if *his* kin were dead. *His* kin not theirs. He dances as if he were alone in the world, as if the dance were a completely private affair. Yet the irony is that he's *supposed* to dance as if his kin were dead. This is not a case of "the bitter smile beneath the painted grin," of "laugh, clown laugh," of an artist alien and suffering in a noncomprehending society, forced to go through his act in spite of unhappiness. The dancer of the land, performing a traditional dance, reaches the height of his art when the traditional pose and motions seem to rise out of individual bereavement, when he seems to dance as if, out of all the people there, his kin alone were dead and he chilled yet frantic with sorrow.

As in tragedy, this representation causes pleasure to the audience. The people praise his art, the old fiddler fiddles with laughing eye and lip. There's an expression here of tragic zest, tragic ecstasy in the lightning tread of the dancer, the merriness of the music and the pleasure of the spectators.

One might even say that the juxtaposition of the dancer's energy with his cold death-like expression suggests the effect of tragic catharsis. However, the energy does not come to an end in "calm of mind all passion spent." The tension between death and activity continues to the end of the poem. Nor is there any cathartic experience for the audience who, at least so far as we, perhaps they, can tell, are merely admiring skill. That is all the poem tells us they are doing.

Turning now from the poem as a type of dance, let us look at it as a representation of a particular man doing a particular dance on a particular night. What do we know of this dancer as an individual which would support the idea that a personal tragedy is the subject of the poem? The dancer is tall; his face is white. Stanza one tells us that he has a look of death on his face. Is he pale with melancholy, or is he unwell, a doomed man? Or is this the pallor of one who, being a dancer, has to be out nights and sees little of the sun? In this country setting, probably not. The light after all is upon him, making his face look white. His eyes are shut against it. Meanwhile it is dark around the walls where the people are. His eyes are withered. He is probably not an old man; yet the withered eyes tell us that he is not a young man. He is perhaps prematurely aged. Or does he seem so merely in contrast to the old fiddler who does not have death on his face? We do not know. His face is a mask, and this is all that we can say about the dancer as a man. "How can we know the dancer from the dance?" I don't think we can in this poem. The poem doesn't say that his kin are dead; it says that he dances as if they were. The next to the last line is ambiguous. Is there really clay in his thoughts, or is he merely dancing as if there were? And does clay in his thoughts mean that he is thinking of death—clay as a symbol of death—or does it mean that his thoughts move slowly, almost do not move at all, in contrast to his feet? There is, figuratively speaking, lightning in his tread, but that does not help us with the ambiguity of "clay in his thoughts." We cannot tell from the poem whether the dancer really has any personal sorrow, or whether he is simply an outstanding dancer.

We are left with a fairly objective picture. His face *is* a mask. We know nothing of what goes on inside. We know only that this is a performance of a traditional dance, a superlative performance in which the effect created is like that of a man who dances "as if his kin were dead."

The poem is told in the third person and from the point of view of an observer who is objective, yet sensitive and perceptive. The same point of view regards "The old fiddler fiddling" and the people sitting and standing round the dark walls. The observer confines himself to objectively noted details and to "As if" (the dancer dances "As if his kin were dead), and this is as far as the observer will go in interpretation. He does not know what goes on behind the mask any more than we.

Does the speaker of the poem see more than does the old fiddler or than do the people standing and sitting around the walls? Do they see that the dancer's face is white as death and that he dances as if his kin were dead? Such a scene, even if one knew that it were only an effect of the dance, would hardly produce the reaction of the fiddler, his laughing eye and lip. But we can't judge him because he is the music, and some of the dancer's effect (in the poem, that is, not in the actual dance form) depends on the contrast with the merry old fiddler. His softly beating foot and merry fiddle go inevitably on with the tune to which the tall doom-faced man dances.

The people praise the art of the dancer. Does the art include looking as if his kin were dead, and if so do they notice that look? One cannot say for sure.

In short it is impossible to know whether the very strong impression that the dancer is wrapped up in thoughts of the grave and is utterly oblivious of his audience as he performs so magnificently is *the truth about the dancer* or *the appropriate effect of the dance.* We can't help feeling that the personal tragedy of the dancer is the subject. But perhaps that is the poet's way of involving us in the scene too. If we knew whether the dancer really did or did not have reason to dance as if his kin were dead, we would cease to be witnesses of the dance alone; our interest would shift to biography. As it is we are in the dark with the other spectators, watching the light on that still face and those lightning-like feet and left free to imagine whatever we will.

THOMAS KINSELLA

'Downstream'

Drifting to meet us on the darkening stage
A pattern shivered; whorling in its place
Another held us in a living cage
Then broke to its reordered phase of grace.

Again in the mirrored night—a liquid mask—
   We sank our oars, bowing both in team;
   The ripples scattered, dying, to their task

Under ghost alders stooped above the seam
   Of calm and current, mowing like the blind.
   We gave our frail craft to the hungry stream,

Grazing the near reeds, letting the banks unwind
   In stealth on either hand. The Wood's dark door
   Opened and shut; the clean sky fell behind;

The channel shrank. Thick slopes from shore to shore
   Lowered a matted arch and moved out roots,
   Full of slant pike, over the river-floor;

The black cage closed about us. Furred night-brutes
   Stopped in the rat-trails, twitching their tiny brushes,
   Or plopped in the reeds, astir between the shoots.

Then I remembered how among those bushes
   A man one night fell sick and left his shell
   Collapsed, half-eaten, like a rotted thrush's

To frighten stumbling children. "You could tell,"
   My co-shadow murmured, "by the hands
   He died in trouble." Then the cold of hell,

A limb-lightness, a terror in the glands,
   Pierced again as when that story first
   Froze my blood: the soil of other lands

Drank lives that summer with a body thirst,
    While nerveless by the European pit
    —Ourselves through seven hundred years accurst—

We gazed on barren earth obscurely lit
    By tall chimneys flickering in their pall,
    The haunt of swinish man—each day a spit

That, turning, sweated war, each night a fall
    Back to the evil dream where rodents ply,
    Man-rumped, sow-headed, busy with whip and maul,

Among nude herds of the damned. It seemed that I,
    Coming to conscience on that lip of dread,
    Still dreamed, impervious to calamity,

Imagining a formal drift of the dead
    Stretched calm as effigies on velvet dust,
    Scattered on starlit slopes with arms outspread

And eyes of silver—when that story thrust
    Pungent horror and an actual mess
    Into my very face, and taste I must!

Then hungry joy and sickening distress
    Met in union by the brimming flood
    And Night devoured a hopeless loneliness . . .

Like mortal jaws, the alleys of the wood
    Fell-to behind us, caged upon a ghost
    That glimmered, hidden, with my gift of blood,

Spreadeagled on a rack of leaves, almost
    Remembering. It searched among the skies,
    Calmly encountering the starry host,

Meeting their silver eyes with silver eyes
    —An X of wavering flesh, a skull of light
    That dimmed in our wake and guttered to a close.

Then the current, pausing in its flight,
    Swerved on pliant muscle; we were sped
    Through sudden calm into a pit of night:

The Mill-Hole, whose rocky fathoms fed
    On moss and pure depth and the cold fin
    Turning in its heart. The river bed

Called to our flesh from under the watery skin
    And, breathless, our shell trembling across the abyss,
    We shipped our oars in dread. Now, deeper in,

Sheathed in obscurity, a quiet hiss
    Fluttered against the rock, a folded crest
    Shifted in sleep, betraying with feathered kiss

A soul of white with darkness for a nest;
    Some creature wore the night so tranquilly
    I lifted up my eyes. There without rest

The phantoms of the overhanging sky
    Occupied their stations and descended;
    But, for an instant, to the starlit eye,

The slow, downstreaming dead, it seemed, were blended
    One with those silver hordes, and briefly shared
    Their order, glittering. And then impended

A barrier of rock that turned and bared
    A varied barrenness as toward its base
    We glided—blotting heaven as it towered—

Searching the darkness for a landing place.
                    (Kinsella, "Downstream")[1]

This poem is a description of a trip downstream by boat at night. There are two men together. The stream winds into a thick woods where the trees shut off the view of the sky and the channel narrows. The noise of animals in the rat trails alongside the stream reminds the speaker "how among those bushes/ A man one night fell sick" and died, and his gnawed and rotted body frightened children who stumbled upon it. Being at the very spot, this woods, makes the speaker relive the thrill of fear and distress which the incident first made him feel.

It was during World War II that the incident occurred; "the soil of other lands/Drank lives that summer with a body thirst."

But the war—and death—were not fully real to the speaker, an Irishman (Ireland remained neutral throughout the war) and very young at the time (Thomas Kinsella was only sixteen when the war ended). The Irish had been through seven hundred years accurst—the seven hundred years of English rule. Free since 1922 and unwilling to endanger her shores by siding with her former oppressor, the little country perched on the edge of Europe watched the conflict with an objectivity, if not a detachment, unavailable to the participants.

> While nerveless by the European pit
>
>   ·   ·   ·   ·   ·   ·   ·
>
> We gazed on barren earth obscurely lit
>   By tall chimneys flickering in their pall,
>   The haunt of swinish man—each day a spit
>
> That, turning, sweated war, each night a fall
>   Back to the evil dream where rodents ply,
>   Man-rumped, sow-headed, busy with whip and maul,
>
> Among nude herds of the damned. . . .

"The European pit" suggests sitting on the edge of a pit watching rats fighting at the bottom of it. I suppose the "tall chimneys" refer to factories in regions like the English Midlands, frantically (and in some cases greedily) turning out war products. In the lines which follow, the image of rats in a pit merges with the image of rat-shaped demons punishing man. The picture evoked is worthy of Dante's *Inferno*, and one should note that the rhyme scheme of "Downstream" is the *terza rima* made famous in Dante's poem. Since the poet speaks of "swinish man" and the rodent-demons are "man-rumped," "sow-headed," it would seem that the concept is that of the brutishness of men being punished by the brutishness of other men in war.

The boy knew that soldiers were dying everywhere, but his thought of death was still an immature one. He had vaguely accepted death as the customary thing that happens to old people and to soldiers. Death as he had conceived it was distanced by a formal funereal quality which protected his young emotions.

> It seemed that I,
> Coming to conscience on that lip of dread,
> Still dreamed, impervious to calamity,
>
> Imagining a formal drift of the dead
> Stretched calm as effigies on velvet dust,
> Scattered on starlit slopes with arms outspread
>
> And eyes of silver. . . .

The "formal drift" of the dead (Down the river of time, one supposes) suggests a funereal procession; "effigies" suggests tombs; and "velvet dust" suggests the lining of coffins. So that death to this young boy was not a raw fact. He was shielded from the thought of it by all the traditional trappings with which society wraps death to make it bearable. But suddenly the incident of the man dying in this woods and being half-eaten by rats forced the raw fact of death into the boy's consciousness.

> . . . that story thrust
> Pungent horror and an actual mess
> Into my very face, and taste I must!

The next three lines give us the effect on the boy of this coming, in war time, to a vivid consciousness of the reality of death. These lines are powerful but puzzling, and tantalizingly brief.

> Then hungry joy and sickening distress
> Met in union by the brimming flood
> And Night devoured a hopeless loneliness. . . .

First of all the lines present the boy's vicarious reliving of the event of the man's death. "Hungry joy" would apply quite literally to the appetite of the rats, and "sickening distress" to the condition of the dying man. This appetite and this condition did meet in union by the "brimming flood" of the river. The stricken man no doubt felt a "hopeless loneliness" which ended as that night of his death passed: "And Night devoured a hopeless loneliness." . . . The word "devoured" would apply literally as well as metaphorically since the body was found "half-eaten."

But this stanza does not present merely the reenactment of the man's death in the boy's mind, or even the boy's vicarious reliving of that death as if it were his own. It presents as well the consequence, the effect which this experience had on the boy, his reaction to it. Thus the "sickening distress" is not only the stricken man's illness but also the boy's fear, disgust and pity on hearing the story. His "hungry joy" is more difficult to account for. The awareness of death, for a youth, may, however, be an initiation into life. This death is real; the youth is at last living real life. This horror is not the conventional death which his elders have told the youth about or which he has had to face only when protected by the formality of funerals. The direct facing of death may make life more vivid, more immediate, more genuine, and may give a tremendous impetus which might be described as a "hungry joy." The phrase "brimming flood" suggests life at the full. The hungry joy, then, is a hunger for vivid life and the expectation of having found it. The horror of death and the hunger for life (which hunger, since it is a hunger for the passage of time, is in some sense a hunger for death) meet "in union by the brimming flood" of the boy's emotional growth.

"And Night devoured a hopeless loneliness" intensely conveys both the boy's identification with the dying man and the boy's own fear of death—perhaps with the added sense that it took a whole night for him to master the feeling which the story aroused in him. But also the line seems to say that the feeling was mastered, that the awesome finality of universal death, perhaps symbolized by the capitalized "Night," overwhelmed his sense of personal loneliness and fear and freed him of it.

At any rate, in the next lines the boat has passed out of the wood where the man died and the speaker's emotion subsides, but he still recalls the body as if it were lying there, its eyes reflecting the stars.

> Like mortal jaws, the alleys of the wood
>> Fell-to behind us, caged upon a ghost
>> That glimmered, hidden, with my gift of blood,
> Spreadeagled on a rack of leaves, almost
>> Remembering. It searched among the skies,
>> Calmly encountering the starry host,
> Meeting their silver eyes with silver eyes
>> —An X of wavering flesh, a skull of light
>> That dimmed in our wake and guttered to a close.

The "distress" of the man who "died in trouble" is over with his life. As the poet passes out of the woods where the death occurred, he sees in his mind's eye the dead man lying there, his eyes "Calmly encountering the starry host," and now that the death agony is over the dead man seems to reach that acceptance and reconciliation which was less realistically imagined in the boy's earlier immature dream in which the dead were "Scattered on starlit slopes with arms outspread/And eyes of silver. . . ." The agony over, the dead man seems once again united with some kind of cosmic order. His dead eyes regard the stars calmly, "Meeting their silver eyes with silver eyes."

But what about those who are still alive? The next lines provide an image of a live surface trembling over an abyss to suggest the sense of danger and death which possesses the speaker. The dead are reconciled, the living tremble. The images suggest life above death.

> Then the current, pausing in its flight,
>> Swerved on pliant muscle; we were sped
>> Through sudden calm into a pit of night:
>
> The Mill-Hole, whose rocky fathoms fed
>> On moss and pure depth and the cold fin
>> Turning in its heart. The river bed
>
> Called to our flesh from under the watery skin
>> And, breathless, our shell trembling across the abyss,
>> We shipped our oars in dread.

The phrase "our shell trembling across the abyss" gives the sense of life against death—"shell" can be taken as the boat itself or as a reference to the bodies of the speaker and his companion. (The word has been used earlier: "A man one night fell sick and left his shell/Collapsed, half-eaten, like a rotted thrush's/To frighten stumbling children.") The river bed, in this deep spot, seems hungry to swallow them. However, their fear is not of the death agony, the fear of dying; it is rather the fear of death itself—the abyss of infinite darkness which one imagines to ensue after the process of dying. We have moved from an evocation of the dying man's agony, through a presentation of the way the calm after death seems to reconcile his pain with cosmic order, to this contemplation of the abyss of death—symbolized by the "Mill-Hole"—from the point of view of the living.

But within this "depth" of death there is life. The images of a fish, "the cold fin/Turning in its heart"—and of a swan, "a quiet hiss . . . a folded crest," are evoked. The "cold fin" sounds ominous, perhaps partly by association with the phrase "cold fear." The swan, on the other hand is made into an image of hope: "A soul of white with darkness for a nest." Utter blackness turns out to be a "nest" for utter whiteness. Devil and God, Judas and Christ, are joined in the swan image. At the very heart of one's contemplation of death is the discovery of life. And not only of life but of life in keeping with purpose and divine order in the universe. Thus the presence of the swan somehow makes the poet look up and see the stars, their motions symbolic of that order.

> Some creature wore the night so tranquilly
> I lifted up my eyes. There without rest
>
> The phantoms of the overhanging sky
> Occupied their stations and descended. . . .

The phrase "without rest" is reminiscent of John Milton's well-known sonnet "On His Blindness" in which he reconciles himself to his inability to serve God actively because of the loss of his eyesight. [God's] "state/Is kingly: thousands at his bidding speed,/And post o'er land and ocean without rest;/

They also serve who only stand and wait" (Milton, *Poetical Works*, pp. 189–190). But the stars are not seen as angels in Milton's poem, nor as "phantoms of the overhanging sky" which occupy their stations and descend. The stars are indeed identified with the heavenly host in a much later poem, George Meredith's "Lucifer in Starlight," which may have been in the poet's mind. "On a starred night Prince Lucifer uprose" and, "Tired of his dark dominion" in Hell, soared above earth, which was, however, "Poor prey to his hot fit of pride," and flew higher, towards Heaven.

> Soaring through wider zones that pricked his scars
> With memory of the old revolt fom Awe,
> He reached a middle height, and at the stars,
> Which are the brain of heaven, he looked, and sank.
> Around the ancient track marched, rank on rank,
> The army of unalterable law.
>   (Meredith, *Poetical Works*, pp. 181–82)

Whether these are deliberate allusions or chance similarities, it seems significant that in the three poems one moves from unquestioned faith in the thousands that at God's bidding speed, through the much more secularized, scientific and deterministic conception of "the army of unalterable law," to the quite tenuous and tentative "phantoms of the overhanging sky." A phantom is something that has only an apparent existence, but it may either be completely illusory or may refer to some reality —as, say, the ghost of Hamlet's father was in some sense real enough, even though Horatio called out to it, "Stay illusion!" The use of the word "phantoms" for what has earlier in the same poem been called the "starry host" implies a connection between the stars (and the cosmic order they represent) and the dead.

> But, for an instant, to the starlit eye,

> The slow, downstreaming dead, it seemed, were blended
> One with those silver hordes, and briefly shared
> Their order, glittering.

Calling the stars "phantoms" already blends their "silver hordes" with the "downstreaming dead." It at the same time, however, underlines the tentative and provisional nature of any statement which the poem makes about the dead. "It seemed," at any rate, that, "briefly," those who die were seen by the speaker to be united to cosmic purpose. Death, then, may not be meaningless, although part of an order and a plan beyond man's comprehension.

Who are these "downstreaming dead"? All men, one supposes, especially those who were dying in the war. But since the "starlit eye" to which this brief vision appears is the speaker's own eye, and since he has spoken earlier of the eyes of the deadman, and of all the other dead, being silvered by the reflecting starlight, the speaker himself, though still alive, becomes the representative of the dead. It is he and his companion who are literally boating down the stream as all men are figuratively streaming down to death. For a moment the wheeling of the heavens seems to give order and meaning to this mortal process and to descend mercifully to man.

This vision past, we return to actuality, and the speakers approach the shore where they intend to land and to take up their active lives again. In this return there will be no vision of cosmic order to sustain them. They return to a life something like the "barren earth obscurely lit" of an earlier stanza. As they approach shore a towering rock (the mill dam?) rises before them, shutting out the symbolic stars and presenting a barren and difficult front. Such is the exterior presented by the world in which they, and we, must find a "landing place."

And then impended

A barrier of rock that turned and bared
A varied barrenness as toward its base
We glided—blotting heaven as it towered—

Searching the darkness for a landing place.

Thus far in this analysis, originally written as an introduction to exercise questions on the poem, I have deliberately omitted calling attention to certain image patterns which I wished the students to discover for themselves. These image-patterns are, however, of climactic significance in my reading of the poem. For example, there are many more images of hunger or thirst, eating or drinking in the poem than I have noted above. Even the "cold fin" turning in the heart of the Mill-Hole is potentially something to be caught and eaten. The word "mess"— as in the "actual mess" of the dead body which "that story thrust . . ./ Into my very face, and taste I must!"—may mean "meal" as well as "unpleasant mixture." The word suggests "mass." The boy's encounter with death is thus put in terms of a Eucharistic meal.

In order to underline the imagery of the Eucharist, I tried to get the students to see an implied connection between the man who died, or his corpse, and the traditional figure of the Crucified. I asked:

> What is communicated by the line, "An X of wavering flesh, a skull of light"? The "skull of light" may suggest that the dead man is for the speaker a kind of *memento mori* ("Remember that you have to die"). Skulls were frequently placed on the desks of medieval scholars and clerics to remind them constantly that their souls should be ready to meet death. But the X is puzzling. Of course, the spreadeagled body does make an X where it lies. But perhaps there is some meaning beyond the merely descriptive. Here are some uses of the letter X which the dictionary gives. See if any of them are relevant: the letter considered with regard to its shape, hence identified with a cross; in algebra, used as the symbol for an unknown or variable quantity, hence something unknown or undetermined; used to stand for a person's name when the name is unknown or to be left undetermined; in writing the name Christ, especially in abbreviations, X represents the first letter of Greek ΧΡΙϹΤΟϹ (Christos), hence it is used as an abbreviation of the syllable *Christ*.

And unless that should fail to help them see the poem as an initiation into the Lord's Supper of experience, I asked also: "Is there any special significance or allusion in these phrases: 'You could tell . . . / . . . by the hands/He died in trouble' and 'betraying with feathered kiss'?"

Eating and drinking, figuring the assimilation and transformation of experience, seem important not only in this poem but in all of Kinsella's work. There is an astonishing variety, from the "grief-chewers," the priests and acolytes of "Office for the Dead" (Kinsella, *Nightwalker,* p. 13), through the "Dog-faces in his bowels,/Bitches at his face," the scholars and critics of "Death in Ilium" (Kinsella, *Nightwalker,* p. 50), to the "human taste" in "Nightwalker" (Kinsella, *Nightwalker,* p. 69) and the "ordeal-cup" and "delicate distinct tissue" of "Phoenix Park" (Kinsella, *Nightwalker,* pp. 76, 82). The rationale is offered in the "Prologue" to *Wormwood*: "This bitter cup is offered, heaped with curses, and we must drink or die. And even though we drink we may also die, if every drop of bitterness—that rots the flesh—is not transmuted. . . . But if we drink the bitterness and can transmute it and continue, we resume in candour and doubt the only individual joy—the restored necessity to learn. Sensing a wider scope, a more penetrating harmony, we begin again in a higher innocence to grow toward the next ordeal" (Kinsella, *Nightwalker,* p. 28).

In "Downstream" the eating and drinking images seem especially related to the Eucharist as a central symbol.

Robert Frost

ROBERT FROST

'The Thatch' and 'Directive'

Of the two distantly related poems discussed here, one has received multitudinous interpretation and praise while the other is scarcely mentioned by most of the writers on Frost. "Directive" was singled out soon after its inclusion in *Steeple Bush* (1947) as "a summing up of Frost's attitude towards New England and towards existence in general" (O'Donnell, "Frost and New England," p. 711).[1] Later it was accepted as one of Frost's "greatest" and "supremely accomplished" poems (O'Donnell, "Frost at Eighty-Eight," p. 218), "the major poem of Frost's later years" (Brower, *Constellations,* p. 226).

"The Thatch," on the other hand, has been neglected by most of Frost's critics. Frost himself omitted it (and several others) from the 1946 Modern Library *Collected Poems,* and although it has been asserted that "One can hardly think of the poet without thinking of these [omitted poems]" (Mertins, *Intervals,* p. 38), most critics have not, in fact, thought of "The Thatch" when they thought of Robert Frost.[2]

I have chosen to dwell on it because it is a poem which is easy to ignore, but which if attentively read contains one of Frost's most devastatingly controlled effects. I have long thought it one of Frost's most deeply disturbing poems, and although it cannot rival "Directive" in range or complexity of either art or wisdom, it does present more vividly than any other of Frost's poems the raw hurt which love inflicts feelingly and which death later inflicts unfeelingly. This raw hurt is somewhat sealed over with philosophical acceptance by the time of "Directive," so that the scene of domestic tragedy which is at the center of many of Frost's poems, especially those which are about abandoned homes, may here be contemplated in a rather early ("The Thatch") and a late ("Directive") treatment. I shall, however, perhaps illogically, treat the more familiar poem first.

DIRECTIVE

Back out of all this now too much for us,
Back in a time made simple by the loss
Of detail, burned, dissolved, and broken off
Like graveyard marble sculpture in the weather,
There is a house that is no more a house
Upon a farm that is no more a farm
And in a town that is no more a town.
The road there, if you'll let a guide direct you
Who only has at heart your getting lost,
May seem as if it should have been a quarry—
Great monolithic knees the former town
Long since gave up pretense of keeping covered.
And there's a story in a book about it:
Besides the wear of iron wagon wheels
The ledges show lines ruled southeast-northwest,
The chisel work of an enormous Glacier
That braced his feet against the Arctic Pole.
You must not mind a certain coolness from him
Still said to haunt this side of Panther Mountain.
Nor need you mind the serial ordeal
Of being watched from forty cellar holes
As if by eye pairs out of forty firkins.
As for the woods' excitement over you
That sends light rustle rushes to their leaves,
Charge that to upstart inexperience.
Where were they all not twenty years ago?
They think too much of having shaded out
A few old pecker-fretted apple trees.
Make yourself up a cheering song of how
Someone's road home from work this once was,
Who may be just ahead of you on foot
Or creaking with a buggy load of grain.
The height of the adventure is the height
Of country where two village cultures faded
Into each other. Both of them are lost.
And if you're lost enough to find yourself
By now, pull in your ladder road behind you

And put a sign up CLOSED to all but me.
Then make yourself at home. The only field
Now left's no bigger than a harness gall.
First there's the children's house of make-believe,
Some shattered dishes underneath a pine,
The playthings in the playhouse of the children.
Weep for what little things could make them glad.
Then for the house that is no more a house,
But only a belilaced cellar hole,
Now slowly closing like a dent in dough.
This was no playhouse but a house in earnest.
Your destination and your destiny's
A brook that was the water of the house,
Cold as a spring as yet so near its source,
Too lofty and original to rage.
(We know the valley streams that when aroused
Will leave their tatters hung on barb and thorn.)
I have kept hidden in the instep arch
Of an old cedar at the waterside
A broken drinking goblet like the Grail
Under a spell so the wrong ones can't find it,
So can't get saved, as Saint Mark says they mustn't.
(I stole the goblet from the children's playhouse.)
Here are your waters and your watering place.
Drink and be whole again beyond confusion.

(Frost, *Poetry,* pp. 377–79)[3]

There is no easily identifiable location for "Directive," but every nonurban New Englander will probably feel free to associate the poem with a particular spot.[4] I associate it with a scene from my own place of residence, Amherst, Massachusetts, which is much less rural than the New Hampshire and Vermont scenes which Frost usually wrote about, but which is still New England and which, moreover, is associated with Frost, who was once a teacher at Amherst College and who later returned annually to lecture and to talk with students. Frost's appreciation of the outskirts of Amherst may be seen in his comments on nearby Pelham. Pelham

is the kind of town I should have wanted to magnify anyway . . . just one high old street along a ridge, not much
to begin with and every year beautifully less. The railroads
have worked modern magic against it from away off in
the valleys and the woods have pressed in upon it until
now there is nothing left but the church . . . a few houses
. . . and here and there a good mowing field of about the
size of a tea-tray in the sky. (Frost, "Burroughs," p. 11;
quoted by Nitchie, *Human Values,* p. 120)

I live near the northeastern edge of Amherst. Until very
recently there have been very few houses beyond mine before
one comes to woods which surround the reservoir for the town
water supply. It is a nice place to walk, and in fine weather I
have strolled there. Right around the reservoir the trees are
white pine planted not many years ago and there is newness
also in the dam which created the reservoir and in the traces of
bulldozers and other mechanical equipment used on the gravel
road. But a little further from the reservoir the woods become
high and dense and full of hardwoods which are of quite respect-
able age. The general effect is of wilderness interrupted very
recently by the present generation in their search for water.
In my repeated walks down a particular road, however, I was
struck by the presence of a large catalpa tree. It struck me as
odd that way out there in the woods there should be a big old
catalpa—usually only a cultivated tree this far north. Later came
the realization that there was a whole long line of these trees,
which I had not at first noticed because of the younger growth
around them. They had not grown there haphazardly but were
arranged at exact intervals and in an exact straight line. Suddenly I realized that I was walking down a principal street of an
old village, that all the few gigantic old deciduous trees were
related to the layout of ancient dwellingplaces and that younger
trees had grown up over what had been lawn and pasture, the
open spaces between the dwellings. You can imagine the con-
striction of the heart as I realized that I was in the midst of
an ancient settlement now almost completely obliterated. I
realized then the significance of a small ancient cemetery not

far up that road—a cemetery no longer used, although someone takes care of it. And I poked into the woods far enough to
see the outlines of the foundations of former houses. The huge
trees still stretched their shading arms over and through the
younger growth. Except for that, however, one never would
have noticed that there had been houses there.

I do not pretend that this private reminiscence helps at all
with the poem. It is just testimony that the experience Frost
is talking about is easy to have in New England. Perhaps the
reader has had it.

> Back out of all this now too much for us.[5]

In "Directive" the poet takes the reader up into hills where
the ruins of two abandoned towns may still be seen. The journey, then, is a journey back in time.[6] We are reminded of the
wear on the rocky road of iron wagon wheels of the old days
but also of the marks made by the glacier in the ice age. We
go back not just in history but even back to the geological formation of the land. We also go back in time from adulthood to
childhood and end up drinking from the mountain stream with
a broken drinking goblet from a children's playhouse. There is
also the image of following a river back up to its source. This
process of going back is a process of getting lost.

> . . . a time made simple by the loss
> Of detail. . . .
> . . . if you'll let a guide direct you
> Who only has at heart your getting lost. . . .
> . . . two village cultures faded
> Into each other. Both of them are lost.
> And if you're lost enough to find yourself
> By now. . . .

Losing and finding. There is also the image of hiding something:[7]

> I have kept hidden in the instep arch
> Of an old cedar at the waterside
> A broken drinking goblet like the Grail
> Under a spell so the wrong ones can't find it,

> So can't get saved, as Saint Mark says they mustn't.
> (I stole the goblet from the children's playhouse.)

If confusion is a state of being lost, then at the end of the poem the guide has led us to where we are lost no longer.

> Here are your waters and your watering place.
> Drink and be whole again beyond confusion.

Of course, confusion is associated as well with the present moment of history—"all this now too much for us." Another image of the confusion of modern life is that of "the valley streams that when aroused/Will leave their tatters hung on barb and thorn." We must reject the confusion of the valley streams for the brook "Cold as a spring as yet so near its source,/Too lofty and original to rage."

The process by which we achieve the blessed state of being beyond confusion is apparently a process of loss and of getting lost. This process is at the same time one of rising to heights. The moment of greatest height and the moment of greatest loss coincide in the poem:

> The height of the adventure is the height
> Of country where two village cultures faded
> Into each other. Both of them are lost.

This is also the moment when we should be lost enough to find ourselves.

The poem then is one about the achievement of peace of mind, of wholeness, of getting saved. The means of achieving this may be interpreted in different ways: one thing Frost seems to suggest is that we go back for our values to an earlier, simpler, more well-oriented age—that of our forefathers. The poem presents a conservative view of values. One is reminded of the poem just before "Directive" in the volume *Steeple Bush* which also uses the metaphor of the flooded valley streams to stand for the confusion of the present times. One may think of the boulders in the torrent as great nations or great institutions. Frost says he saved himself from the general confusion by "one step backward taken" which is exactly what he did when he became the poet of rural Vermont and New

Hampshire, places where one still feels in distant contact with the first settlers:

> Not only sands and gravels
> Were once more on their travels,
> But gulping muddy gallons
> Great boulders off their balance
> Bumped heads together dully
> And started down the gully.
> Whole capes caked off in slices.
> I felt my standpoint shaken
> In the universal crisis.
> But with one step backward taken
> I saved myself from going.
> A world torn loose went by me.
> Then the rain stopped and the blowing,
> And the sun came out to dry me.
>
> (Frost, *Poetry,* pp. 376–7)

The last lines are perhaps a bit optimistic. The "rain" has hardly stopped, and the confusion still rules. However, Frost's answer to the situation is "one step backward taken." The next poem, "Directive," begins "Back out of all this now too much for us."

But "Directive" means much more. The poem is not just about going back in time to find conservative values, it is about loss, about how to face loss. For example, how do you face the fact of the ruin of the house in which you loved a wife and raised a family, when as in "The Thatch"

> Its life of hundreds of years has ended
> By letting the rain I knew outdoors
> In onto the upper chamber floors.
>
> (Frost, *Poetry,* p. 253)

How do you face the tragedies and deaths of loved ones? Your own death?

It is to answer these questions that our poet guide takes us up and back to where we can see where two whole villages, in fact two whole "cultures," are lost—the word "cultures," especially in the context of the references to the prehistoric ice age, carries connotations of whole civilizations of past times.

We are made to feel the reality, the very presence, of these long dead people: they seem to watch us from forty cellar holes, and one of them "may be just ahead of you on foot/Or creaking with a buggy load of grain." Of course he is just ahead of us in the sense that we will soon be dead too, which is a "cheering song" indeed! We not only feel the presence of these people as society watching us and as fellow workmen. We are also made to follow that road home to the children's playhouse and to the belilaced (Did Frost pronounce this *belilacked* or *belilāced?*) cellar-hole, now slowly closing like a dent in dough —an image redolent of the homely country kitchen. We are made to feel the reality of the family lands of these long dead people and to weep both for the playhouse and then for the house in earnest. Then we are perhaps ready to drink from the cup which is like a grail, to drink from a "lofty and original" source, to drink out of the children's cup, "for of such is the kingdom of heaven."

The process is one of learning about human solidarity. As in the poem "The Tuft of Flowers" from the 1913 volume *A Boy's Will,* " 'Men work together,' ... / 'Whether they work together or apart.' " And just as in that poem the speaker "went to turn the grass once after one/Who mowed it in the dew before the sun" (Frost, *Poetry,* pp. 32–33), so in this poem the reader is invited to follow after another worker, only this time they are separated by the space of lifetimes rather than the space of a morning. Nevertheless this dead fellow worker is "just ahead of" us, we are all together in facing death.

The growing awareness of human solidarity is a process of mounting up to the height where all cultures fade into each other, that is, become one in death. The image is a remarkably paradoxical one. The cultures become each other, become indistinguishable, become one. Yet they do this in the process of death, of disappearing. We are reminded somehow that Frost held very strongly for the individuality of peoples. Yet we, in contemplating their death and our own, may find relief from our sense of loss, which is after all loneliness, in the sense of human solidarity. We are not alone. All men become one for us in the realization that we share their death.

This is one means by which the guide helps us to endure and accept loss. Another way is the process of our getting lost ourselves:

> . . . if you'll let a guide direct you
> Who only has at heart your getting lost. . . .

What does getting lost mean here? First, as has been said, we must get lost from contemporary culture, get out of the confusion of the modern world. Go away from towns into rural areas back nearer to nature, and also go back in time. This may mean that we will be less fitted to make a killing in the stock market or to become successes. We may be lost in that sense. But we may find ourselves. For another thing we all shall be lost in the same way that the village cultures were lost, that is we shall all die and be forgotten. Looked at this way our guide begins to seem like a sinister old man carrying a scythe. He will take us back in time to show us ages in which we did not exist and hint at a future when all trace of our lives will be gone.

But we are to get lost in another way too. Like the two village cultures on the mountain we are to fade into oneness with others. At the same time we are to realize our own nothingness. This unity is a fading away, yet it is also the height of the adventure. We are then to get lost in the sense of transcending the ego, of freeing ourselves from individual self concern. The line "And if you're lost enough to find yourself" echoes the Biblical paradox "He who would save his life shall lose it, but he who would lose his life for my sake shall find it."

Thus the poem does move out of the present, "Back out of all this now too much for us," to assert traditional Christian values. I say Christian because of the explicit references to St. Mark and to the Grail. These references tip us off to one of the structural elements in the poem. "Directive" is Robert Frost's equivalent of *The Waste Land* in that it seems to use the same basic theme of the "serial ordeal" a knight must face in his pursuit of the vision of the Holy Grail.[8] Eliot's protagonist is the modern consciousness seeking a way to salvation in the modern world, and the strange experiences he comes upon are all tests in that quest. Thus in Frost's poem one passes through a series of really nightmarish experiences before one reaches the height of the mount. And even then there are secrets to be discovered.

First, the aim. We are to be led back to a sort of blessed community reachable in a specific place and time—not our place or time. We have a search back like that in Eliot's *Four Quartets* and paradoxes like those in *Ash Wednesday*. The house is no more a house, the farm is no more a farm, the town is no more a town, but nevertheless this place mysteriously exists, is reachable by getting lost, and when we are there we shall find true community with all men, and by losing our-serves shall find ourselves.

Next, the terrors and labors of the way. It is uphill work, like Dante's climb up the mount of Purgatory, but like Dante, we have a good guide. The road is a rocky one; it may seem as if it should have been a quarry. But the road is personified, "Great monolithic knees." Like the knight of old we find giants in our path. Not only the owner of the great monolithic knees, but also the "enormous Glacier/That braced his feet against the Arctic Pole." We not only see the chisel marks[9] he left but we can feel his presence here now.

> You must not mind a certain coolness from him
> Still said to haunt this side of Panther Mountain.

The coolness expresses a certain distaste of the past for the present, of the original molder of the landscape for those who have since messed it up. The coolness also carries that sense of getting lost in the past, of being absorbed into the coldness of death.

Panther Mountain is itself a rather redoubtable-sounding monster in our path, like the leopard which barred Dante's path up Mt. Zion.

Next is the serial ordeal

> Of being watched from forty cellar holes
> As if by eye pairs out of forty firkins.

A firkin is a small wooden vessel or cask, hardly to be compared in size with a cellar hole. Perhaps each foundation has two cellar windows which look like eyes staring at the passerby. At any rate this is another gigantic image, for the creatures whose "eye-pairs" are imagined must be large to make the cellars seem like small casks.[10]

One must not mind these imaginary terrors which arise from the loneliness of the place, one must press on toward one's goal.

The loneliness and dread are underlined by the advice to "make yourself up a cheering song." The terrors past, one is led forward by a new guide, heading home just ahead of you, another creature of the past and of imagination. Having resisted all terrors and reached the top of the mount, one cuts off connection with one's past life by metaphorically pulling up the ladder. Then one is shown various symbols: the shattered innocence of the children's dishes, the house that is no more, and one weeps for these things. After this broken and contrite moment, one is led, as Virgil led Dante to the river Lethe, as the Grail Knights went to the ritual footwashing, to water for cleansing and baptism. Here are your waters and your watering place. The Grail is hidden to all except those who have lost themselves in the way the poem recommends. But the knight who has passed through his ordeals and vigils, humbled himself and become like a little child, is ready to receive it.

I have overdone it a bit, but the poem does have hidden in it, like the signs the knight must recognize and interpret, all sorts of suggestive hints. Moreover Frost almost explicity warns us that the poem is a parable:

> I have kept hidden in the instep arch
> Of an old cedar at the waterside
> A broken drinking goblet like the Grail
> Under a spell so the wrong ones can't find it,
> So can't get saved, as Saint Mark says they mustn't.

These lines are the equivalent of Yeats's "I have a marvellous thing to say,/A certain marvellous thing/None but the living mock" from "All Souls' Night" (Yeats, *Variorum Poems*, p. 471).

In the passage from The Gospel according to Saint Mark Jesus has just told the parable of the sower who went forth to sow. His disciples, when he is alone, ask him the meaning of the parable. He answers, "Unto you it is given to know the mystery of the kingdom of God but unto them that are without, all these things are done in parables: That seeing they may see, and not perceive; and hearing they may hear, and not understand; lest at anytime they should be converted, and their sins should be forgiven them" (Mark IV: 11–12).

Who are the *wrong ones*? They are those who won't allow themselves to get lost, so that therefore they can never find themselves and get saved. Relevant texts would be "I came not to call the righteous, but sinners to repentance" (Mark II:17); "Seek and ye shall find" (Matthew VII:7); "Many be called but few chosen" (Matthew XX:16).

But if the *I* of the poem is Frost the poet, his hiding of the Grail under the cedar is like his embodying precious conceptions in his poems. Only to those who will live with the poems and know them intimately can they speak directly. To the rest they will seem to contain calculated obscurities and in fact *will* contain calculated obscurities.

One must, as the disciples followed Christ and Christ only, be willing to put up a sign CLOSED to all but the speaker of the poem, then make oneself at home with speaker and poem. A poem demands total commitment—that is, a free and dedicated reading—from those who would truly know it and use it as a guide to the aesthetic vision just as religious commitment must be a total one to lead to the religious vision. In any case this last section of the poem from "If you're lost enough to find yourself/By now" on, is full of images of a private secret cult.

It is all playfully done. To pull in a ladder road and put a sign up closed to all but a friend is to emulate children playing in tree-houses. But the one, the I, of the poem, is a very mysterious person. On one level he is obviously the poet, but on another he suggests the deity.

The game is a game of mystery, of finding the clues, following the trail, discovering the hidden treasure. Frost is the most public of poets. What poet of such high quality in this century has been able to speak to multitudes as he has? Not Yeats certainly. And yet this late poem contains secrets and an aesthetic of secrecy and of mysterious symbols worthy of the great magician himself.

We have not considered the title: my dictionary defines "directive" thus: "something that serves to direct, guide, and usually impel toward an action, attainment or goal; *specifically* an authoritative instrument issued by a high-level official body or competent official." The title is playful, and sly. Frost is pretending to an authority over us which is religious and moral as well as artistic. But I wish especially to note that a "directive" is a written document of some detail. Here the poem itself is the "Directive," written with authority, written to *us* specifically—not for everyone—providing description of each step which we are to take. That is, if the word is a noun. If it is an adjective then it simply means "serving to point direction," a humble tone much more in line with such apologies as "if you'll let a guide direct you." The choice is ours. Frost means to keep us guessing about the title too.[11]

THE THATCH
Out alone in the winter rain,
Intent on giving and taking pain.
But never was I far out of sight
Of a certain upper-window light.
The light was what it was all about:
I would not go in till the light went out;
It would not go out till I came in.
Well, we should see which one would win,
We should see which one would be first to yield.
The world was a black invisible field.
The rain by rights was snow for cold.
The wind was another layer of mold.
But the strangest thing: in the thick old thatch,
Where summer birds had been given hatch,

Had fed in chorus, and lived to fledge,
Some still were living in hermitage.
And as I passed along the eaves
So low I brushed the straw with my sleeves,
I flushed birds out of hole after hole,
Into the darkness. It grieved my soul,
It started a grief within a grief,
To think their case was beyond relief—
They could not go flying about in search
Of their nest again, nor find a perch.
They must brood where they fell in mulch and mire,
Trusting feathers and inward fire
Till daylight made it safe for a flyer.
My greater grief was by so much reduced
As I thought of them without nest or roost.
That was how that grief started to melt.
They tell me the cottage where we dwelt,
Its wind-torn thatch goes now unmended;
Its life of hundreds of years has ended
By letting the rain I knew outdoors
In onto the upper chamber floors.

(Frost, Poetry, pp. 252–53)[12]

The bleakness of "The Thatch" is in inverse ratio to the pleasure with which Frost recalled the days in England when he first was recognized as a poet. "I had nearly a perfect life over there—a romance such as happens to few" (Sergeant, p. 352).[13] At thirty-eight Frost had left his position as a teacher of psychology at Plymouth, New Hampshire, and sailed to England to write. The Frosts arrived in London on or about September 14, 1912, and settled in a farm cottage in Buckinghamshire. Soon Frost's first voume, *A Boy's Will* (1913), was accepted for publication by David Nutt and Company. Frost became acquainted with a number of young writers. To be near these he moved to the Gloucestershire-Herfordshire border in the spring of 1914, first living at Little Iddens, Ledbury. Lascelles Abercrombie and Wildrid Gibson lived near. Other

writers Frost knew there were Rupert Brooke, John Drink-
water, William Henry Davies, and especially Edward Thomas,
with whom he developed a deep friendship.

This idyllic period came to an end with the advent of World
War I. Thomas went off to become a soldier. The Frosts moved
in September 1914 to share Lascelles Abercrombie's double-
cottage The Callows, which he liked to call The Gallows, at
Ryton Dymock, where they were of course beset with worries
about their future course as Americans in a foreign country in
a state of war. This was the cottage which is the scene of "The
Thatch."[14] Frost describes it in a September 17, 1914, letter to
Sidney Cox: "We are in another old house, this time under a
very ancient thatch: the bottom layer of straw is rye—perhaps
put on two or three hundred years ago" (Frost, *Letters,* p.
136).[15] An account by a friend[16] says that the cottage was
thatched almost all the way to the ground, which helps to explain the action of the poem (Mertins, *Frost,* p. 116).

The exact terms of the domestic quarrel which initiates the
action of the poem are, I suppose, not important. One recognizes the universal domestic quarrel. John Crowe Ransom had
reflected it in "Lady Lost" and had presented it in "Two in
August," both published in *Two Gentlemen in Bonds* (1927)
the year before Frost's poem appeared.[17] According to Jean
Gould the quarrel was over whether the Frosts should leave at
once for America (as Elinor wished) before sailing got any
more dangerous or whether they should stay (as Robert wished)
until his success in America was assured by his increasing pres-
tige in England (Gould, p. 142). Gould stresses the normalcy
of Frost's conflicts, Lawrence Thompson the abnormalcy.
Thompson's account of Frost's friendship with Edward Thomas,
a man whose marital problems Frost understood by their analogy with his own, includes the fact that Frost had, at least once,
shown Elinor a loaded revolver and threatened to kill himself
and/or her. The theme of escape and return which Thomas
pleased Frost by comprehending in the arrangement of the
poems in *A Boy's Will* is extended by Thompson to Frost's relations with Elinor. The return, of course, was never certain.

"Even after moving to The Gallows," writes Thompson of the occasion of "The Thatch," Frost "hurt himself in his childish attempt to hurt his wife for her solicitude" (Thompson, *Early Years,* p. 464). The escape-return pattern is to be found in "The Thatch" with the bitter twist added that the nest to which one returns is ultimately found rifled.

The Frosts sailed from Liverpool for the States on February 13, 1915. Edward Thomas was killed in action Easter Monday 1917, as Rupert Brooke had been at an earlier date. Frost stayed away from England for many years. In 1925 Frost mentioned in his letters the possibility of going to Europe. In one to John Haines on July 21, he reminisces about Leddington and Ryton. The contemplation of this journey may well have eventually produced "The Thatch," some time before the Frosts actually sailed to Europe early in August 1928 (Frost, *Letters,* p. 349). In early September[18] the Frosts visited the Haineses in Gloucestershire and were taken to their old haunts. Without relying on what "They tell me," Frost could see for himself that the rain he had known outdoors was now coming in onto the upper chamber floors of the cottage where he and Elinor had dwelt. Haines wrote, "We took him also to the outside of the Gallows, but he did not go in, and the place was then getting dilapidated, the Gallows in recent years deteriorated and much of the place was more or less fallen down and was so when I took R F to see it in 1928" (Mertins, *Frost,* p. 176).[19] In 1957 Frost visited the region again. This time there was worse than rain: a deluge of *Life* magazine photographers "to follow and photograph the poet where once there had been companion poets" (Mertins, *Frost,* p. 345).

"The Thatch" falls into three sections. The first sets the scene of the domestic quarrel:

> Out alone in the winter rain,
> Intent on giving and taking pain.
> But never was I far out of sight
> Of a certain upper-window light.
> The light was what it was all about:
> I would not go in till the light went out;

It would not go out till I came in.
Well, we should see which one would win,
We should see which one would be first to yield.

These opening lines with their bare forthrightness, do not conceal the ridiculousness of one of man's most ridiculous situations: I say *man's* because it is usually the male who manages to get in the more ridiculous situation. The husband has apparently walked out of the house in a huff, but has no place to go except to walk around the house in the rain. And of course he doesn't really want to go anywhere. He wants the wife to admit that she was wrong, that she can't live without him, to plead with him with abject tears, until in spite of his fully justified sense of indignation, out of pity for her—the weaker vessel—he condescends to come back to bed. I am caricaturing, but Frost's speaker is intent on giving and taking pain, on giving pain by refusing to go into the house till his wife turns off the light so that he won't have to look at her or speak to her (though I suspect that he will be all the angrier if she really does turn over and unconcernedly go to sleep). He is intent on taking pain not only by suffering in the wet and cold but also by savoring the pleasure of feeling unappreciated and unjustly treated.

But never was I far out of sight
Of a certain upper-window light.

He really wants to see that light, to know she is there awake. Also he perhaps wants to be seen, or at least to have her peer out, looking for him, and to take satisfaction in the thought that she cannot see *him* in that darkness.

In any case, that light is his center—it is "what it was all about"—and the world outside has no attractiveness for him:

The world was a black invisible field.
The rain by rights was snow for cold.
The wind was another layer of mold.

He is, then, almost buried by the wind. Light and warmth inside, darkness and cold outside.

The tone of self-mockery—mockery of the childish self-centeredness of each of the quarrelers, controls the real pain expressed. The lines have a doggerel repetitiousness and sing-song quality which makes the whole painful business faintly ridiculous:

> The light was what it was all about:
> I would not go in till the light went out;
> It would not go out till I came in.
> Well, we should see which one would win,
> We should see which one would be first to yield.

I don't want to exaggerate the comic quality of such lines. The tone is one of faintly ironic candor.

One or the other *will* yield, though the yielder is usually the winner in such affairs. (The man usually wins the war and loses in the treaty negotiations afterwards!) Both are dramatizing, playing a game, seeing "which one would win." The "light" is not really what the quarrel is about, but it is symptomatic of the pettiness of such a quarrel between two people who have committed themselves to each other to the extent of having four children as the Frosts had done.

> I would not go in till the light went out;
> It would not go out till I came in.

Putting it so indirectly preserves anonymity and impersonality. He does not say until "she" put out the light, but till the light went out. The awkward indirection of "*It* would not go out till I came in," putting "*It*" for the light which is put for the lady, helps to dramatize the ridiculousness of the quarrel. But as we have seen the light does stand for the lady, and the world is very dark without her. Thus in a back-handed way Frost revives one of the oldest of metaphors: "But soft! What light through yonder window breaks? / It is the East, and Juliet is the sun!" At any rate the Lady won't turn out the light. She insists on his making up with her and coming to bed.

The lines:

> The world was a black invisible field
> The rain by rights was snow for cold.
> The wind was another layer of mold.

are a transition to the second section of the poem. The speaker becomes aware of the cold dark winter world around him, so far and so different from that interior world of light and warm domestic battle upstairs in the house. But it is not just that he has been thrown, or has thrown himself, into outer darkness. That darkness is peopled by other lives, other sufferers, whose peace he disturbs in his angry walking. Suddenly there impinges on his hot anger, on this private emotional self-indulgence on which he is so "Intent," the cool awareness of these other lives:

> But the strangest thing: in the thick old thatch,
> Where summer birds had given hatch,
> Had fed in chorus, and lived to fledge,
> Some still were living in hermitage.
> And as I passed along the eaves
> So low I brushed the straw with my sleeves,
> I flushed the birds out of hole after hole,
> Into the darkness. It grieved my soul,
> It started a grief within a grief,
> To think their case was beyond relief—
> They could not go flying about in search
> Of their nest again, nor find a perch.
> They must brood where they fell in mulch and mire,
> Trusting feathers and inward fire
> Till daylight made it safe for a flyer.
> My greater grief was by so much reduced
> As I thought of them without nest or roost.
> That was how that grief started to melt.

Here we have some of the accurate observation which has made Frost known as a nature poet. But as always he is really more concerned here with the human dimension. The objectivity and intelligence by which he understands in detail what is happening to these birds are also the means by which the speaker escapes from his self-concern and is able to give up his anger and pride and to go back into the house—as one assumes he does:

> That was how that grief started to melt.

The speaker doesn't just respond with a vague consciousness of birds, he understands the very point of the nesting cycle at which he interrupts them. They are "in hermitage," the nesting cycle is in fact completed. The young birds have been given hatch, fed in chorus, and they have lived to fledge. Most have flown away to begin the cycle again elsewhere. The birds who are left are old pensioners living "in hermitage." "Hermitage" has the sense of "hideaway." Also the numerous small holes in the thatch may be compared to numerous cells in a monastery. The phrase "in hermitage," then, has connotations of celibacy.

The image of the birds thus is in meaningful comparison and contrast to the domestic situation of the speaker. Like them he has been driven from his nest, his cottage, or at least has left it, but unlike them he and his family are in the midst of the cycle of love and procreation, while the winter birds have finished their yearly cycle. Realization of this fact, by the keen observer of nature, is an unvoiced reminder that his and his wife's own life cycle will, in a few years, run to the same point as that of the birds, the children will have flown, and one or the other may be living alone in aged celibacy, in hermitage. This sudden impingement on his consciousness of an image of a later point in the life cycle than the point at which he stands, has a cooling effect on his anger and a melting effect on his pride.

The other point of contrast between himself and the birds is that whereas he, play-actor as he is, can return upstairs to light and warmth and love whenever he has conquered his pride, there is no return that night for the birds. Frightened out of their hermitage nests,

> They must brood where they fell in mulch and mire,
> Trusting feathers and inward fire
> Till daylight made it safe for a flyer.

We move from the partly imagined and self-created obstacle which prevents the speaker from returning to his room to the real impossibility of the birds' finding their way back to their nests. And with the speaker's awareness of this situation, we find in him a tenderness, an ability to imagine objectively and sympathetically the genuine troubles of other beings with which we would not have credited him in the first lines of the poem. That he would be aware of the birds' plight shows both remarkable keenness of observation and tenderness of heart. In fact the situation is a bit ironic. He doesn't mind torturing his wife—who of course well deserves it!—but he has a real sympathy for the birds, and rather than drive more of them out of their nests, he goes back in to his wife.

I have again caricatured the situation. That is not the way it is put in the poem. The tone of this second section is in fact much more serious than that of the first. In the first section the speaker refrains from taking his own trouble completely seriously, but in the second section he does take the birds' trouble seriously. Because after all, he can get back, they cannot.

This daring equation of the human level and the ornithic level, underlined by phrases like "in chorus," "in hermitage," "their case was beyond relief," and "safe for a flyer"—locutions usually applied to human beings—is the basis for a new seriousness with which the poet presents his own grief.

Lovers' quarrels may be ridiculous, but they are painful, and especially so among couples of middle age who thought they had learned how to live together. (Frost was forty and in his twentieth year of marriage.) The poet gets us to accord a new importance to his difficulty, by the comparison with the plight of the birds. Surely the plight of a man must be regarded—at least by men—as more important than the plight of a bird, even though one is emotional, the other physical.

Moreover the speaker gives his trouble new dignity by giving it a new word: "grief." We had thought it was anger and stubbornness—"Well, we would see which one would win." But now it is suddenly "grief," and it is harder for grief to be ridiculous than for anger. Moreover, "grief" implies not only that he is suffering, genuinely suffering, but that he intensely regrets what has happened. He is sorry. Not that he is immediately ready to make up. Anger and grief can be combined. One can be sorry that an impossible situation has arisen without ceasing to be indignant. In fact grief is necessary, I think, to give anger dignity. We don't respect a man who is choleric; we do respect a countenance more in sorrow than in anger but expressing

both, like that of Hamlet's father. Therefore when the poet puts
"grief" where we had expected "anger," we realize the seriousness and pain of this quarrel in middle age.

The idea of grief is cleverly introduced by means of an idi-
omatic expression:

> It grieved my soul.

This, being merely a manner of speaking, is not too strong a
way of putting his momentary pity for the birds. But having
taken up the idea, the poet elaborates it, playing with words,
elaborating the mere manner of speaking:

> It started a grief within a grief,
> To think their case was beyond relief.

We still do not know how seriously he is taking the grief of
this lover's quarrel, or how much dignity he attaches to it, but
we do know that he takes the minor grief of the birds' plight
seriously, and the other grief is greater than that.

But our attention is on the birds who

> . . . must brood where they fell in mulch and mire
> Trusting feathers and inward fire.

"Inward fire" contrasts with the fire and warmth in the house,
yet recalls them. Thus while our attention is shifted from the
main problem we are still considering analogues of it.

When the poet shifts back to his own trouble, he can simply
refer to it as "My greater grief," as if that had all been established, and go on.

> My greater grief was by so much reduced
> As I thought of them without nest or roost.
> That was how that grief started to melt.

The poet has never asserted the greatness of his grief. Even here
he only refers to it as greater than his grief for the birds, not as
great in itself. Thus he avoids sentimentality and embarrassing
self-pity or any form of self-assertion. Our attention is really
still mainly on the birds, not on him.

The language subtly assumes that his grief is great. In the lines

> My greater grief was by so much reduced
> As I thought of them without nest or roost

that "As" seems on a first reading to be a subordinating conjunction, which could be replaced by a "when," and the "so" seems like a colloquial intensifier: That is, "My greater grief was reduced by such a great deal when I thought of them without nest or roost." But no, there is exact measurement here: "My greater grief was reduced by exactly so much as I thought of the birds without nest or roost." This exactness implies a limitation to the reduction. His grief was reduced by so much and no more. A substantial grief, reduced only to a limited extent by this distracting concern for the birds, is implied.

> That was how that grief started to melt.

The grief that is left is still substantial, like a big block of ice, but the slow but accelerating process of melting pride starts with this reminder that there are some who cannot, if they would, go back, and are "without nest or roost."

The third section begins without a break. It starts with the second line of a couplet:

> That was how that grief started to melt.
> They tell me the cottage where we dwelt,
> Its wind-torn thatch goes now unmended;
> Its life of hundreds of years has ended
> By letting the rain I knew outdoors
> In onto the upper chamber floors.

In these last five lines Frost gives the *coup de grace*. This brief laconic dismissal of the subject, with its shattering implications, comes with a great shock, yet all its elements have been thoroughly prepared for: Section one: the ridiculous quarrel; Section two: the melting, healing tenderness brought about by sympathy for the little birds turned out of their nests; Section three: hindsight years after—"They tell me," the impersonal they, like the voice of the generations, of time. They, English friends, perhaps, tell him that the cottage—that cottage, which with its thatched roof full of nests was itself the nest of the speaker's family—is an empty ruin.

"Its life has ended." There is double syntax here. First, the life of the house is over, and second, its life has ended "By letting the rain I knew outdoors/In onto the upper chamber floors." It was of course in that upper chamber room that someone waited and refused to put out the light. All are gone now. The house is an empty ruin. There are two effects: First, the rain coming in onto those upper chamber floors seems a real invasion, a desecration, a violation of the deepest and most sacred feelings of love. That last line, which has lain in wait for us throughout the build-up of the poem, strikes us like a blow.

But there is a further effect. The rain did not force its way in, it was let in. The feelings of guilt about the quarrel, above all the weaknesses and mistakes with which we sully love, the feeling of weariness with the way we let our lives be ruined, is expressed in those lines. The rain, which is the pain he insisted on taking, the rain which "was snow for cold" in "a black invisible field" broken only by the window light, has, through neglect—and not the neglect of maintaining the house only—now spread through the whole abandoned structure. After the self-deprecating humor and tenderness of the first part of the poem, this image of one's life all gone by and one's love over with, not without lingering guilt, is stark indeed.

> Its life of hundreds of years has ended
> By letting the rain I knew outdoors
> In onto the upper chamber floors.

To go back, there is another, I should say an additional, way of reading the middle section of the poem. It is "the strangest thing" that although the world "was a black invisible field," nevertheless

> In the thick old thatch,
> Where summer birds had been given hatch,

> Had fed in chorus, and lived to fledge,
> Some still were living in hermitage.

In the midst of that blackness he unexpectedly discovers life of which he had not been conscious, life which has inward fire to trust to. This is a hopeful sign. Even though his quarrel with his wife reveals the world to be a dark place there is still hope. The cycle represented by the birds may be a cycle of love as well as of life. The human love too has "been given hatch,/ [Has] fed in chorus, and lived to fledge," has gone through a cycle of fulfillment and departing. Yet still some lonely remnant of that love is living in hermitage. This reading may not work very well in the passage itself, but when one comes to the end of the poem, when all is gone and the thatch probably is not even useful for nesting anymore, one is reminded that in spite of the fact that the earlier moment was the end of a cycle it was not the end of everything. The moment visualized at the end of the poem *is* the end of everything, and that angry moment in the cold rain seems real happiness by comparison.

In "The Thatch" we have one of Frost's favorite subjects, the abandoned house. Even in his early poems he was considering what the end of the road would be like:

> Out through the fields and the woods
>   And over the walls I have wended;
> I have climbed the hills of view
>   And looked at the world, and descended;
> I have come by the highway home,
>   And lo, it is ended.

These lines from "Reluctance," the last poem in Frost's first volume, echo the melancholy feminine endings, beautifully handled, of

> Its wind-torn thatch goes now unmended;
> Its life of hundreds of years has ended. . . .

"Reluctance" ends,

> Ah, when to the heart of man
>> Was it ever less than a treason
> To go with the drift of things,
>> To yield with a grace to reason,
> And bow and accept the end
>> Of a love or a season?
>>> (Frost, *Poetry,* pp. 29–30)

There is no acceptance in "The Thatch," just the stark fact of ruin, death, and emptiness.

George Nitchie finds "The Thatch" to be one of a group of poems in which there is "an erotic relationship that, revealing ambivalence, is transformed sometimes into something rich and strange but more often into something close to nightmare in its destructive equating of love and cruelty." In "The Thatch", "the speaker has descended into his own unconscious and has to a degree mastered the ambivalent chaos that confronts him there; the poem is a kind of night journey in miniature." Nitchie adds, and is the only critic I know of to make the connection, "Something of the same pattern appears in . . . 'Directive'. . . ." (Nitchie, p. 100). Reuben Brower, without using the Jungian term "unconscious," finds a similar pattern in much of Frost. "The connection between the road, the wood, the journey into lostness, and the discovery of what is most his 'own' and most 'true' for him is deep and permanent in Frost's poetry—and we may guess—in his life . . ." (Brower, pp. 230–31).

Brower is close to the center of Frost's work here, and Nitchie too, although he himself finds the "self-mastery" of "The Thatch" rare in Frost (Nitchie, p. 101). I suppose that a "night journey" need not be taken at night or a wilderness journey into the woods. Surely the basic pattern of which these critics speak is the embracing concept of all of Frost's best work. It may be found in the little poem which Frost put at the beginning of his collections:

> I'm going out to clean the pasture spring;
> I'll only stop to rake the leaves away
> (And wait to watch the water clear, I may):
> I sha'nt be gone long.—You come too.

"Directive" repeats the invitation of "The Pasture" to come out and "clean the pasture spring," except that the spring is now a long way "over back." Frost rakes away the leaves of years and centuries and waits for clear water. Like "The Pasture," "Directive" is very tender in tone.

As we have seen, even the title is the gently humorous irony of a spiritual guide who doesn't take himself too seriously but who is eager to share the experience of regained innocence. In both poems the guide counsels concern for "what little things could make [children] glad":

> I'm going out to fetch the little calf
> That's standing by the mother. It's so young
> It totters when she licks it with her tongue.
> I sha'nt be gone long.—You come too.
>
> (Frost, *Poetry*, p. 1)

This concern it is that leads us to the lofty and original spring, frees us from the lower reaches of life where destructive rages hang their tatters among symbols of pain given and taken ("barb and thorn").

The action of "The Thatch" starts in these violent lower reaches. Its subject is rage, its characters "Intent on giving and taking pain." Instead of giving us a generalized benediction like "Directive," the earlier poem demonstrates how, in a specific conflict situation,

> The notion of some infinitely gentle
> Infinitely suffering thing
>
> (Eliot, *Complete Poems*, p. 13)

—or as close as pragmatical Frost will get to Eliot's ideal— makes the heart contrite and restores wholeness. Yet we must not exaggerate the degree to which the heart of the speaker in "The Thatch" is contrite. His grief has "started to melt," no more, up to the last five lines. Those lines too are cold and grim and unhappy. The relic of the conflict is still there.

Part of the grimness of this poem results from the fact that there is no "You" in it. The "We" of "Directive" is "You and I." "The Pasture" calls "You come too." But the "We" of 'The

Thatch" is really third person in reference: when the speaker refers to "the cottage where we dwelt" he means "She and I" not "You and I." He is not speaking to his loved companion but to an impersonal audience or to himself. "She" appears in the poem only as the personage symbolized by that "upper window light." "The Thatch" is a lonely poem, and the speaker stands alone in it from beginning to end. His insistence that the life of the house in which they had dwelt had ended seems almost a way of threatening both self and wife with the destruction he envisions as ultimately inevitable anyway. It is almost as if he takes satisfaction in the future ending of their love by natural causes. Yet this is only part of the complex tone which Frost's tact and economy have created. The dominant impression one gets is that the vision of an ultimate desolation restores the speaker's perspective, restores home and love to their true value.

In "The Pasture" the invitation to a journey to clean the spring and then to return to ordinary life is issued simply and casually as to a child or a young companion. (It could even be a love poem.) Life and attitudes are as yet uncomplicated. "The Thatch," too, though on the passion-bound level of middle-life, has as its subject an experience of cleansing and renewal. The foray into anger and the return out of it again comprise a clarifying experience, and the speaker supposedly returns to his wife a chastened and better husband. In "Directive" the desolation which is not hinted at in "The Pasture" and which looms so terrifyingly in "The Thatch" is accepted as norm. The cycle is over. The point has been reached where, like the birds of "The Thatch" one cannot return to the nest. The problem is to make oneself "at home" in this desolation. The guide of "Directive" presents as his credentials the fact that he himself is already "at home" enough in this high region—which is the end of time, of history, and of personal life—to play host. He invites us to settle down where we are, to make the desolation itself home. We have made our journey. All that is necessary to realize this is to accept the cup. The guide speaks directly to us, his "We" is "You and I," but there is no conflict. "The Pasture" is pre-conflict, "Directive" post-conflict. There is no wife any more for him to fight with. The person he addresses need not listen to him unless he wants to. The guide himself speaks out of friendship freely and not from compulsion. Only if we wish need we bind ourselves exclusively to this guide "who only has at heart [our] getting lost." But in this last of a series of journeys and returns, only if we accept, at bitter cost, the freedom in emptiness which he has to offer, can we at last make ourselves "at home."

Hart Crane

HART CRANE

Hart Crane's Technique

Every poet distorts accepted idiom and syntax and finds rich images and metaphors in order to enforce attention and to widen implication. But Hart Crane carried these techniques to an extreme, often astonishing and confusing the reader. Term and referent become indistinguishable. One cannot tell the central point from the circumference to which imagery has expanded it. One is afraid that there are many centers and many circumferences, arcs whose circles are not completed within the poem's subject or whose center-points lie outside that subject, thus disintegrating the poem's total effect.

When Crane succeeds in staying on the cosmic side of those borders the bounds of his creation are of immense proportions; but unfortunately his frequent excursions beyond those borders into chaos do not enlarge the domain of form. Within the same poem certain syntactical tricks and certain images stay within bounds, while others, constructed along similar lines, go too far. The poems are so complex that almost no instance is quite paralleled by another.

Incomplete or amorphous syntax is one of the most frequent and effective devices used in modern poetry to give the contemporary sense that in our lives choice has surrendered to chance. Pound's "Canto I" (a paraphrase of *The Odyssey,* Book XI) begins "And then went down to the ship" (Pound, *Cantos,* p. 3). A subject for "went" is never explicitly provided, although the clipped epistolary or ship's-log style may aid in implying one. This incompleteness of syntax functions to support the world-view implicit in *The Cantos.* It is dramatically appropriate—one feels as if he had broken in on a continuing conversation or monologue. Pound's Ulysses seems caught in a meaningless flux without beginning or goal. The syntax is distorted to present a psychological process.

Crane's "Voyages II" starts off:

And yet this great wink of eternity,
Of rimless floods, unfettered leewardings,
Samite sheeted and processioned where
Her undinal vast belly moonward bends,
Laughing the wrapt inflections of our love;

Take this Sea, whose diapason knells
On scrolls of silver snowy sentences,
The sceptred terror of whose sessions rends
As her demeanors motion well or ill,
All but the pieties of lovers' hands.

(Crane, *Complete Poems,* p. 36)

The syntax is incomplete. We never learn what, "And yet," the sea does. The poet breaks off and begins again in the imperative: "Take this Sea." Does he mean, "And yet take this Sea," that is, "Nevertheless take this Sea?" Obviously, but the syntax is still distorted and with it, inevitably, the logic of the statement. We conclude the logical content of the above paraphrase when we interpret "yet" as "nevertheless." It may also be read as "still," and then too one may infer a connection between the stanzas: "Continue to take this Sea." But both meanings could have been made clear without cutting short the syntactical pattern. What Crane is really after is the emphasis on "yet" which the lack of predication causes. "Yet" is in tension with "wink" and has several meanings here: And still, in spite of time and death (time and death being carryovers from "Voyages I") this Sea "is." The mind leaps to complete syntax and logic by assuming the presence, in meaning at least, of the verb "to be." To the reading "this Sea is," "wink" (by one of its connotations: a friendly wink) adds a further idea: and is friendly, "Laughing the wrapt inflections of our love."

"Wink" as an image for the sea suggests indulgence, good-nature, and yet a certain lack of seriousness, independability, both because of what a wink means and because it lasts but a moment. The sea is like an eye, aqueous, rimmed, curved slightly with the curvature of the earth. But the eye opened is eternity. The wink is the sea. The eye is closed. The sea is eternity with the veil of time over it. To mix the figure, it has the opaqueness of things seen in a glass darkly.

The image connects interestingly with the last line: "The seal's wide spindrift gaze toward paradise." A "spindrift gaze" is certainly one veiled by the thick spray raised by storm. It parallels a wink in being like the open eye of eternity. In other words, the sea is all the paradise an animal like the perfectly adapted seal can know. But the man can know perfect adaptation or paradise only through death. "Seal's" is both itself and a compromise between "sea's" and "soul's." The soul's blind gaze is answered in death. The soul is bound in time, but also in awe. The sea is time, and the soul is blindly adrift in it and gazing to paradise. The sea's "spindrift gaze toward paradise" is that of time waiting for its cessation, the end of the wink. The seal is a figure representing both human and nonhuman. Limitedly perfect, enjoying an earthly eternal Now, yet blinded and subject to death. The human being longs for death because of his incompleteness in life. Obviously the last line complicates rather than drops the image of the first line.

There is a paradox in the first line. Time, symbolized by the sea, is but a wink of eternity. "And yet" time and the sea seem to run on timelessly.

A naive enthusiast might say that the incompleteness of sentence structure in stanza one and the sudden use of the imperative in stanza two give one a feeling of the sea, its unbeginning and unending rhythms, its rushes and sudden changes, that the movement of the syntax parallels the movement of the sea. This is not quite true. It is the words themselves that tell us about the

> . . . rimless floods, unfettered leewardings,
> Samite sheeted and processioned where
> Her undinal vast belly moonward bends,
> Laughing the wrapt inflections of our love.

The incomplete syntax certainly gives us an impression of something started, not finished, begun again, taken many ways, but still not finished. The syntax is qualifying the implications of the words. These processions never really get anywhere. This love is not completely secure. To the good-nature implied in "wink" and in "Laughing the wrapt inflections of our love" is added a sinister changeableness and inconsequentiality. The syntax warns us in advance that this is not a sentimental poem about the sea and love. Because of it we suspect from the beginning that only in "the vortex of our grave" is answered "The seal's wide spindrift gaze toward paradise." The syntax thus exploits certain implications already latent in the "wink" image and in the sinisterly ambiguous "wrapt." Proper prediction and completed logic function here by their absence to influence a conclusion about the nature of the declaration being made: It is to be severely qualified in the direction mentioned. I feel that syntax has been distorted with superb effectiveness in this poem.

Just as a distortion of syntax may have a calculated effect even though it presents insoluble difficulties to the reader who demands subjects for verbs, unambiguous reference for pronouns, and so forth, so Crane's chain-reaction series of metaphors may be effective without being analyzable in terms of concrete reference. Sometimes it is important, as Crane seemed to think it was in the line "The calyx of death's bounty giving back" in "At Melville's Tomb," for one to get the exact reference of the metaphor: "This calyx refers in a double ironic sense both to a cornucopia and the vortex made by a sinking vessel" (Crane and Monroe, "Discussion," p. 420). At other times whatever metaphorical reference may have been in the poet's mind may have disappeared so completely in the poem that it is useless to speculate upon the matter; one can only deal with the implications derivable from the word itself in its context. This method of analysis has been brilliantly exemplified by R. P. Blackmur in his treatment of the phrase "New thresholds, new anatomies!" from Crane's "The Wine Menagerie":

> We see that thresholds open upon anatomies: upon things to be explored and understood and felt freshly as an adventure; and we see that the anatomies, what is to be explored, are known from a new vantage, and that the van-

tage is part of the anatomy. The separate meanings of the words fairly rush at each other; the right ones join and those irrelevant to the juncture are for the moment—the whole time of the poem—lost in limbo. (Blackmur, p. 132)

In the various manuscript versions of "Atlantis" we can trace the history of an image based on horseback riding and the use of spurs to the point where nothing is left of that reference but the word "slit." Crane is trying to get the impact on the reader of so many complicated related metaphors that only the total complex, not only understood image, makes its impression on the mind. Here, in the final version, are the lines concerned:

> Sheerly the eyes, like seagulls stung with rime—
> Slit and propelled by glistening fins of light—
> Pick biting way up towering looms that press
> Sidelong with flight of blade on tendon blade
> —Tomorrows into yesteryear. . . .
> (Crane, Complete Poems, p. 115)

How would one explain the imagery of the second line? If the eye is figured as a fish it could not be "slit" by a fin. If it is not a fish, it could not be propelled by a fin. One does not pause to worry about this dilemma, however, if one is thinking about looking at the shining bridge. The light both pierces one's eyes and attracts them. The line is effective.

Earlier versions reveal an origin for "slit." Among the "Worksheets, Spring and Summer, 1926" are found the following drafts.

> Sheerly the eyes are poured in avenues
> [decrees] [the *threshing*] [winnowing]
> Up towering *syncopations, leaning* press
> Of blade on tendon blade, inevitably
> [altar]
> Whose *verdant* looms and shuttles, drawing love,

[er] [blazing]
Build shimm ∧ ing up *the* conquering script;
[And terror] [shimmering] [*up*] [build]
Lo, *confidences* of *all* youth, beatitudes
[*th*] [testaments]
In sinuous music hewn of mythic words,—
The dance is chosen, the steep ways evoked! . . .

(Weber, p. 433)[1]

[flung *up* and poured]
Sheerly the eyes are *poured in* avenues
That shuttle upward (so the towering press
Of string on string leads on) and so incline
Beyond memory, O verdant cresting tides,
So shimmering of all youth, so dyed with love—
The steep dance chosen and the ways evoked;
Yea, as this shine refers,—beatitudes
In sinuous shafts commemorate of all Spring. . . .

(p. 434)

[out]
Sheerly the eyes *are* poured in avenues,
[Up] [Of]   [*and*] [*the*] [through]
Up towering looms, *whose* winnowing sidelong press
[gleams]
Of blade on tendon blade some altar *gleans,*
[*Whose*]   [*love*] [wefting]   [rise]
[With] *With* shuttles *fluttering* love and terror, *lifts*
The scriptural ciphers of *how young* a world [how young,] . . .

(p. 434)

[Picked *threadingly*]   [bightingly]
Sheerly the eyes are poured in avenues,—
[biting] [those]
Up towering looms, *the winnowing sidelong* press
Of blade on shuttle blade what *dread subsumes*
[sidelong dread] . . .

(p. 435)

Sheerly the eyes are spilled in avenues,

Picked bitingly up towering looms whose press
Of blade on shuttle blade what sidelong spurs . . .

(p. 435)

Sheerly the eyes are spilled in avenues,
[looms]
Picked bitingly up towering *avenues* that *crest* rake

(p. 435)

Sheerly the eyes are spilled in avenues,
Raked bitingly up towering looms that press
(O sidelong press of blade on shuttle blade)
All themes into that *cipher* that dreadful cipher
All themes into that dreadful cipher soar,
O love, that only you *can guess* may . . .

(p. 435)

[spilled]
Sheerly the eyes are *poured* in avenues,—
Picked bitingly up towering looms whose press
Of blade on shuttle blade what sidelong *dread* spurs
Medley of love and terror ciphers there . . .

(pp. 435–436)

Sheerly the eyes are spilled in avenues,
Picked bitingly up towering looms that press
(O sidelong spurs of blade on shuttle blade!) . . .

(p. 436)

Sheerly the eyes are spilled in avenues,
Picked bitingly up towering looms that press
[(Swiftly a seagull chides the *rain of* reins of light)]
(O sidelong spurs of blade on tendon blade!) . . .

(p. 436)

Sheerly the eyes, like seagull's stung with rime
[black]
And starlight riding the reins of light
Pick bitingly up towering looms that press
(O sidelong spurs of blade on shuttle blade!)
Tomorrows into yesterday, and *soar* [*thread*] [delve] . . .

(pp. 436–437)

Sheerly the eyes, like seagulls stung with rime
And starlight, riding *the* black reins of light,
Pick bitingly up towering looms that press
    [*the*] [with]
(*O* sidelong∧flight of blade on shuttle blade!) . . .

(p. 437)

Among the "Lines Sent to Waldo Frank, August 3, 1926" we find:

Sheerly the eyes, like seagulls stung with rime
And startryst, riding the black fins of light
Pick biting way up towering looms that press
Sidelong with flight of blade on tendon blade.

(p. 438)

The line "Slit and propelled by glistening fins of light" may have been meant as an amalgamation of fish and riding imagery. "Slit and propelled"—at least "Slit"—may refer to spurs. The seagull is "stung with rime" (analogous to a horse being pricked by spurs). The eyes are spurred up the way presented by the bridge by the sharp moving lines of light. These lines of light act both like spurs on active heels and like fins on an active fish. A horse picks its way "bitingly" when spurred, whereas these words do not seem to apply to a seagull or a fish (unless the fish is thought of as rising to a bait which it nibbles.) "Press/Sidelong" is a spur as well as a loom metaphor. In "Sidelong with flight of blade on tendon blade," earlier "O sidelong spurs of blade on shuttle blade" (Weber, p. 436), Crane has, by altering "spurs" to "flight," changed the horse metaphor to the seagull metaphor. "Tendon," which would go with either of the animal images, does not strictly correspond with the loom image. It is a metaphor for "shuttle." In other words, not only are the eyes seagulls, horses, fish, and shuttles, but the "tendon blades," the shuttles, are, by the use of the anatomical adjective, metaphorically wings, spurs, and fins.

Crane is not after an image from any one living creature, beast, bird, or fish, but is after an amalgamation of imagery from swift things of land, air, and water in order to make the bridge a symbol of the individual's union with life. He wishes to achieve a complex total impression without calling attention to scattered details. Thus it does not matter where "slit" comes from. The word is given a new significance by its context. That significance may be clearer if we do not attempt to visualize the metaphor than if we do.

On the other hand, when syntax and metaphor are both opaque how is the reader to read? Or when the metaphors suggest a developed figure but continually seem to drop that figure, or to work with it most awkwardly, how is the reader to know when to continue to think along certain lines and when to be sensitive only to each successive image as it strikes him? In "Lachrymae Christi" the lines "Let sphinxes from the ripe/Borage of death have cleared my tongue/Once and again" exemplify the former problem (Crane, *Complete Poems,* p. 20). One does not know whether "Let" is an adjective or a verb. Furthermore, one does not know what "sphinxes" have to do with "borage." The line is about as clear as Nimrod's "Rafel mai amech zabi almi" in Dante's Inferno. (Canto XXXI).

A reading of "The Broken Tower" exemplifies the second problem. There seems to be no consistently developed image of casting or manufacturing in the poem, nor perhaps one of flood, and yet the reader is constantly led to suspect the presence of such figures to account for the unstopped meaning-echoes of certain words. "The Broken Tower" is much like Crashaw's later work in being complexly emblematic and in mixing boldly figures which have no possible affinity except through the ideas each represents. Yet Crashaw's images change from phrase to phrase, not with each word as Crane's do. The result in Crashaw is less concentration than in Crane but more opportunity for the reader to follow the intellectual process of the poem. The poem proceeds by a psychological association which is never separated from a logical thought pattern. Furthermore, since the scaffolding of the poem is explicitly logical, images may leave off at any point. The logic will supply the continuity until the next image gets going.

Crane's images have too much responsibility. They must supply the continuity when syntax and logic abdicate. As a result metaphors which have been dropped are picked up again in embarrassing contexts. For one association which was intended or which works there may sometimes be at least one other which was not intended or which dissipates rather than enriches the total effect. In an emblematic type of poetry it would seem to be necessary to keep at least the "logically rigid significations"[2] of words. It is difficult to attend to the abstract rather than the concrete significance of a puzzling metaphor, while at the same time depending on a later echo of some aspect of its concrete significance to achieve poetic organization.

Of course any poem which hangs together has a logical (along with a psychological) structure. In Crashaw the two are equally evident. In Crane, the logical structure is hidden, most indirectly hinted at through psychological symbols. It is to be discovered. If found, it will prove to be as sound within its scope as Crashaw's. Sometimes, however, it cannot be found.

Lack of logic in the texture is the means of throwing the reader off the track in his search for logical structure, and psychological association in texture is the means of making the reader look for a psychological poetic organization. The reader is to feel the logic as marginally as a reader of eighteenth-century philosophical poetry is to feel the process of emotion and psychological association. Examples of both types of poetry often fail to achieve wholeness because of weaknesses inherent in the techniques.

The thread of connection of a Hart Crane poem is to the individual words as a resourceful host is to a large and various group of talkative guests, when he attempts, in the middle of a lively and seemingly endless discussion, to herd them all in to dinner. Even as the host has them by the elbow, many guests turn at the doorway, not heeding what he says, and speak energetically and cheerfully back into the room. The destination beyond the doorway, the dining room or whatever, is like the meaning of the poem. To get the bumptious words, without which there would be no dinner party, past the door, is the poet's attempt at connection. It is not always successful, and often Crane's poems are more like the excited prelude to a feast than like the feast itself. This is because in our time the wedding guests have neglected to come to the feast and Crane has had to send out into the highways and byways to gather in celebrants. That is, established systems of belief and the traditional ways of expressing those systems no longer accord with the psychology which the poet wishes to present.

Nevertheless, poetry must contain a kind of logic, because the mind is partly logical and because poetry is written with the full mind. Poetry is not a stream of associations, nor is it a logical syllogism, but it contains both in a superior organization.

'Repose of Rivers'

The willows carried a slow sound,
A sarabande the wind mowed on the mead.
I could never remember
That seething, steady leveling of the marshes
Till age had brought me to the sea.

Flags, weeds. And remembrance of steep alcoves
Where cypresses shared the noon's
Tyranny; they drew me into hades almost.
And mammoth turtles climbing sulphur dreams
Yielded, while sun-silt rippled them
Asunder . . .

How much I would have bartered! the black gorge
And all the singular nestings in the hills
Where beavers learn stitch and tooth.
The pond I entered once and quickly fled—
I remember now its singing willow rim.

And finally, in that memory all things nurse;
After the city that I finally passed
With scalding unguents spread and smoking darts
The monsoon cut across the delta
At gulf gates . . . There, beyond the dykes

I heard wind flaking sapphire, like this summer,
And willows could not hold more steady sound.

(Crane, Complete Poems, p. 16)

"Repose of Rivers exemplifies a difficulty which differs from
that of much of Crane's work. One of Crane's undoubted successes, this poem is an example of how a slight misreading may
throw the reader completely off. Here the danger is that one
may mistake the persona, the "I" who speaks the poem. Since,
in other poems, Crane's speaker is usually the poet himself

as poet or lover or sufferer, it is natural for the reader to assume that such is the case here. One recent critic commenting on "The pond I entered once and quickly fled—" identifies the "I" with Crane, here supposedly recalling an incident of his youth (Quinn, p. 33). Another spends several pages showing how the poem recapitulates Crane's writing career (Lewis, pp. 211–15). A third finds the poet in a swamp surrounded by cypresses. (He does not mention mosquitoes) (Hazo, p. 39).

Actually, and this is very important to realize, the speaker of the poetry is not Crane but a river. The title suggests the subject: "Repose of Rivers." What is it that is the repose of rivers? Why, the sea. The poem is an account, by a river, of the river's cycle of existence. A river has its source in the hills, descends to the plains, passes large cities near its mouth and empties into the sea, where it loses its individual existence. The river is an old symbol for time and human life, as the sea is an old symbol for death or eternity. Thus the sea is both a goal and the value of the river's life's journey. Further, rivers are both infinitely old and perpetually new. If a river could speak, it could tell of events older than the history of man. Yet the river is a good symbol for regeneration since the water it pours into the sea at the end of its life span is drawn up into clouds, is evaporated by the action of the sun, and descends as rain in the regions of the river's source. Thus the river has lived many times, and if it had a memory it would recognize, on coming to the sea, that it had been there before. Crane's river does this.

The critics find significant relations between this poem and Crane's life. Actually, however, the success and value of the poem stem from Crane's thorough escape from himself into this river persona. Admittedly the theme of memory and of losing oneself in an infinite element are familiar ones in Crane's other poetry. But he has universalized them by speaking through the river, a symbol which relates to something deep in all of us, not something personal to Crane. As T. S. Eliot put it in "The Dry Salvages," "The river is within us, the sea is all about us" (Eliot, *Complete Poems*, p. 130).

The opening stanza of Crane's poem is a marvelous evocation, through the sound and rhythm of wind, trees, grasses, and water currents, of the flat delta marshes just before the river is united with the sea. The river has been there many times before, but only now recollects. The lines

> I could never remember
> That seething, steady leveling of the marshes
> Till age had brought me to the sea

may suggest the human feeling "I have been here before" which one may have at the approach of life's end, but can hardly refer to anything personal in the life of twenty-seven-year-old Crane.

Realizing that the river speaks, the reader can relate the rest of the details of the poem to items in the river's history: the "steep alcoves" of its mountain source, so deep "they drew me into hades almost," the "black gorge," and the beaver pond of the foothills, the city of the lowlands, and finally the gulf. This is not to say that the lines do not work symbolically as well as descriptively. The "noon's/Tyranny" certainly suggests a fear of life. The lines,

> The pond I entered once and quickly fled—
> I remember now its singing willow rim

are very poignant. Entering the pond is a foretaste of the river's death in the sea, so that the river quickly flees. Yet, since this death is also the consummation of its life, the river remembers with satisfaction the pond's "singing willow rim," now that it has reached the willow rim of that final pond of ponds, the ocean, where it will merge with all other waters.

The only difficult lines tell how

> . . . mammoth turtles climbing sulphur dreams
> Yielded, while sun-silt rippled them
> Asunder . . .

These lines may present simply an aquatic detail—a picture of turtles, perhaps huge prehistoric turtles from some earlier millenium of the river's life, climbing a yellow mudbank or swimming in yellow water as the sunlight creates so intense a brilliance that the turtles seem rippled asunder by the water—an optical illusion. Or the rippling asunder refers to the extinction of this species at some period of the river's ageless history. Or (least likely) the sulfur and sunsilt may be meant to suggest a lava flow which consumed the turtles at some previous geologic period which the river survived. (I suppose that this phenomenon—"giant turtles" being caught in lava flows and consumed—could happen even in the present in the actively volcanic Galápagos Islands, which Crane had read of in Melville's "The Encantadas, or Enchanted Isles," 1854).

Certainly this dissolution of the turtles,—like the mowing, the "leveling," the drawing into "hades," the "black gorge," the fleeing from the "pond," the "scalding unguents"—is a foreshadowing of the death which is continually escaped until age brings one—the river—to the sea, where suddenly it is recognized that this death which one was fleeing is the value which one is pursuing: "How much I would have bartered!" The monsoon is the wind of winds, the sea the water of waters —and the moment of entering the sea in the monsoon season is the consummation and rebirth of the river's existence.

Does Hart Crane have a particular river in mind? The "delta/At gulf gates" clearly sounds like the Mississippi delta and the Gulf of Mexico. The city is probably New Orleans, the "City storied of three thrones" of Crane's "The River." In that poem the Mississippi, "Meeting the Gulf, hosannas silently below."

HART CRANE

'At Melville's Tomb'

Often beneath the wave, wide from this ledge
The dice of drowned men's bones he saw bequeath
An embassy. Their numbers as he watched,
Beat on the dusty shore and were obscured.

And wrecks passed without sound of bells,
The calyx of death's bounty giving back
A scattered chapter, livid hieroglyph,
The portent wound in corridors of shells.

Then in the circuit calm of one vast coil,
Its lashings charmed and malice reconciled,
Frosted eyes there were that lifted altars;
And silent answers crept across the stars.

Compass, quadrant and sextant contrive
No farther tides . . . High in the azure steeps
Monody shall not wake the mariner.
This fabulous shadow only the sea keeps.

(Crane, *Complete Poems*, p. 34)

"At Melville's Tomb" is an elegy for Herman Melville, who is buried in Woodlawn Cemetery, New York. Crane explained certain lines of the poem in the well-known letter to Harriet Monroe (Crane and Monroe, "Discussion"). But much of the poem's difficulty dissipates if we assume that Crane, like many elegists, follows a technique of allusion, filling his poem with echoes of the life and work of the poet he elegizes. If one has read *Moby Dick* one should immediately recognize that this poem is written out of a thorough assimilation of Melville's work and is surrounded by an aura of Melville reminiscences. The "he" of the poem is of course Melville, who, Crane is saying, often contemplated the phenomenon of death at sea, who felt the immensity of the sea and of the numbers drowned since the world began, and who sought meaning in it. To the poet or novelist or philosopher the drowned bones, ground to particles by the action of the water, would seem to leave messages, "bequeath/An embassy," from the dead to the living. These messages, like the pieces of bone, "Beat on the dusty shore and were obscured." The bones become pulverized, and the meaning of death is too much for either our understanding or our attention. "Numbers" suggests the vast hordes of people who have drowned, suggests also the numbers on "dice" and the now-obscured identity of the bones, the message they express, and the whole idea of chance and fate. The sea rolls the bones as dice are rolled in the hand or in a box, and it throws the ground pieces on the shore as one throws dice. But whereas one can read the dice, the bones are nameless, and the meaning of death beyond comprehension. The rhythmic effect of these lines is marvelously suggestive of wave rhythms, starting out at sea, "beneath the wave, wide from this ledge," and moving into the shore. It may be that the searching motion is partly achieved by making the reader look for the referent of "beneath the wave," the only puzzling ambiguity of syntax in the lines. This phrase can modify either "bones" or "he." The bones are, of course, "beneath the wave" when, drowning at sea, they bequeath their embassy which is so attenuated before it reaches land. But Melville's imagination is also "beneath the wave" and "wide from this ledge" of the safe land when, on his intellectual voyage, he visualizes the never-ending deaths of people who still had things to say. The ambiguity enables us to think of Melville as an omniscient author's intelligence contemplating both the drowning at sea and the washing up upon the shore, both the individual deaths and the infinite repetition of death.

The last three stanzas seem to visualize an actual shipwreck and, as Joseph Warren Beach has pointed out (Beach, pp. 191–92), are full of echoes of *Moby Dick,* especially of the final chapter, about the sinking of the *Pequod.* In the line "And wrecks passed without sound of bells" there is an ambiguity of meaning in "passed." Melville's omniscient imagination visualizes wreck after wreck passing by beneath the wave. They also pass away, that is, sink. The latter image relates to the chief image of stanzas two and three, the whirlpool made by a sinking vessel. In the lines,

> The calyx of death's bounty giving back
> A scattered chapter, livid hieroglyph,

there is implicit the figure of a cornucopia pouring out "bounty," as the whirlpool made by the sinking vessel brings up pieces of wreckage. "Calyx," the circle of sepals below the petals of a flower, ironically turns this image into that of a blossoming, the circle of white wreckage flowering up from the whirlpool. Similarly in "Voyages II" we have the lines

> . . . sleep, death, desire,
> Close round one instant in one floating flower.

"The portent wound in corridors of shells" introduces another image, that of the windings of a shell, say a conch shell, which have a spiral shape similar to that of the cornucopia or the whirlpool. "The portent wound in corridors of shells," if one holds one to his ear, is the hum of his own veins multiplied in the shell and so calls up again the mystery of life and death. You too will die, is what the shell says. To call pieces of wreckage a "chapter" or "hieroglyph" is to refer, as in "embassy," to the messages the dead may have had for the living and to the meaning—incomplete, mysterious—which the living may derive from contemplating those deaths. In the case of Melville, in particular, the deaths gave back "A scattered chapter" or two, since his novels emerged from such contemplation. The "livid hieroglyph" may just possibly be a recollection of the tattooing on the body of Queequeg, the cannibal harpooner.

> And this tattooing had been the work of a departed prophet and seer of his island, who, by those hieroglyphic marks, had written out on his body a complete theory of the heavens and the earth, and a mystical treatise on the art of attaining truth; so that Queequeg in his own proper person was a riddle to unfold; a wondrous work in one volume; but whose mysteries not even himself could read,

though his own live heart beat against them; and these mysteries were therefore destined in the end to moulder away with the living parchment whereon they were inscribed, and so be unsolved to the last. (Melville, *Moby Dick, p.* 476)

After his recovery from a fever, Queequeg carves these same "hieroglyphs" onto the coffin which he had had made for him when he thought he was dying. He uses the coffin for a sea chest. Then, when the ship's life-buoy is lost, Queequeg's coffin takes its place. After the ship goes down, Ishmael the narrator alone escapes drowning, buoyed up by that coffin life-buoy which shoots up beside him. Quite literally in that case the sea gives back a "livid hieroglyph."

Stanza three seems to refer to the moment when the whirlpool subsides after the ship has sunk and when the survivors are left floating in the water, probably to drown, though in Ishmael's case to be saved.

So, floating on the margin of the ensuing scene, and in full sight of it, when the half-spent suction of the ship reached me, I was then, but slowly, drawn towards the closing vortex. When I reached it, it had subsided to a creamy pool. Round and round, then, and ever contracting towards the button-like black bubble at the axis of that slowly wheeling circle, like another Ixion I did revolve. (Melville, *Moby Dick,* pp. 565–66).

In stanza three "coil" again parallels the spiral shape of the whirlpool, and along with "lashings" and "malice" suggests that the whirling water is like a great serpent which, lashing its tail, has encircled men and ship in its coils. Moby Dick, who has sunk the *Pequod,* is associated in the book with "Leviathan the piercing serpent, even Leviathan that crooked serpent" (Isaiah), that is with Evil incarnate, Satan, the serpent of the Garden of Eden. The "lashing" of Moby Dick's tail is certainly to be feared: "The White Whale . . . rushing among the boats with open jaws, and a lashing tail, offered appalling battle on every side . . ." (Melville, *Moby Dick,* p. 549).

"Head on, he came churning his tail among the boats; and once more flailed them apart; spilling out the irons and lances from the two mates' boats, and dashing in one side of the upper part of their bows . . ." (Melville, *Moby Dick,* p. 559).

The words "coil" and "lashings" also call up images of the whale line which in this last chapter takes Ahab out of his boat with a noose around his neck and which earlier has been compared to a malicious serpent.

> Thus the whale-line folds the whole boat in its complicated coils, twisting and writhing around it in almost every direction. All the oarsmen are involved in its perilous contortions; so that to the timid eye of the landsman, they seem as Indian jugglers, with the deadliest of snakes sportively festooning their limbs. . . . The graceful repose of the line, as it silently serpentines about the oarsman before being brought into actual play—this is a thing which carries more of true terror than any other aspect of this dangerous affair. (Melville, *Moby Dick,* pp. 278–80)

At the very end of *Moby Dick* the lashings are indeed charmed and the malice reconciled after the death of the great Captain Ahab. "For almost one whole day and night, I floated on a soft and dirge-like main. The unharming sharks, they glided by as if with padlocks on their mouths; the savage seahawks sailed with sheathed beaks" (Melville, *Moby Dick,* p. 566). No doubt, during that night, Ishmael's "Frosted eyes" often "lifted altars" as he prayed for survival. But while reminiscent of the end of *Moby Dick* the stanzas are not about Ishmael, who lived, but about those who died, in the *Pequod* and in many other ships. The eyes of these less fortunate mariners were "Frosted" not only in the sense of reflecting light but also in the sense of being frosted over in death after a last upward drowning glance. The figure is not so unusual that it has never been used before. In Dante we read concerning the martyred Saint Stephen that "ever of his eyes made he gates onto heaven," that is, his last living glance upward was full of saving prayer.

The mysterious "silent answers" that "crept across the stars"

are the last that the dying man sees. Death itself is a "silent
answer." After all have sunk beneath the surface, only the
stars remain above it.

Since the poem is an elegy upon the dead Melville, one inevitably associates his death with that of those whose "Frosted
eyes . . . lifted altars" and one associates the answers he won
with the "silent answers" that "crept across the stars."

The last stanza is completely elegiac in mood. "Compass,
quadrant and sextant contrive/No farther tides" recalls Ahab's
breaking the quadrant and also his making a new compass. The
lines say several things—that the quest (Melville's or Ahab's)
is a desperate, final one from which there is no turning back,
no returning to shore; that the voyage is over, that is, Melville
is dead; finally, that human ingenuity will never think up
works of greater scope than Melville's. Melville is the drowned
mariner whom the "Monody" of the wind, "High in the azure
steeps," shall not wake. And the word "Monody" is especially
appropriate here since it is the title of a poem which Melville
wrote to the memory of a dead friend, Nathaniel Hawthorne.[1]

"This fabulous shadow"—Melville—" only the sea keeps."
Even though he is buried on land, Melville's true element is
the sea, since he wrote about it. But also the lines suggest that
in some sense Melville lives on, in his work or as some eternal
principle. The last line of the poem has been prepared for in
the first line with the ambiguity of syntax there which enables
us to read that it is Melville who is "beneath the wave," seeing
death from that vantage point. "This fabulous shadow" which
is "beneath the wave" is again reminiscent of *Moby Dick*. Melville was indeed a fabulous writer of fables, but his most fabulous fable was Moby Dick himself, whose shadow looms im-
pressively out of the water at various points in the book. One
of the most effective passages is the following:

> . . . Ahab could discover no sign in the sea. But suddenly
> as he peered down and down into its depths, he profoundly
> saw a white living spot no bigger than a white weasel,
> with wonderful celerity uprising, and magnifying as it
> rose, till it turned, and then there were plainly revealed

> two long crooked rows of white, glistening teeth, floating up from the undiscoverable bottom. It was Moby Dick's open mouth and scrolled jaw; his vast, shadowed bulk still half blending with the blue of the sea. (Melville, *Moby Dick,* p. 539)

Crane ends his elegy by identifying the great novelist with his vast creation, Moby Dick, who may be swimming yet somewhere in this little fishbowl of a globe. For the whale too is immortal.

> In Noah's flood he despised Noah's Ark; and if ever the world is to be again flooded, like the Netherlands, to kill off its rats, then the eternal whale will still survive, and rearing upon the topmost crest of the equatorial flood, spout his frothed defiance to the skies. (Melville, *Moby Dick,* p. 458)

'For the Marriage of Faustus and Helen'

"For the Marriage of Faustus and Helen" is Crane's first major poem. It uses the mythical method of ordering contemporary experience which, by the time Crane's poem was finished early in 1923, had been exemplified by both James Joyce's *Ulysses* and T. S. Eliot's *The Waste Land,* though Crane's conception preceded both the completion of *The Waste Land* and the full publication of *Ulysses.* As he wrote in a January 5, 1923, letter to Gorham Munson, Crane wished, in "Faustus and Helen," to "take Eliot as a point of departure toward an almost complete reverse of direction." His would be "a more positive, or . . . ecstatic goal." "I feel," he wrote, "that Eliot ignores certain spiritual events and possibilities as real and powerful now as, say, in the time of Blake" (Crane, *Letters,* p. 114–15).

In reading "Faustus and Helen" it is important for one to catch the tone in which Crane, evoking a "very real and absolute conception of beauty," as he wrote in "General Aims and Theories" (1925, published 1937), builds "a bridge between so-called classic experience and many divergent realities of our seething, confused cosmos of today, which has no formulated mythology yet for classic poetic reference or for religious exploitation" (Crane, *Complete Poems,* p. 217). It is well to remember that Crane, as he wrote in "Legend," was

> . . . not ready for repentance;
> Nor to match regrets.
> (Crane, *Complete Poems,* p. 3)

Neither Faustus nor Helen were conventionally proper people. Both must have been condemned by those who were. Yet each lived in myth as the ideal of the future—Helen as abstract beauty, Faustus as the questing imagination. The marriage of Renaissance Faustus to the wraith of Classical Helen was a daring and evil thing in Marlowe's *The Tragical History of*

Doctor Faustus and could not, in any version of the myth, be a marriage sanctioned by society. It is, on the contrary, a defiance of social codes. Doctor Faustus chooses Helen rather than the salvation offered by orthodoxy.

Therefore the title "For the Marriage of Faustus and Helen" has about it a certain deliberate flouting of accepted ways of thought and behavior, as if one should cry, "Here's to the two bad ones!" At any event it is not certain that the marriage of "this abstract 'sense of beauty' " and "the poetic or imaginative man of all times," as Crane called Helen and Faustus in a February 7, 1923, letter to Waldo Frank (Crane, *Letters*, p. 120), actually takes place in the poem. The poem's title is not "The Marriage of Faustus and Helen" but *"For* the Marriage." Rather than a prothalamion, this may be a poem "towards" or "in favor of" the marriage of poet and beauty, the actual consummation of which never takes place. Such a subject would be close to Crane's own experience. On December 10, 1922, a month before finishing "Faustus and Helen" Crane wrote to a friend, "Life is meagre with me. I am unsatisfied and left always begging for beauty" (Crane, *Letters*, p. 108).

His gift of humor has not left him in writing "Faustus and Helen" (*Complete Poems*, pp. 27–33). There is gaiety in the title and in the epigraph—taken from a scene in Ben Jonson's *The Alchemist* in which Sir Epicure Mammon is fooled and fleeced. In good-natured double-talk the epigraph invites the reader to join with the poet-alchemist

> . . . *to raise the building up*
> *Of Helen's house against the Ismaelite. . . .*

that is, of abstract beauty against the bigoted, money-making Philistines of the age. (It is well to remember that Subtle, the hilarious fake alchemist of the Jonson comedy, is in the same alchemical profession as Doctor Faustus and is scornfully called a "Faustus" by one who would expose him.) The epigraph cannot help but imply that Crane refuses in this poem to take himself entirely seriously, a hint which we will do well to heed as we proceed into part I. (Crane, *Complete Poems*, pp. 27–29).

> The mind has shown itself at times
> Too much the baked and labeled dough
> Divided by accepted multitudes.

Not the "baked and labeled" attitudes to which workaday, money-grubbing society is committed, but the guilty flashes of unconventional thoughts and desires, the "equivocations" flashed out by "smutty wings," may lead the mind—for example the minds of office-workers in the "stacked partitions" of the skyscrapers—toward beauty, as they undoubtedly led Paris, a proper guest in proper Menelaus's dull home, to think about running off with Helen.

The second stanza of part I contains a fused image of "numbers" from "stock quotations" and "baseball scores" and "numbers" of sparrows on the streets, gutters and sidewalks of New York.

> The mind is brushed by sparrow wings;
> Numbers, rebuffed by asphalt, crowd
> The margins of the day, accent the curbs,
> Convoying divers dawns on every corner
> To druggist, barber and tobacconist,
> Until the graduate opacities of evening
> Take them away as suddenly to somewhere
> Virginal perhaps, less fragmentary, cool.

"Numbers, rebuffed by asphalt" calls up images of newspapers (financial and sport sections most visibly) drifting into the gutters, "the margins of the day," and of sparrows alighting on the curbs. ("Margins" is, of course, a stock market term.) The mind, filled with these newspaper "numbers" which regulate business and pleasure is at the same time "brushed by sparrow wings," moved by vague intimations of flight to a life of fuller satisfactions. If these uses of "numbers" seem contradictory— one related to the limiting environment, the other to the flight to the ideal—the contradiction is only momentary. "Numbers" are involved in the proportion and harmony necessary to ideal beauty, are related to the eternal Platonic ideas or forms which govern that proportion and harmony, and are the basis of the scientific and mechanical achievements by which the present society will rivet its eye to Helen's "plane."

"Numbers" also applies, of course, to the numbers of people getting up and going to work, crowding the margins of the streets and crowding peeps at the financial and sports sections into the margins of their time. The vague intimations of beauty, vague rebellions and desires of flight, also crowd the margins of their time, unconscious wishes coming to the surface during pauses in their limiting and confining daily tasks. These little glimpses are the only spiritual margins, as opposed to financial margins (in the sense of profit) which people can claim, and these brief moments of spiritual margin or profit are crowded and invaded by the jostling numbers of other city-dwellers.

At the end of the day, however, all these clear labels, separating partitions, accented curbs and limitations, are obscured by the "graduate opacities of evening" and with an out-of-school "graduate" feeling one can ignore, be opaque to, the categories of daytime life. The "divers dawns" which make one man a druggist, one a banker, and another a tobacconist, are, with the other "numbers," obscured, and all men become the same again, simply men come home to rest and renew themselves. "Virginal" intrudes the vague desire suggested in "smutty wings," but now in a purified, more essentialized form, free of the adulteration of the business world (of wealthy Menelaus?).

But this repetitive cycle of dull struggle and self-deceived rest, the day and night of most people, "the world dimensional," is not for our protagonist, our Faustus who wishes, like Paris, to carry off Helen. He is "twisted by the love of things/irreconcilable." He wants "abstract beauty" and he wants to hold it in his arms in a concrete embrace. Only in madness, drunkenness, or some kind of mystical exultation is this possible. Here the poem confirms the hint of stanza two where the numbers with which the mind was filled began to move with wings as sparrows. All the ordinary curbs, rules, limitations of life seem suddenly dissolved.

And yet, suppose some evening I forgot

> The fare and transfer, yet got by that way
> Without recall,—lost yet poised in traffic.

The poet gets by without "the fare and transfer." He passes sure-footedly through murderous traffic. Yet he is "lost" in some mind-freeing sensation as if under the influence of alcohol or drugs. The equivalent of this condition, in the Faustus legend, would be the magic of Lucifer or Mephistopheles which sets aside scientific law for Faustus' benefit.

In this state he travels, on a street-car, from the quotidian to the absolute. Helen, a girl across the aisle, her hands counting the nights, is still half engrossed in the "numbers" of her day; these fragmentary concerns are still flickering in her eyes.

> Then I might find your eyes across an aisle,
> Still flickering with those prefigurations—
> Prodigal, yet uncontested now,
> Half-riant before the jerky window frame.

> There is some way, I think, to touch
> Those hands of yours that count the nights
> Stippled with pink and green advertisements.
> And now, before its arteries turn dark
> I would have you meet this bartered blood.
> Imminent in his dream, none better knows
> The white wafer cheek of love, or offers words
> Lightly as moonlight on the eaves meets snow.

The word "prefigurations" and the phrase "half-riant" suggest that she invites his attention, flirtatiously hinting things to come. He hopes to touch those counting hands and move her from daytime concerns to those of night and love. "Lightly as moonlight on the eaves meets snow" links with "Virginal perhaps, less fragmentary, cool" above. The "white wafer cheek of love" is a spiritually genuine communion contrasting with the mock-Eucharist of "the baked and labeled dough / Divided by accepted multitudes." In the next stanza the girl's blush, responding to the man's attention, and their reciprocal excitement, suddenly express the need of all men for beauty, the need prefigured in the equivocations of smutty wings.

> Reflective conversion of all things
> At your deep blush, when ecstasies thread
> The limbs and belly, when rainbows spread
> Impinging on the throat and sides . . .
> Inevitable, the body of the world
> Weeps in inventive dust for the hiatus
> That winks above it, bluet in your breasts.

All the activities of man's "inventive dust" become a clamoring for the ideal, the perfection which life can never give, the "hiatus," gap or lack, which "winks above" "the body of the world." The image is puzzling, but I take it that the Idea is the separation of the actual from the ideal, this separation being symbolized by the empty blue sky above the earth. The implicit idea of a cleavage between the ideal and the actual suggested to Crane the figure of the cleavage between Helen's breasts. The blue sky, the separation between the actual and the ideal, becomes the bluet in the breasts of Helen, the ideal.

The daydream ends here. Crane is no longer supposing that he has met Helen as a girl on a streetcar. She is above and he is below, as far from seeing ideal beauty as ever. Yet the device has succeeded in moving our mind's eye from street to sky, from actual to ideal. The poet now lifts his arms from ephemeral earth to deified Helen. He accepts that living hands are

> . . . too alternate
> With steel and soil. . .

to hold onto the ideal. To gain this beauty nothing less than the sacrifice of all man's energy and attainments is required.

> I meet you, therefore, in that eventual flame
> You found in final chains. . . .

The burning of Troy, the recapture of Helen, figure forth the cost of attaining beauty. One must be willing to go through the whole tragic cycle. Crane unhesitatingly accepts that the destruction of his society and his own destruction in that "eventual flame" are the ultimate price of serving ideal beauty. But Helen is untouched, unchanged, through all the destruction and accusation:

... No captive then—
Beyond their million brittle bloodshot eyes;
White, through white cities passed on to assume
That world which comes to each of us alone.

The image here must be a triumphal procession in which the re-
captured Helen is displayed as a captive. At the same time it
becomes a triumphal procession of Helen herself as conqueror,
having destroyed city after city and age after age by her beauty.
She is the unattained goal of every heart. She is the beauty in
which the value of life inheres and which can only come to
each man individually.

In the last four lines, Helen is broadly identified with ideal
beauty as expressed through modern technological society. "Accept a lone eye riveted to your plane," Crane puns, thinking of
the "higher plane" of ideal beauty but also of the airplane
which appears again in part III. His image of his own humility,
"Bent axle of devotion," is almost comic, but works with "plane"
to express these spiritual concepts in mechanical terms. The
glance of Crane's "lone eye," the eye of a seer and poet, has left
earth in order to orbit about this new heavenly body and to be
a lesser companion in the train of timeless beauty.

Accept a lone eye riveted to your plane,
Bent axle of devotion along companion ways
That beat, continuous, to hourless days—
One inconspicuous, glowing orb of praise.

Critics complain of a shift of tone from part I to part II
(Crane, *Complete Poems,* pp. 30–31), but the shift is natural.
Part I evokes beauty and moves from the actual to the ideal,
whereas part II re-embodies the ideal in the actual.

Brazen hypnotics glitter here;
Glee shifts from foot to foot,
Magnetic to their tremolo.
This crashing opéra bouffe,
Blest excursion! this ricochet
From roof to roof—

> Know, Olympians, we are breathless
> While nigger cupids scour the stars!

Here, Crane wrote to Gorham Munson (January 14th, 1923),
we have "Dance, Humor, Satisfaction." (Crane, *Letters,* p.
116). In "General Aims and Theories" he explained that he
had transferred the "Dionysian revels" of Helen's "court and
her seduction . . . to a Metropolitan roof garden with a jazz orchestra" (Crane, *Complete Poems,* p. 217). To Waldo Frank
he wrote (February 7th, 1923) that part II was "the Dance
and sensual culmination" and the "acceleration of the ecstasy of"
part III (Crane, *Letters,* p. 121). In Crane's three-part for-
mula of "Evocation," "Dance," "Catharsis," one should almost
substitute "Desecration" as the second term. The ideal must be
evoked, then desecrated by the limited mortal attempt to realize
it. Then there must be suffering and renewal so that the whole
process may start again. To Crane, a homosexual given to passing loves, this was the all too familiar pattern of passion: high
anticipation; inadequate possession; satiety, disillusion, and a
new commitment. It was his way of life.

The mood of part II is that of a hilarious good time, adoles-
cent high jinks become a credo and affirmed in the teeth of
death itself.

> While titters hailed the groans of death
> Beneath gyrating awnings I have seen
> The incunabula of the divine grotesque.

All but the last stanza is impressionistic, the roof-garden scene
as apprehended by one of the dancers who is moved by the music to a point where (as in part I) scientific law seems set aside:

> And you may fall downstairs with me
> With perfect grace and equanimity.
> Or, plaintively scud past shores
> Where, by strange harmonic laws
> All relatives, serene and cool,
> Sit rocked in patent armchairs.

This graceful fall, to the accompaniment of music, is not only
part of the dance, but also the fall of Helen, her seduction. The

"relatives" who are "rocked in patent armchairs" are people, chaperones of some sort, who don't really know what's going on. (In the Helen myth, Menelaus and Agamemnon were complacent "relatives" until Paris escaped with the girl!) But the word also means "relatives" as opposed to the *absolute* beauty Crane is attempting to embody. "Relatives" are also the relative major and minor keys of music, for Crane was eager to get into words the effect the new music had on him.

Along with imagery of the Fall of Man, we have imagery of satiric "metallic paradises" in which "cuckoos clucked to finches." Crane may be thinking of flappers and their "sugar daddies," the latter probably being both "cuckolds" and a bit "cuckoo." The "canters," "banters" of a "rooster," and "cuckoos" and "finches," all of course being sounds from the orchestra, give a background of animal lusts to these "metallic paradises."

> O, I have known metallic paradises
> Where cuckoos clucked to finches
> Above the deft catastrophes of drums.
> While titters hailed the groans of death
> Beneath gyrating awnings I have seen
> The incunabula of the divine grotesque.
> This music has a reassuring way.

Though "catastrophe" and "death" are behind the scene, the speaker seems to say, let us play the game out to the end.

> The siren of the springs of guilty song—
> Let us take her on the incandescent wax
> Striated with nuances, nervosities
> That we are heir to. . . .

There is no apology for Helen here. She is the only Helen there is and the only Muse for Crane. If she were not guilty—that is, if she did not put beauty before truth or goodness, at least as society sees them—how could she be absolute beauty? Guilty song is, by the same reasoning, the only song there is and is worth the guiltiness. Crane's Muse *was* a siren. All genius destroys established form. It breaks up the old, hopefully in order to remold and recreate, but assuredly it does break up the old.

When Helen appears, Paris or Faustus must run off with her, whatever the disastrous consequences, because if this did not happen, nothing would happen. The new beauty must be pursued, whatever the social catastrophe that follows. Let us take her then, on the "incandescent wax" of the dance floor, an incandescence that relates to "that eventual flame" of burning Troy and the "Repeated play of fire" of World War I. "She is still so young" because she is new, the new beauty of the new age.

> We cannot frown upon her as she smiles,
> Dipping here in this cultivated storm
> Among slim skaters of the gardened skies.

In part III (Crane, *Complete Poems*, pp. 32–33) "this cultivated storm" of the roof-garden dance floor becomes the "cultivated storm" of World War I, modern equivalent of the Trojan War.

> Capped arbiter of beauty in this street
> That narrows darkly into motor dawn,—
> You, here beside me, delicate ambassador
> Of intricate slain numbers that arise
> In whispers, naked of steel;
> religious gunman!
> Who faithfully, yourself, will fall too soon,
> And in other ways than as the wind settles
> On the sixteen thrifty bridges of the city:
> Let us unbind our throats of fear and pity.

Paris, the "Capped arbiter of beauty" who chose Aphrodite as beauty queen over Hera and Athena and so won Helen of Troy for his own, is here beside Faustus in the form of a World War I airplane pilot. When above in his plane, he is a helmeted "arbiter of beauty," deciding what targets below shall not be destroyed. When walking the streets in uniform, including cap, he gratuitously judges the girls. He is the eternal soldier, representative of the generations that have died in man's attempt to capture Helen, ideal beauty. This pilot too, as Faustus fell for and with Helen in part II, "will fall too soon," when his plane crashes. "Let us unbind our throats of fear and pity," Faustus-Crane cries to him, deliberately recalling the terms of tragic catharsis.

The three following stanzas describe the air warfare of World War I:

> We even,
> Who drove speediest destruction
> In corymbulous formations of mechanics,—
> Who hurried the hill breezes, spouting malice
> Plangent over meadows, and looked down
> On rifts of torn and empty houses
> Like old women with teeth unjubilant
> That waited faintly, briefly and in vain:
>
> We know, eternal gunman, our flesh remembers
> The tensile boughs, the nimble blue plateaus,
> The mounted, yielding cities of the air!
>
> That saddled sky that shook down vertical
> Repeated play of fire—no hypogeum
> Of wave or rock was good against one hour.

Then Crane comments:

> We did not ask for that, but have survived
> And will persist to speak again. . . .

This utterance, the obscure lines which follow seem to say, is to take place "before" the remaining streets, those that have not known absolute destruction:

> before
> All stubble streets that have not curved
> To memory, or known the ominous lifted arm
> That lowers down the arc of Helen's brow
> To saturate with blessing and dismay.

Crane is actually thinking, the letters reveal, of the streets that are dwarfed by the edge of Brooklyn Bridge, whose curve no doubt suggested

> ... the ominous lifted arm
> That lowers down the arc of Helen's brow. ...

Since earlier lines in this section picture the airplane falling

> ... in other ways than as the wind settles
> On the sixteen thrifty bridges of the city

we probably have, in the lines beginning "All stubble streets," a fused image of the plane descending in a crash or in an attack, and the downward curve of the bridge, bridge and plane being mechanical forces of the new age which both bless and dismay.

The lines beginning "A goose, tobacco and cologne—" remain obscure.

> A goose, tobacco and cologne—
> Three-winged and gold-shod prophecies of heaven,
> The lavish heart shall always have to leaven
> And spread with bells and voices, and atone
> The abating shadows of our conscript dust.

If a reminiscence by Samuel Loveman can be trusted, we may have a hint as to Crane's intent. "He used to get his lines in the oddest way. . . . He once showed me a clipping, saying, 'I'm going to use this.' A Negro was arrested for stealing a goose, tobacco and cologne" (Loveman, pp. 21–22). I take it that Crane was pityingly amused at the man's version of the good life and his trust and enterprise in seeking it. After all, God helps those that help themselves. Perhaps Crane wanted a tone of boisterous, defiant assertion, of a ridiculous but heroic challenge— all the more heroic for being ridiculous—thrown in the face of loss and death. The mood is perhaps the one of "gaiety and quest" in "Chaplinesque" which does not prevent the sensitive clown from hearing "a kitten in the wilderness" (Crane, *Complete Poems,* p. 11).

In the next lines, the references to Anchises, father of Aeneas, and to Erasmus, remind us of two great beginnings out of the "blown blood and vine" of former civilizations—that of Rome and that of modern Europe. Just so the pilot, the eternal soldier, the young man of the present (who is also the recalled "brother-thief" Paris), is urged to "Delve upward" into the air for the wine of the new age.

> Anchises' navel, dripping the sea,—
> The hands Erasmus dipped in gleaming tides,
> Gathered the voltage of blown blood and vine;
> Delve upward for the new and scattered wine,
> O brother-thief of time, that we recall.

The last eight lines are an eloquent hymn to the modern spirit. Play out the game to the end, they say. We have to seek beauty in our time in our own new way. This way, like all ways, leads to tragedy and death. Just as Paris took Helen in spite of what would happen and caused the destruction of Troy, which in turn caused the building of Rome (through Aeneas), so America chose to create a great mechanical civilization out of which came the World War. Nevertheless this new, though also transitory society is worth the cost, and we shall go on to build it laughing in the face of pessimism. As in "Lachrymae Christi" the imagery of joy blends with imagery of crucifixion. "It is Dionysian in its attitude," Crane wrote to Frank (February 7th, 1923), "the creator and the eternal destroyer dance arm in arm . . ." (Crane, *Letters,* p. 121). Whatever is lost, the work of the imagination spans a height "beyond despair" surpassing the petty interested formulations of "bankers, schoolmasters, and clergymen" (Yeats, *Variorum Poems,* p. 205).

> Laugh out the meager penance of their days
> Who dare not share with us the breath released,
> The substance drilled and spent beyond repair
> For golden, or the shadow of gold hair.
>
> Distinctly praise the years, whose volatile
> Blamed bleeding hands extend and thresh the height
> The imagination spans beyond despair,
> Outpacing bargain, vocable and prayer.

The phrase "Laugh out" is consistent with the gaiety of tone of the whole. Yet this gaiety, it need hardly be said, is not a mere healthy, chest-beating optimism, but a gaiety beyond tragedy. "Ecstasy," not "happiness," is the word Crane gives to the tone of part III (Crane, *Letters*, p. 116). Early in the process of writing that part, in a letter (August or September, 1922) to Gorham Munson, he had paraphrased Samuel Butler to the effect that " 'No one has ever begun to really appreciate life, or lived, until he has recognized the background of life as essentially Tragedy.' It is from this platform of perception," adds Crane, "that I conceive every artist as beginning his work" (Crane, *Letters,* p. 99).

So did W. B. Yeats:

> As life goes on we discover that certain thoughts sustain us in defeat, or give us victory, whether over ourselves or others, and it is these thoughts, tested by passion, that we call convictions. Among subjective men (in all those, that is, who must spin a web out of their own bowels) the victory is an intellectual daily recreation of all that exterior fate snatches away, and so that fate's antithesis; while what I have called "the Mask" is an emotional antithesis to all that comes out of their internal nature. We begin to live when we have conceived life as tragedy" (Yeats, *Autobiography,* p. 116).

Had Crane lived, had his own tragedy not been complete six years earlier than the publication in 1938 of Yeats's "Lapis Lazuli," he would have admired the expression of his own theme by the only poet of his time who could give it more triumphant and convincing expression:

> All perform their tragic play,
> There struts Hamlet, there is Lear,
> That's Ophelia, that Cordelia;
> Yet they, should the last scene be there,
> The great stage curtain about to drop,
> If worthy their prominent part in the play,
> Do not break up their lines to weep.

They know that Hamlet and Lear are gay;
Gaiety transfiguring all that dread. . . .

. . . All things fall and are built again,
And those that build them again are gay.
                    (Yeats, *Variorum Poems,* p. 565–66)

HART CRANE

'The Dance'

The swift red flesh, a winter king—
Who squired the glacier woman down the sky?
She ran the neighing canyons all the spring;
She spouted arms; she rose with maize—to die.

And in the autumn drouth, whose burnished hands
With mineral wariness found out the stone
Where prayers, forgotten, steamed the mesa sands?
He holds the twilight's dim, perpetual throne.

Mythical brows we saw retiring—loth,
Disturbed and destined, into denser green.
Greeting they sped us, on the arrow's oath:
Now lie incorrigibly what years between . . .

There was a bed of leaves, and broken play;
There was a veil upon you, Pocahontas, bride—
O Princess whose brown lap was virgin May;
And bridal flanks and eyes hid tawny pride.

I left the village for dogwood. By the canoe
Tugging below the mill-race, I could see
Your hair's keen crescent running, and the blue
First moth of evening take wing stealthily.

What laughing chains the water wove and threw!
I learned to catch the trout's moon whisper; I
Drifted how many hours I never knew,
But, watching, saw that fleet young crescent die,—

And one star, swinging, take its place, alone,
Cupped in the larches of the mountain pass—
Until, immortally, it bled into the dawn.
I left my sleek boat nibbling margin grass . . .

*Then you shall
see her truly
—your blood
remembering
its first
invasion of her
secrecy, its
first encounters
with her kin,
her chieftain
lover . . . his
shade that
haunts the
lakes and hills*

I took the portage climb, then chose
A further valley-shed; I could not stop.
Feet nozzled wat'ry webs of upper flows;
One white veil gusted from the very top.

O Appalachian Spring! I gained the ledge;
Steep, inaccessible smile that eastward bends
And northward reaches in that violet wedge
Of Adirondacks!—wisped of azure wands,

Over how many bluffs, tarns, streams, I sped!
—And knew myself within some boding shade:—
Grey tepees tufting the blue knolls ahead,
Smoke swirling through the yellow chestnut glade . . .

A distant cloud, a thunder-bud— it grew,
That blanket of the skies: the padded foot
Within,—I heard it; 'til its rhythm drew,
—Siphoned the black pool from the heart's hot root!

A cyclone threshes in the turbine crest,
Swooping in eagle feathers down your back;
Know, Maquokeeta, greeting; know death's best;
—Fall, Sachem, strictly as the tamarack!

A birch kneels. All her whistling fingers fly.
The oak grove circles in a crash of leaves;
The long moan of a dance is in the sky.
Dance, Maquokeeta: Pocahontas grieves . . . .

And every tendon scurries toward the twangs
Of lightning deltaed down your saber hair.
Now snaps the flint in every tooth; red fangs
And splay tongues thinly busy the blue air . . .

Dance, Maquokeeta! snake that lives before,
That casts his pelt, and lives beyond! Sprout, horn!
Spark, tooth! Medicine-man, relent, restore—
Lie to us,—dance us back the tribal morn!

Spears and assemblies: black drums thrusting on—
O yelling battlements,—I, too, was liege

To rainbows currying each pulsant bone:
Surpassed the circumstance, danced out the siege!

And buzzard-circleted, screamed from the stake;
I could not pick the arrows from my side.
Wrapped in that fire, I saw more escorts wake—
Flickering, sprint up the hill groins like a tide.

I heard the hush of lava wrestling your arms,
And stag teeth foam about the raven throat;
Flame cataracts of heaven in seething swarms
Fed down your anklets to the sunset's moat.

O, like the lizard in the furious noon,
That drops his legs and colors in the sun,
—And laughs, pure serpent, Time itself, and moon
Of his own fate, I saw thy change begun!

And saw thee dive to kiss that destiny
Like one white meteor, sacrosanct and blent
At last with all that's consummate and free
There, where the first and last gods keep thy tent.

                    *   *   *

Thewed of the levin, thunder-shod and lean,
Lo, through what infinite seasons dost thou gaze—
Across what bivouacs of thine angered slain,
And see'st thy bride immortal in the maize!

Totem and fire-gall, slumbering pyramid—
Though other calendars now stack the sky,
Thy freedom is her largesse, Prince, and hid
On paths thou knewest best to claim her by.

High unto Labrador the sun strikes free
Her speechless dream of snow, and stirred again,
She is the torrent and the singing tree;
And she is virgin to the last of men . . .

West, west and south! winds over Cumberland
And winds across the llano grass resume

Her hair's warm sibilance. Her breasts are fanned
O stream by slope and vineyard—into bloom!

And when the caribou slant down for salt
Do arrows thirst and leap? Do antlers shine
Alert, star-triggered in the listening vault
Of dusk?—And are her perfect brows to thine?

We danced, O Brave, we danced beyond their farms,
In cobalt desert closures made our vows . . .
Now is the strong prayer folded in thine arms,
The serpent with the eagle in the boughs.

(Crane, *Complete Poems,* pp. 70–75)

In "The Dance" Crane fuses imagery related to nature and
the Indian with imagery related to industry and the white man.
Crane wrote of this section of *The Bridge,* "Here one is on the
pure mythical and smoky soil at last! Not only do I describe the
conflict between the two races in this dance—I also become
identified with the Indian and his world before it is over . . ."
(Crane, *Complete Poems,* p. 251). The contrast between red
and white in line one begins this "conflict" and the questions of
lines two and seven look forward to the later, answering, identification. The white protagonist imaginatively identifies "with
the Indian and his world" at the moment which corresponds to
the suffering and death of the Indian brave and to the crushing
of the Indian as a people. (The "winter king" may recall the
white Aztec god Quetzelcoatl, who returned as the white conqueror Cortez. Through him Crane may fuse the Indian and the
white man into one male principle informing the "red flesh"
of the continent.)[1]

The first two stanzas describe the yearly cycle of the seasons
—running from winter, through spring and summer, to autumn—the natural clock and calendar that measured the life of
this ancient race. These stanzas also describe the beginning and
ending of the Indian period on this continent. The Indian did
squire "the glacier woman down the sky" in that primitive man
moved south with the ice age and, as the glacier retired, enjoyed the height of civilization in the southwest. The "glacier
woman" must be identified, like Pocahontas, with the American

soil. At this spring and summer period of his national cycle she gives herself fully to the Indian. But as the maize dies, so that age passed, and the second stanza, although obscure, presents the autumn of the Indian's history and of the year. The stanza may present only a search for water, which can be read as either bitterly frustrated or successful. But perhaps we see, in the second and third lines of the stanza the Indian of a later age rediscovering and examining without full comprehension relics of the great Aztec civilization. Or perhaps the "prayers" that "streamed the mesa sands" are gold dust and we are seeing the discovery of gold by the Indian before the white man's advent. In "Indiana", the next section of *The Bridge,* Crane attaches a religious symbolism to gold:

> We found God lavish there in Colorado
> But passing sly.
>
> The pebbles sang, the firecat slunk away
> And glistening through the sluggard freshets came
> In golden syllables loosed from the clay
> His gleaming name.
>
> (Crane, *Complete Poems,* p. 76)

"The stone," comes after "die", and suggests the idea of a gravestone. Perhaps the exhausted land, eroded to the rock, may be thought of as the gravestone of the corn-woman of more fruitful days. In any event stanza two ends with the image of the defeated Indian metamorphosed into the evening star which is found elsewhere in the poem.

In stanza three the protagonist speaks as a present-day man looking back to the days when the Indian, being pushed westward into the wilderness, was still close enough to us to send "Greeting . . . on the arrow's oath." Now the gap of time and the history that has occurred are incorrigible obstacles to our gaining an instinctive and natural relation to the land. Such a relation is nostalgically celebrated in stanza four in the symbol of Pocahontas's nuptials. As the "glacier woman" she has been squired down the sky by the Indian, but the actual Pocahontas married John Rolfe, a white man. So that in remembering these nuptials the protagonist looks back to a time when the white man had a relationship with the continent almost as natural as that of the Indian. Yet there was a veil upon *his* Pocahontas even then. And the "broken" or intermittent play of happy bride and bridegroom becomes the "broken" or destroyed play lost with the destruction of the Indian and regretted by lonely contemporary man.

Note how Crane has enriched the description of Pocahontas with details which connect her with the landscape: The "bed of leaves," the "veil" which later is a cataract gusting "from the very top" of some spot in the Adirondacks (stanza eight), and the "brown lap." Her "flanks and eyes hid tawny pride" as the land hid tawny Indians and animals.

Beginning with stanza five the poet's attempt to identify imaginatively with the Indian is figured as his protagonist's journey when he, a white man, "left the village for dogwood." Crane cleverly leaves the period of this "village" unspecified, although it is contemporary with or later than the period of water-power, since he speaks of "the mill-race." It may be a country village in the present. The poet begins to be aware of intimations in the landscape of Pocahontas' recurrence and ever-presence. The moon is her "hair's keen crescent running."

In the next stanza the "laughing chains the water wove and threw" recall the "broken play" of bride and bridegroom and link with other sections of *The Bridge,* "the chained bay waters" of the "Proem" and the "Catskill daisy chain in May" of "Van Winkle." To learn "to catch the trout's moon whisper" is to begin to succeed in getting back to the Indian imaginatively.

Liberated from chronology by having "Drifted how many hours I never knew," the poet-protagonist experiences the whole rise, fall, and metamorphosis of the Indian as the passing of a night and the rising of the morning star. The dawn into which that Indian-star bleeds is the present, in which the Indian has become a principle—alone because the land he knew, his Pocahontas, has passed. Yet at the same time that dawn is the Indian past, "the tribal morn" (stanza fifteen) which the poet has at last succeeded in winning imaginatively. He chooses "a further valley-shed" (stanza eight), passing up and over that which separates him from his vision of the Indian. He cannot stop as his imaginative journey takes him closer and closer to what his letter to Kahn called the "pure mythical and smoky soil." The "One white veil" which "gusted from the very top," no doubt a high waterfall, is the first veil to be lifted from his bride-land, of which he is to have new knowledge at last.

The vision is achieved when he "gained the ledge" and sees the whole panorama of the land before him, wearing Pocahontas' "inaccessible smile," inaccessible because the hills are steep and because immediate, vital knowledge of nature is lost in the past, or else is an impossible ideal in any age.

Up to this point what the protagonist has reported could actually have happened; he could have loosed a canoe and gone wandering. But what happens in the rest of the poem is, except for the continuity of the Adirondack landscape, purely visionary, the knowledge of the Indian (and of man of his own time) gained by the poet from this Pisgah height of vision.

The poet now speeds rapidly over "bluffs, tarns, streams," all the obstacles between himself and identification with the Indian, and, as happens in dreams, suddenly finds himself to be "within some boding shade." The way this is put, "I . . ./. . . knew myself within some boding shade—," may hint that by identifying with the Indian he "knew himself" as he had not before. "Boding shade" is one of those absolutely brilliant inventions of Crane which convey many meanings in a concentrated form. To know yourself suddenly in "some boding shade" is to feel both sheltered and threatened. You are suddenly in the dark, a dark which bodes no good for you, perhaps because you are a white man caught near Indian "abodes." Perhaps the abodes themselves are threatened, perhaps by your coming, the white man's coming. Certainly the whole place seems to brood over problems like these, and the chill which struck when you found yourself within that "boding shade" seems to have "boded shade" throughout the whole region, for now a symbolic storm cloud gradually darkens the sky and broods forebodingly over the Indian village.

Crane fuses the mountain storm—a phenomenon which could be of the present—with the Indian dance going on in this village of the past, with the wars of whites on Indians and of Indians on Indians, and with the industrial conquest of the continent. Stanzas ten through twenty have a double movement, backwards in time to the essential life of the Indian as expressed in his dance, and forward through a violent history to the subjugation of the Indian. The death of Maquokeeta is the culmination of both movements. It is the human sacrifice that ends the dance (as in Aztec ceremonies), it is the death of warriors in the various battles of early history, and it is the final collapse of Indian power. It is at this original and final moment, just before the Indian's apotheosis, that Crane is able at last to identify with the Indian and to cry that he, too, "buzzard-circleted, screamed from the stake" and "could not pick the arrows from [his] side" (stanza seventeen).

This double movement is accomplished partly by a remarkable fusion of images that relate to the life of the Indian with images that relate to the white man and industrial expansion. This fusion already assumes the identification of white man and Indian before Crane proclaims it.

The beat of the imagined Indian dance moves the poet at the deepest, most primitive level, "—Siphoned the black pool from the heart's hot root!" (stanza eleven). It takes him away back to the age of savage man. Yet the word "Siphoned" suggests an industrial process and links the dance with the present.

The "distant cloud," the "thunder-bud" which "grew" is the threat of the white man's coming. The Indian dance and the storm are presented in the vocabulary of the white man's civilization. A line like "A cyclone threshes in the turbine crest" combines two visual images: the circular shape of an Indian headdress (which is a crest) and the circular whirling of a wind in the trees on the crest of a hill. The storm in the trees is the advance of the white man who chops down all those trees and, in the process, destroys the life of the Indian: "—Fall, Sachem, strictly as the tamarack!" This destruction of the forest makes way for agriculture and "threshing" machines, and for industry, the "turbine." A turbine is a rotary motor just as a cyclone is a circling wind, and moreover a turbine has vanes remotely like the feathers on the circular headdress. The images dramatize the conflict of Indian and white man at the same time that they identify the two. Underneath all is the circle image basic to *The Bridge,* the symbol of God of which the arcs of the bridge are a part and which appears whole in "Ave Maria" where God himself is the dancer:

> This disposition that thy night relates
> From Moon to Saturn in one sapphire wheel:
> The orbic wake of thy once whirling feet,
> Elohim, still I hear thy sounding heel!
>
> (Crane, *Complete Poems,* p. 51)

The forests go down ("The oak grove circles in a crash of leaves"), and the war between Indian and white man intensifies. The images of "lightning", "flint," and "red fangs/And splay tongues" that "thinly busy the blue air" present the storm, the shooting of flintlocks, and the sparking of electric motors. The lightning is "deltaed" down the brave's hair because Maquokeeta means "Big River"[2] and through this reference to the Mississippi Crane suggests that this dance of history informs the whole continent. The images of serpents' fangs and tongues hark back to the "wide tongues" of the serpent Mississippi in the preceding section, "The River," and look forward to the metamorphosis of the Indian in stanza nineteen of "The Dance"—

> ... snake that lives before,
> That casts his pelt, and lives beyond!

—and his becoming "pure serpent, Time itself."

In his motion backward in time the poet has passed through the period of the Indian wars back to the pre-white "tribal morn." In his motion forward he has arrived at the time when the Indian, pressed westward to the "sunset's moat," has been destroyed and deified, become, to twist Crane's description of a poem, "self-evident as an active principle in the reader's consciousness henceforward" (Crane, *Complete Poems,* p. 221).

After the storm imagery Crane turns appropriately to images of "rainbows," "fire," "noon," and of violently rushing liquid: "lava," "cataracts." The Adirondack scene after a storm, with the sun come out and the streams full, remains as the fundamental sketch or outline which Crane's dream vision fills in. The end of the storm is death: the death of the Indian sacrificed or murdered at the stake, overcome in earlier times by volcanic eruptions, or shot by the flaming cataracts of the white man's guns. (Gunpowder could be explained to the Indians only in terms of volcanoes.) The poet is successful in identifying, not with the *life* of the Indian, but with his death. The destruction of the Indian has been a human sacrifice out of which there may come renewal of life.

Of the coda, the last six stanzas, Crane writes:

> Pocahontas (the continent) . . . survives the extinction of the Indian, who finally, after being assumed into the elements of nature . . . persists only as a kind of 'eye' in the sky, or as a star that hangs between day and night—'the twilight's dim perpetual throne' (Crane, *Complete Poems*, p. 251).

The questions asked in the next to the last stanza seem to subsume a larger question: Is a relation to nature as valid as was the Indian's still possible for man on this continent? The questions are not answered, but the last stanza presents the Indian as the ideal on which the hope may be based.

> We danced, O brave, we danced beyond their farms,
> In cobalt desert closures made our vows . . .
> Now is the strong prayer folded in thine arms,
> The serpent with the eagle in the boughs.

The "we" refers to Crane and the Indian, with whom he has succeeded in becoming identified. The vows they take are (primarily) marriage vows to Pocahontas. Crane, by identifying with Maquokeeta, is able to "know" the continent as a man "knows" a woman. Several images are fused: the Indian's act of praying erect, arms folded; his embracing of Pocahontas; the folding of his arms in death; and various other "closures." The "prayers forgotten" of stanza two are now, more positively, the "strong prayer," the prayer with which "To Brooklyn Bridge" ends, which "Ave Maria" is, the prayer for a humanly significant American culture.

Under this positive meaning, however, lurks a good deal of

irony. The image of Maquokeeta's folded arms contrasts with
the opening image of the glacier woman's sprouting arms, the
"burnished hands," the later images of the birch tree's "fingers"
flying in the wind and of the "hush of lava wrestling" Maquokeeta's arms. The images progress from primal affirmation
through wary exploration, anxiety, and vain struggle, to resig-
nation and death.[3]

The "vows" remind one of treaties made with the Indian by
the white man. The many relevant meanings of "closures" [4]—
primarily desert enclosed places, perhaps cobalt blue at evening,
in which Maquokeeta has embraced Pocahontas—have among
them the concluding of treaties. Many of these treaties pushed
the Indian further west and south, into the desert. They enclosed, limited him, bound him in enclosures, reservations. Then
when these lands proved valuable after all for oil or minerals—
including cobalt?—the treaties were broken, the "closures" were
"desert" in another sense.

But the positive meaning is dominant. In another "closure,"
the serpent of time and the eagle of space are united. The
"strong prayer" of the Aztecs had been fulfilled when they came
upon an eagle grasping a serpent upon a stone cactus and knew
that there they were to build their great city, Tenochtitlan. The
sun was an eagle, and his strong ray was a serpent of light
through whom he—Huitzilopochtli—conquered. The sun was
fed with the blood of sacrificial victims like Maquokeeta. At the
end of the poem the eagle and the serpent, the sky and the earth,
ideal and actual, are linked at last. "The serpent with the eagle
in the boughs" shows a reconcilement of the American eagle
with the soil from which it later too precipitately departed—at
the beginning of "the space age"—and to which it therefore
was likely to be rejoined too suddenly and catastrophically—cf.
the crash of the "eagle-bright" plane in "Cape Hatteras." If we,
like the founders of Tenochtitlan, are to fulfill a positive destiny,
we too must see the serpent *with* the eagle. From Mexico, June
13, 1931, Crane wrote, "Humanity is so unmechanized here
still, so immediate and really dignified" (*Letters,* p. 371). Identification with the Indian can give us a true grasp of our place
on the continent.

E.E.Cummings

E.E. CUMMINGS

anyone and noone

anyone lived in a pretty how town
(with up so floating many bells down)
spring summer autumn winter
he sang his didn't he danced his did.

Women and men (both little and small)
cared for anyone not at all
they sowed their isn't they reaped their same
sun moon stars rain

children guessed (but only a few
and down they forgot as up they grew
autumn winter spring summer)
that noone loved him more by more

when by now and tree by leaf
she laughed his joy she cried his grief
bird by snow and stir by still
anyone's any was all to her

someones married their everyones
laughed their cryings and did their dance
(sleep wake hope and then) they
said their nevers they slept their dream

stars rain sun moon
(and only the snow can begin to explain
how children are apt to forget to remember
with up so floating many bells down)

one day anyone died i guess
(and noone stooped to kiss his face)
busy folk buried them side by side
little by little and was by was

all by all and deep by deep
and more by more they dream their sleep
noone and anyone earth by april
wish by spirit and if by yes.

Women and men (both dong and ding)
summer autumn winter spring
reaped their sowing and went their came
sun moon stars rain

(Cummings, *Poems,* pp. 370–371)

If one substitutes for anyone and noone the letters A and B, or Mr. A and Miss B, then this poem reads like a simple story of Mr. A, who was loved loyally and sacrificially by Miss B alone among all mankind. But if one takes the poem as it is, then all sorts of complexities develop, or should develop. To call our hero "anyone" implies that this is the story of any individual taken as individual, that is, valued in himself as opposed to his value as a member of the group. The poem then becomes a celebration of individual experience and worth—the way we feel our own lives—versus social experience and worth—the way we feel the lives of others. There is or seems to be a difference of intensity. Whereas anyone "danced his did," that is, lived fully, the someones and everyones "did their dance," that is, just went through the motions. There is a further nuance. "Anyone" is one who regards himself as just anyone; whereas "someones" are people who think well of themselves, who are someone, as we say. Everyones are formidable dowagers who set the standard for all. Thus ironically they are people in the mass, people no different from others, representative of all mankind like Everyman, but in the bad sense that one is not getting an individual but "the world," in spiritual terms, or *le monde* in social. There is also the sense that no one is being left out, every one is being married. Low and conventional aims are fully achieved and there is no longing left over, no yearning for something higher left unsatisfied.

Someones and everyones live on a lower plane. They sleep their dream. Taken as social beings, then, asserting our places in the group as someones and everyones, we are rather pompous, living unimaginative limited lives in a mechanical fashion. Taken as humble indivdiuals, not as asserting our place in the group but as living our private mental lives, we are able to have higher satisfactions. Anyone "sang his didn't," cheerfully expressing in music or poetry whatever drives were frustrated in practical life. People in the mass are not without pluck. They "laugh their cryings." But humor, the social way of dealing with life's disappointments, to grin and bear it, is not as creative as the individual's way, which is to make art of it. Anyone "sang his didn't." And what he was able to accomplish in action was a triumphant dance.

But what about noone? Noone complicates the poem even further. To say that Miss B loved Mr. A "more by more," that she "laughed his joy she cried his grief," that his "any was all to her," that when he died she kissed his face, and was buried at his side, all that is one thing. But to say that noone loved anyone is to say something much different indeed. It is to say that there is no love in the world. And to say that noone loved anyone "more by more" is to say that things are getting worse all the time. Yet these are ideas which the tone of the poem seems to reject, stanza four taken by itself for example, expressing the loyalty of a true love.

It is this paradox, that anyone is both loved and not loved, which, in good old new-critical and Cleanth Brooksian fashion, I assert is at the center of the poem and is what gives the poem interest and life. The question in my mind, however, is, does Cummings really work out both sides of the paradox or is the trick of calling the girl noone a trick only?

Noone is a fine name for the patient Griselda type who is our heroine. The name suggests not just ordinary humility but a dedicated subjugation of self. The lady lives only in his life, laughing his joy and crying his grief. She represents that extra-ordinary Desdemona-like ability of woman to attach herself firmly to an extravagant and wheeling stranger of here and everywhere, to live his life, that ability without which the institutions of marriage and the family would soon come to a grinding halt. The lives of the other married couples (representing marriage in the conventional and social dimensions) go rather mechanically through the daily rhythm and the rhythm of the dance of a whole lifetime: "(sleep wake hope and then) they/said their nevers they slept their dream."

On the other hand the ideal love of noone for anyone has its orthodox reward of union in death: "all by all and deep by deep/and more by more they dream their sleep." The tense changes to present. The story of the someones and everyones is over with death; they have slept through their dream of life. But the deathsleep of anyone and noone is only a dream. It is not really death. They "dream their sleep." Or it is a sleep that is full of dreams, a vivid afterlife. The following two lines express physical recurrence and spiritual affirmation, even the idea of resurrection: "noone and anyone earth by april/ wish by spirit and if by yes." The remarkable thing is that it has been anyone who has been loved in this fashion. Anyone at all may be given such love. Anyone in his individual aspect, that is. (It would be interesting, in stanzas seven and eight, to observe the various meanings of "by," such as "beside," "after," "replaced by," "in the name of.")

Another reading of the poem comes to light when we reflect further on the fact that the object of noone's affection is called anyone, anyone at all. In this reading noone represents, not the loyalty of the loving wife, but the ability to live selflessly for others generally. Well, not generally because it is "his" grief, as opposed to "their" cryings. She represents the ability to love any human being, any *individual,* which is a far different and more difficult thing than to love a vague humanity en masse without looking too closely at the sordid particular specimens. This saintly lady does the more difficult thing. She feels increasing love for *any* of these imperfect specimens. She is like Matilda in the earthly paradise in Dante's *Purgatorio,* who "makes her will of the will of another, soon as it is disclosed by outward sign" (Canto XXXIII, Carlyle-Wicksteed translation).

Is this reading not inconsistent with the story of a happy marriage deduced above? But Cummings has never said that noone and anyone are married. "Someones married their everyones," but the relation of noone to anyone has been left ambiguous. It can be the relation of a saint-like person, Lady Noone, to any of her fellow mortals taken as an individual soul of infinite worth. The seventh and eighth stanzas are so suggestive of the idea of the married couple buried side by side that they are hard to interpret in this new manner. But they can be; the love of a saint for any of God's human creatures surely goes with the creature to death and beyond. Nevertheless I cannot convince myself that the stanzas work as well on this level as on the other. Am I to be blamed then for trying to read too much into the poem and thus twisting and straining it? It was not I who named one of the characters anyone. If Miss Noone loves anyone more by more, she does, that's all. She loves anyone, any person at all. It takes sainthood to do that. For any one must mean all ones, if not the everyones: "all by all and deep by deep/ and more by more." Another possible dimension of meaning, that of divine love, is made difficult by "she": Only one who is no body loves anyone. No one truly loves the individual soul but God. But "she" puts aside this meaning. Cummings' Unitarian ancestors would surely keep him from Mariolatry.

But perhaps the difficulty is that we are letting loose all the meanings of anyone while still keeping one meaning of noone tied down, and this meaning is the principal one, its only denotation: no one, no person.

"Women and men (both little and small)/ cared for anyone not at all."

Noone, on the other hand, loved him "more by more."

Do these two statements, put as if they meant opposite things, really mean the same thing: that each person dies unloved? Logically they do. Yet the detailed portrait of noone counteracts that meaning. The lady both does and does not exist. One effect is to make her like an imagined sweeetheart invented by our hero Mr. Anyone to compensate for his loneliness and the fact that "Women and men" care for him "not at all." Thus she would stand for the private world of ideals or fantasies with which we supplement the limited psychic satisfaction of our public life.

Another way of looking at the matter is that anyone gets along very well with no one to bother him. "Women and men (both little and small)", insignificant and narrow-minded, care for him not at all, but he goes along dancing his did (or does) at a great rate, fully content that he is loved by no one at all. Fully content, that is, with his own psychic adventures, and not demanding or asserting petty recognitions. The intense expression of growth-in-love of the next to the last stanza is, in this reading, really the oneness of the soul's knowledge of itself.

The most poignant lines in the poem are: "one day anyone died i guess/ (and noone stooped to kiss his face)." In these lines taken by themselves the bare fact of death and of aloneness in death is unglossed. The "i guess" looks back to the children's forgetting and forward to the burying "little by little." It also, however, introduces the assertions of the eighth stanza. If it is only a guess, perhaps anyone did not die but still lives. The poem introduces the idea of lovelessness only to pull quickly away from it. Three times the word noone is used, and each time the poem quickly gets away from it into details that make it seem the opposite of what it really denotes, giving to airy noone a local habitation and a name.

Probably the best interpretation emerges if we observe the structure of the poem. The poem breaks into two-stanza units. In stanza one we are given anyone and his love of life. The locale of the poem is a town, and in the poem the individual is posed against his town. It is a "pretty how" town. How pretty a town it is! Yet, pretty? How? One would do well to look into that prettiness a little further.

When one does look, one finds the group united against the individual. "Women and men" both large and small?—no, "both *little* and small." "Emerson said, 'The God who made New Hampshire/ Taunted the lofty land with little men'" (Frost, *Poetry*, p. 166). "Little" in this sense, intensified by "small," is what these people are like. They sow their "isn't," their dead ideas, and reap the "same" old conventional conclusions. The first two stanzas contrast singing and dancing anyone with the men and women of the town.

The third and fourth stanzas make one sentence about the children and noone. There is the Wordsworthian (and New

Testament) idea here that children are closer to innocence and perceive spiritual truths more directly than do adults. These children perceive "that noone loved him more by more," that is, that he was unloved in the town, but that nevetheless he thrived on this rejection. His life was surrounded with love in spite of it or because of it. The children understand that there are values in his life beyond those that make an obedient townsman.

In stanzas five and six the ordinary lives, the lives of the men in the group, come to their dull conclusion and the children grow up to be as dull and imperceptive as their parents. Snow can explain how—the cold touch of time.

In stanzas seven and eight the unloved individual has his death and apotheosis.

In stanza nine the rhythms of life continue as before.

The individual as individual is necessarily set against society and against other people as members of society. It is in the individual's unique responses that the value of life inheres. One does much what others have always done, but with a difference, and one does it oneself, one's own way, with one's own feelings. These unique responses are always distrusted and feared by the group. The group needs communication and regularity of behavior in order to function as a group and so necessarily rejects what is most individual about the individual. But what is comprehended by all is no longer alive, no longer a living idea or feeling. These are old commonplaces but I think they place anyone in relation to the "Women and men" of the town.

The individual, who necessarily cannot be loved by the group, is the only one surrounded by love of vital quality, the only one who is related to life, spirit, affirmation.

In this interpretation anyone is loved by noone, that is, no one of the group. The group rejects the individual, but, truly understood, this is the best thing it could do for him, and it surrounds his life with fostering love, love which fosters unique, not group, experience. I think this interpretation is not inconsistent with the insistent metaphor of 'noone' as loyal mate. The best thing anyone has, the thing which will stick with him till death and perhaps beyond death, is his uniqueness, his difference from the group, his inassimilability to the group. His loneliness is the most precious thing a man has, the most dangerous to lose. It should love him "more by more."

Does this interpretation account for the stark statement that noone loved anyone, or the even starker one that children guessed that noone loved anyone?: "(but only a few/ and down they forgot as up they grew)." Children guessed the lovelessness of their society and that each person is quite alone. This is half the poem, the "noone" half. But children also guessed the other half, the "yes" half, that this loneliness, this uniqueness, is what makes man alive, allows him to grow, to live now: "when by now and tree by leaf/ she laughed his joy she cried his grief." The seventh and eighth stanzas are the richest in presenting this paradox, opposing as they do the concepts "noone" and "yes.":

> one day anyone died i guess
> (and noone stooped to kiss his face)
> busy folk buried them side by side
> little by little and was by was
>
> all by all and deep by deep
> and more by more they dream their sleep
> noone and anyone earth by april
> wish by spirit and if by yes.
>
> Women and men (both dong and ding)
> summer autumn winter spring
> reaped their sowing and went their came
> sun moon stars rain

E.E. CUMMINGS

'Poem'

Always wonderfully kind to new literary ventures, E. E. Cummings gave a poem for Volume I, Number I, of *The Massachusetts Review* (Fall, 1959, I, 154–155). Shortly after he had sent the poem, he wrote again, enclosing a preferred version, and asking for the return of the first. I returned it, but, struck by the art or genius shown in some very minor alterations which nevertheless transformed the poem, I kept an accurate copy.

(Earlier version)	(Version in *The Massachusetts Review*)
it's	it's
so damn sweet when Anybody yes; no	so damn sweet when Anybody— yes;no
matter who, some	matter who, some
Total (preferably blonde of course) or	total (preferably blonde of course)
on the other	or on the other
well: your Oldest pal for instance (or	well your oldest pal for instance (or
,why	;why
Even i suppose one 's wife)	even i suppose one 's wife)

—does doesn't says unsays
  looks smiles*

or simply Is what
makes you feel you
aren't

6 or 6

teen or 60
million any
bodyelses

but,for once

(ima
gine)

You

—does doesn't unsays says
  looks smiles*

or simply Is
what makes
you feel you
aren't

6 or 6

teen or sixty
000,000
anybodyelses—

but for once

(imag
-ine)

You

In the printed version the only words capitalized are "Any-body" and "You" (the two persons who have real being on the occasions of which the poem speaks) and "Is," the state-of-being verb. There was logic to the first version's capitalization of "Total, "Oldest," and "Even," which all particularize "Any-body." But the way the poem stretches between "Anybody" and "You" and yet joins them, the sentence structure seeming to isolate and unite these individuals in spite of the distance that divides people, is pointed up by the three capitals.

The chiasmus "—does doesn't unsays says" ties the line to-gether better than "—does doesn't says unsays." The first ver-sion is rhetorical and demonstrative. The revised version is suggestive. The order "says unsays" implies a statement fol-lowed by a retraction. By putting "unsays" first, Cummings gains a much subtler effect: understanding without words, mute apology or sympathy. When "says" follows "unsays" what is then "said" is not what has been unsaid but something new, an articulation in words of the previously wordless understanding. Thus we end with the beautiful series "unsays," "says," "looks,"

*The line reading "—does doesn't says unsays looks smiles" should be one single line.

"smiles," in the order of climax, each word representing greater expressiveness.

The revisions of the next three lines place "Is" at the end of the line to strengthen the contrast of meaning with (uncapitalized) "aren't." "what makes," put on a line by itself, has a secondary meaning, "that which is creative"; and "you feel you" has a secondary meaning, "you are aware of yourself as a person, as being," The latter idea is, of course, what the whole poem finally says.

Like "6 or 6" (six of one and a half-dozen of the other— looking almost like a scales printed this way), the three subsequent lines are meant to give the impression of the loss of being we suffer when unrecognized by some "Anybody." The first version

> teen or 60
> million any
> bodyelses

tries to give the paradox of great numbers but lack of identity by isolating "million any" on a line. The decapitation of "any" from "bodyelses" is the split between many wistful hearts and their meaningless experiences. It makes one feel that the bodies and minds of these nonentities may be shuffled without significant loss. The word "bodyelses" may be meant to suggest "bodiless"—unrealized.

The revision is brilliant. It is, of course, what first strikes one in looking at the two versions. Cummings sacrifices the devices mentioned just above for a simpler but amazingly effective one, the row of ciphers, which, in one visual impact, gives the impression of millions of empty lives. It is not just that the poem suddenly adds visual effects to verbal. Actually we do not verbalize "000,000" as "millions." We register the meaning silently; there is a verbal blank at that line; and that silence, that empty space in the verbal continuum which is the poem, stands for the emptiness of lives. Nothing could be more opposite to the word (capitalized) "Is" than the non-word "000, 000." Nothing less "does doesn't unsays says looks smiles" than "000,000."

This version is of a different order from the others. It is the stroke of genius, Cummings' genius, which makes the poem perfectly right and indubitably his.

In "6 or 6" and "teen or sixty" he seems to be playing with secondary meanings of the irrelevance of age to identity. We are ourselves and like to be recognized as ourselves whether the irrelevant flesh be

6 or 6

teen or sixty

Some other touches: "Anybody," a bold declaration, is followed by a little doubt: "yes; no." But then the declaration is affirmed:

. . . no

matter who, some

total . . .

"Stranger" he was about to say, but his not saying it evokes the pun "sum total"—humanity in the large, preferably represented by an individual blonde, who nevertheless must (in order to be universal, "total") be a stranger. Yet how can a blonde be a stranger? One feels a Whitmanian sense of union with all humanity through its blondes.

Or on the other hand "your oldest/pal" or

even
i
suppose
one
's wife)

The word "your" is necessary to look forward to "You." The separation of "one" and "'s" recalls the old locution "one his wife." Your oldest pal or one his wife may be supposed to know one best, be least a stranger, be most an individual to one. The shift is now from "sum total"—humanity—to "one," the individual. "Anybody" amounts to something, whether sum total or unity, when, "for once," he or she recognizes, and so creates, the unity and sum total which is "You." Everything else, every time else, and all the anybodyelses amount to 000,000.

A Dry Tree

The *Dry Tree* When Green:
A Record of Writing Some Poems

Dry Tree is the title of my volume of poetry, and this essay is a fragment of a journal in which I recall and reflect upon my writing of five poems.[1] Although I do not regard myself as a poet of importance, I think that the poems mentioned below are good poems, and I hope that my comments on their genesis may have some interest or even value for writers and readers of poetry. The genesis of poetry is a fascinating subject. Here is one (very fragmentary) record. I quote the poems entire as texts for commentary, but also, of course, with the hope that some one will like them. . . .

    . . . It is interesting and perhaps significant that when I think of the poems I might write I think only vaguely of the themes, the subject matter, the imagery, the emotions to be expressed, and less vaguely of the formal quality, the genre, the general effect. What is most clear and immediate is the *method* by which I would achieve, or evoke, these poems. The method is meditation: the achievement, either by chance or by deliberate cultivation, of a state of mind of unusual stillness combined with unusual alertness—this sounds like Wordsworth—in which abstract ideas and specifically directed emotions seem to have disappeared and some symbol, called up out of the depths of the mind, or simply some object or event in the landscape, occupies all the attention. It (the object or symbol) is (to me, while writing) more interesting, arresting, complex and exciting than any personal thought or feeling. Yet, of course, what I am doing is seeing (or creating) those internal relations in the object which correspond with thoughts and feelings which have ceased for the moment to trouble me consciously but which the symbol is enabling me to interrelate and perhaps reconcile in a new way. (I am not proposing poetry as a therapeutic device. Nevertheless, the feeling one has when one's emotions are forgotten, i.e., caught up in the poetic symbol, is unmistakably joy, even when the poem may not ultimately be successfully completed.)

An elementary example of a symbol's interrelating and reconciling different feelings would be the little poem "Robin." Here the mood of meditation was certainly induced by chance, since I was riding a bicycle when I first conceived the poem. I saw a dead robin in the road. The fascination of death took me because of something in the look of the bird, oblivious to the flies buzzing around it.

> ROBIN
> Here on the road-bed
> Sweet Robin lies,
> Nursing at her red breast
> These gold-green flies,
> Nor cares, for the nursing's sake,
> Whose wings arise
> To touch her breast awake
> And not her eyes.

It is obvious to me now that both the horror and the serene dignity of death, as I had seen it in hospitals where I had worked, combined in this poem with the intense concentration, the oblivion, of sexual ecstasy. Unconsciously my mind supplied—lying in the place of the dead bird—a fused image of the dead bodies which I had prepared for removal from hospital rooms and the body of a loved woman—abstracted, far off, preoccupied with her ecstasy as I touched her, yet no longer conscious of my touch even as her body was responding. Yet I saw no such fused image at the time of writing the poem. Though my experience of death and love was more important to me than my experience of robins in enabling me to write this poem, what I was trying to do, at the time of writing, was to render the robin and the feeling which it—not my own past experience—had aroused.

I seem, in this commentary, to avoid noticing the image of nursing in the poem. There is no nursing going on. The nursing is on the one hand irony for death—the flies at the bloody breast. On the other, I suspect that it was a blind by which I

avoided consciousness that my own sexual experience was involved in my reaction to the bird. Or, if you like, it is a metaphor for the tenderness of love.

I suppose the theme of the poem is dignity and high passion
seen as superior to the ugliness of the mere physical—whether
of death or sex—and also superior to any delusive idealisms,
false paradises. The bird—girl—is oblivious both to the "flies"
and to "wings" that "arise."

Note that part of the effect of this poem is gained by a par-
tially ironic echo:

> SONG
> Hark, hark! the lark at heaven's gate sings
>   And Phoebus 'gins arise,
> His steeds to water at those springs
>   On chaliced flowers that lies;
> And winking Mary-buds begin
>   To ope their golden eyes:
> With every thing that pretty is,
>   My lady sweet, arise!
>   Arise, arise!
>   (Shakespeare, From *Cymbeline,* II, iii, 22–30)

This lady isn't arising! Another echo is that of Scott's "Proud
Maisie" to whom "Sweet Robin" sang of her death in the vocabulary of her bridal:

> PROUD MAISIE
> Proud Maisie is in the wood,
>   Walking so early;
> Sweet Robin sits on the bush,
>   Singing so rarely.
>
> "Tell me, thou bonny bird,
>   When shall I marry me?"
> "When six braw gentlemen,
>   Kirkward shall carry ye."
>
> "Who makes the bridal bed,
>   Birdie, say truly?"—

"The gray-headed sexton
    That delves the grave duly.

"The glow-worm o'er grave and stone
    Shall light thee steady.
The owl from the steeple sing,
    'Welcome, proud lady.' "

                    (Sir Walter Scott)

If my interpretation of my own poem seems far-fetched, let me put in evidence a later poem in which things are somewhat reversed. Instead of using motherhood and love to support the dignity of a bird's death, I use a bird's death to support the dignity of love. In this poem, perhaps liberated by writing the earlier one, I see a direct analogy between the dead bird and a woman.

PINNACLE
(OF. *pinnacle,* fr. LL. *pinnaculum,* fr. L. *pinna,* a feather.).
I took my light love naked in the bed,
Her limbs half-folded like a preening dove.
Her lips took mine as the stretched dove nips its wing,
 The white-bent dove:

Then all given over to her pliant death,
The downed head fallen back, bright eyes at conclusion,
Conceded the breast's whiteness, the limbs free,
The full-struck dove.

O arch and pinnacle, bonnet of the beasts!
I held her risen as the high-choired dove
Holds her unfolded feathers in the sun.
    The light-lost dove.

Here the woman and the emotion she aroused formed the subject. The bird—partly because I had written the previous poem and partly because I have been influenced by such poems of Yeats's as "Leda and the Swan" (Yeats, *Variorum Poems,* p. 441) and the one beginning "A woman's beauty is like a white/ Frail bird . . ." (Yeats, *Variorum Poems,* pp. 784–85)—

was brought in to express the woman. Here again we have both the dead bird—the physical—and wings arising—the spiritual. But this time the wings arising indicate a tribute. The idea is not ironic. It is almost religious.

In this poem too the mood of meditation was induced by chance; it was the aftermath of love. In the above commentary I had meant simply to illustrate briefly that some poems, such as "Robin" and "Pinnacle," came by chance. But my interest in the poems surprised me into more words than I had intended. Now I should like to comment on some poems formed by deliberate meditation.

"Tree" a poem which I have never been able to finish to my satisfaction, was a direct result of a meditation, although as usual the poem came by itself. That is, I had no idea that I was going to write a poem about a tree until it started happening. This is the way it began. I had been reading *The Cloud of Unknowing,* a fourteenth-century book of mysticism which recommends a form of meditation in which one tries to clear one's mind of all thought, all images, and to simply be aware of a sense of love. This, of course, is very difficult to do, but there is no sense in reading *The Cloud of Unknowing* just for curiosity! One either stops reading or tries to do what it recommends. And I tried this form of meditation (as I had every once in a great while over the years since I had first come across the book) one day while on a walk down a country lane. I remember sitting on an ivy-covered stone wall(this was in Ireland) reading the book, and I remember sitting with my back against a tree rapt in this meditation. To me the attempt is like going back to the beginning of things with a sort of primal reddish blackness, full of potentiality, in which creation is about to be sparked off.

Some time later I walked off down the road past a field in which there was a good-sized tree—a linden, I think—a full-foliaged tree—it was midsummer—shaped so as to seem not so much standing on the earth as tugging at it, trying to blow off into the sky—though there was no wind at all.

Walking up and down that road past this tree, I wrote, or started, the following poem:

TREE
Cumulus-boughed,
Parachute,
Ballooning tree,
Tree like a mushroom cloud,
Summer civility,
Swung toward what silent root
High-strung cosmogony
Weighting the billowy shroud
Hangs in activity.

What I was trying to express was the almost agonizing sense that there was a center in that tree somewhere, a center from which emanated all the energy which had created foliage, branches and trunk. I had an actual physical sense of this emanating energy—not just an idea of it. The tree was utterly motionless, and yet its pose and its rich growth made it seem electric with potency.

Obviously my mind had fastened on this tree,—the first notable thing I had looked at after a meditation in which I had tried to clear my mind of all images and just to be aware of the creative principle—as a symbol to which I could attach this feeling, or a complex of feelings which probably flooded in upon me after I had ceased formal meditation.

> —But there's a Tree, of many, one,
> A single Field which I have looked upon. . . .
>   (Wordsworth, Immortality Ode)

Isolated in the center of a field, this healthy tree became the focus of my unconsciously continuing meditation.

What happened was interesting. When I tried to find this center of energy, of supreme life, and to express it, what came into my mind was the hydrogen bomb. I guess it was not far from anyone's mind in 1957 when I wrote this poem. I had no thought of writing a poem about mushroom-clouds, suffering, death. The tree gave me a sense of explosiveness—of being full to the bursting, as we say, of life.

It was not as destruction but as creation that I wished to use the idea of atomic fission. Yet the central image of the poem is that of life "hanging in activity" in the tree, hanging like Christ suffering on the cross (I say Christ rather than Jesus because it is the divine life force that I meant), hanging like a parachutist caught in a tree and kicking—like a hanged man—like a bomb about to explode. "Hanging in activity" of course suggests radioactivity.

The line I had most trouble with is "High-strung cosmogony." By "cosmogony" I meant not the theory but the action of creating worlds. I saw the tree as—like a galaxy—a sort of universe created by a great explosion—full of radiant energy. At the same time I wanted the feeling of potential power, of further explosiveness, and therefore I used "high-strung." (Of course the phrase has the counter suggestion of "strung-up.") But "cosmogony" is, I fear, a dead word—too abstract. I have not been able to bring it alive by putting it in this context. One is still prone to think of the theory, rather than of worlds' being created in a great display of cosmic fireworks.

Into this poem, which was to have expressed creativity, came unwanted, then, the fear, the despair of the atomic age—the sense that we are all about to be blown up, that life—which I had meant to say was ballooning, tugging at the earth in order to soar—is also hanging, caught in its own proliferation, waiting for death.

The center of energy which I had tried to express—the seed, the core—of this ballooning, soaring life, became a weight, the thought of death, that which drags the balloon or the parachute down.

This is probably what happened to my meditation too. I began it like a man of the Renaissance—full of a sense of power to come; I ended it like a man of my own day, full of a sense of power gone by, or of power destroying itself. "Cosmogony"—world-creating energy—waits and weights "the billowy shroud."

None of these cheerful thoughts occurred to me as I wrote the poem! It is just that in trying to express ultimate energy I naturally lighted upon images of life in extremity, life facing death, because it is in trying to avoid death that organisms are aroused to their greatest efforts. Therefore, at the center of the tree, I found the crucifixion.

Maybe part of the matrix of this poem is the sense that we are really afraid—in a religious meditation—that our prayer may be answered, that we may be successful in becoming aware of a reality which will demand of our wills a total commitment. Maybe this is why the image of being caught, like a chutist caught on a limb and kicking, is in the poem.

This is certainly the theme of another poem which again uses the tree as a symbol of energetic life but adds the idea of a bee's nest in a hollow of the tree to stand for the center of energy which I was trying to express in "Tree."

> THE BEE SPACE
> I sped away
> From my swarm in the city
> Droned down a valley
> Drowsed with a tree,
>
> Prised that embrace
> To the bee's space—
> Honeyed interstice
> O sweet comb crevice;
>
> Poised on that comb
> Being from whom came
> Honey tree and valley,
> From whom swarmed the city,
>
> And from that fraught tree
> That disclosed valley
> Fright to the city
> Lined me live away.

This poem says to me, quite simply, "I sought quiet in order to meditate and find the spirit of God, the source of all life, and was so successful as to terrify myself. I feared that if I went any further I should have to give up my will to Him. Therefore I turned and fled back to the distractions of public life so that I might simultaneously forget and preserve my own ego. My small being, confronting Being with a capital B, flew back in fear to hide its smallness in the swarm. The thing is done in terms of bees and a great Bee. The sexual imagery—a great Bee on the comb fecundating all life—was arrived at unconsciously. Expressing life energies, I fell naturally into a sexual metaphor.

Finally I turn to a poem which was not only occasioned by deliberate meditation but which was worked out in detail in a rhythm of conscious and unconscious exploration of religious symbols. Under the influence of Eliot and the metaphysical poets I deliberately worked out the interrelation of my symbols, remembering their traditional significance and their use in these poets.

The occasion of "Mountain Ash" was the sight, in early winter, of a little mountain ash tree heavily laden with berries and snow to which a flock of cedar waxwings came. In the course of two days they stripped the tree clean.

This tree was on the Smith College campus, near the library, and this was where I did my writing in a little faculty study room which had big windows opening out on the gardens. I passed the tree going and coming. As soon as I noticed the tree, and especially after the birds came, I spent a great deal of time watching the scene. I started the poem, worked on it in the little room, and came out every once in a while to check up on my observations and to get new ideas.

The first lines that came were, I thought, a complete little poem like a Japanese haiku. The birds had not yet appeared, or I had not noticed them, but there was a snowfall, and I noticed the berries covered with snow, like a sundae, and I wrote the following:

> Fall-borne fruit of the ash,
> Burn fiercest at the close!
> Offer the year your embers quenched with snow.

I was being very clever, playing with the ideas of ash and embers. I also meant a religious pun on Fall, a pun I'm pretty sick of by this time. I guess the theme was that even if one is fallen one may offer up sacrificially what good one has left.

I showed this poem to a friend as a finished poem, but he responded with the judgment: "A very good first three lines!"

I then went back to work on the poem. I think a line or two about the waxwings—perhaps the lines "The cherry birds all tails and wings in flight, / Sparked yellow and red"—had already come. I think the last lines,

> In the blanched morning
> There is no complaint.
> The ever green
> Whose burden is snow
> Abide
> Nod only

may already have come as a separate poem, a comment on the snowy scene with no reference to the mountain ash at all. The first lines too came separately.

> All visible things that interrupt the light
> Burn to a hazeless blue that winter mourns,
> Hiding its dark in dark.
> Hemlocks that hid in green now hide in snow.
> The earth is white with sky, but sky is heavy with the world.

I don't recall now what I had been reading. Was it *Faust?* Mephistopheles' diatribe against light? I have the sense that I took the first line from some philosophical or mystical prose. Something I came across in chance reading.

These pieces, all a response to the same snowstorm and the coming of the waxwings, I started to forge together into a single poem. The action became the denuding of the ash tree of its berries by the waxwings as a representation of a religious act of sacrifice and renunciation. I tried to tie together close observation of bird and tree with references to religious belief and ritual.

I have come to value most in this poem the close observation of the birds. The religious parallels seem to me now opportunistic, fortuitous, glib. There is one symbol, however, to which I can attach no direct religious equivalent: "That wind made a great rush / When the crow spoke." This still interests me because I do not know what meaning to attach to the wind and the crow, and yet they presented themselves in the actual scene with great drama, and they have a portentous quality in the poem. They mean something emotionally, not just intellectually. What do they mean?

The waxwings are in the ash tree on a bright windy day. Somewhere a crow caws. Then a wind comes, tossing the trees. Most of the birds, perhaps heeding the warning of the crow, leave the tree and fly across the field to a huge low bush. Their colors flash and the tree flashes as the wind moves the clusters of orange-red berries.

The crow speaks. Like evil? Like Satan in the Garden? Like the announcement of the last day? Or like the Angel of the Lord evacuating Adam and Eve from Eden? I don't know and I suspect the image is the stronger for my not knowing. But when the crow speaks everything starts to move. In the wind I may have had in mind Eliot's "cold wind / That blows before and after time" (Eliot, *Complete Poems,* p. 120). The wind at any rate is a cataclysmic event in response to the crows proclamation. The birds, like frightened multitudes, depart. "And pray ye that your flight be not in winter." Mark XIII: 18.

I guess that's the answer. I was thinking of Christ's description of the last day, which brings in other images, such as that of the dry tree. The bird's colors are like sparks igniting the dry tree and the tossing berries are like flames. The ash is like a burned-out soul (after all, the leaves are pretty well withered or gone—only the berries remaining) which is fortunate enough to achieve sacrifice and renunciation before death or in death:

MOUNTAIN ASH
Poem for an Ember Day

And pray ye that your flight be not in the winter.
All visible things that interrupt the light
Burns to a hazeless blue that winter mourns,
Hiding its dark in dark.
Hemlocks that hid in green now hide in snow.

The earth is white with sky, but sky is heavy with the world.
No ashy flake glitters in the sun
As iris blue burned in another blue.

Fall-borne fruit of the ash,
Burn fiercest at the close!
Offer the year your embers quenched with snow.

That wind made a great rush
When the crow spoke.
The cherry birds, all tails and wings in flight,
Sparked yellow and red.
The embers blazed in the ash, blazed up to follow
All visible things that interrupt the light.

Raiders under the thorn seek humbled coverts.
But before the last flametail gutters abashed,
The first flares up with a will in head-down flight,
On the little cross at the fir-crest lists where the wind blows,
Scouts the whitened field to where the lost ash
Flares up a late bright fruit for wintry flight.

The winged return
Flings care upon the wind.
Goes slippery down like noiseless trusting children.
Come to the fruit,
Must break its flight,
Must brake itself in the element where it flew.
Tail to earth, wings to world, crown to sky,
The waxwing stands a Maltese cross on the wind.
Lights in burnt-brown vesture.
Turns bandit eyes.
Crest below claw, bows in snowy conversion
Snatching wine-glowing flesh.
Then turns with fiery beak and red-slashed side
And mounts with wings.

The host flames in a winged return to the ash.
A rending hour crackles in the dry tree.
After, shrunk limbs retain
Glimmers of red, all that was not consumed.

Smoke-thick the dark snows down.
Dark snows down all the earth.

In the blanched morning
There is no complaint.
The ever green
Whose burden is snow
Abide
Nod only.

Pond Image

Like the coating of the eye,
This is the surface of the sky.
The high bird floats with the mite.
The spot of the eye drifts with the bird and the mite
And motes of the mind.
Here one knows unblinded
The sun come out of a cloud,
About whose glare the young growth
Shape uncertainly.
Terror has held them till now.
Their dead chatter in the sun.

Appendix

Freedom,
Joy & Indignation:
Letters from
E. E. Cummings

Edited By Robert G. Tucker and David R. Clark

Hate is a kind of "passive suffering" but indignation is a kind of joy. . . . It is not our business to reply to this & that, but to set up our love and indignation against their pity & hate. . . . (Yeats, *Letters on Poetry*, pp. 126–27).

On January 14, 1963, the Educational Radio Network broadcast *"The Massachusetts Review's* Tribute to E. E. Cummings," an hour-long program produced by station WFCR Amherst.[1] The program included discussion by members of the University of Massachusetts English Depatment who are also on the Editorial Board of *The Massachusetts Review.* But the highlight was the first broadcast anywhere of a half-hour taped radio program which Mr. Cummings recorded in 1954 but which was not considered broadcastable at that time.

This recording was Program Seven in the series *New England Anthology* produced by the Literary Society of the University of Massachusetts for the National Association of Educational Broadcasters under a grant from the Educational Television and Radio Center. A brochure described the series as "an expression in poetry of the American concept of the free man by writers who make use of the New England scene, background or heritage." There were ten programs featuring fifteen New England poets who read, and in some cases discussed, poems they had selected in terms of the series' theme.

When, in 1955, the series was released, fourteen of these poets were heard.[2] But Program Seven was never released. Mr. Cummings told the story, and read the poems on the program, at the YM and YWHA Poetry Center on November 26, 1954:

> some months ago,a number of writers(not excluding our non-hero)were cordially invited to make tape-recordings on the subject of Freedom,with special reference to New

England;& were assured that these recordings—collectively entitled NEW ENGLAND ANTHOLOGY— would be broadcast over the NAEB national network . . . whatever that is

now(as it happens) I love Freedom even more than I loathe radio;so I decided to make a Freedom-recording—provided,of course,I was given the freedom to make one. And to avoid any misunderstanding,I wrote Mr Robert Tucker,the project-supervisor(for this was a socalled project,involving an eastern institution of learning)& stated frankly that my own Freedom-recording would consist of 13 poems—all of which(& please notice this)had been published in various books. I further explained that each of these 13 poems expressed,or tried to express,some aspect of *Freedom as I feel it;*& that consquently no poem could be omitted,nor could my recording-as-a-whole be changed in any way shape or manner.When the supervisor gave me his blessing,I made the recording & forgot all about it

just what happened then,I don't know. But I did learn that (at one moment)every vestige of my recording seemed to have vanished;& also that—after a considerable period of academic Sturm Und Drang—it suddenly reappeared,absolutely intact:whereupon the harried supervisor seized it; & shipped it to Mr John Holt,NAEB Network Manager, Urbana,Illinois

now I find that,in spite of said Freedom-loving supervisor's best efforts,my Freedom-recording will NOT be broadcast. Why? Because,although—in the opinion of the NAEB Network Manager,Mr John Holt,it is (quote)*a fine piece of work*(unquote)it would(quote)*probably cause trouble, possibly with the FCC*(unquote)

so much for(quote)Freedom(unquote) in The Land Of The Free. . .And The Home Of The Slave

I shall now try to read you precisely those 13 poems which

constitute my not-to-be-broadcast Freedom-recording,letting you draw your own conclusions, if any.[3]

The authors of the present article wish to clarify what happened (as an item in the Cummings biography), and to present in context some interesting letters by Mr. Cummings.

On February 19,[4] 1954, Robert Tucker wrote to Mr. Cummings describing the projected series and inviting him to participate. A reply came from his agent Bernice Baumgarten of Brandt & Brandt.

> Mr. Cummings has asked me to answer your letter of February 4th. He would like to work out something for you and he wonders whether it would be possible for you to make use of the tape recordings from his Charles Eliot Norton lectures, particularly the passages comprising page 8 to 13 and page 23 to 34, of the published lectures called "i". These he thinks might work into your program if some way could be arranged for you to take off and re-record those tapes. I think that the Lowell Institute would probably give its consent.
>
> I suggest that you look at the book, which will give you an idea of the passages.[5]

Tucker replied to the effect that the *Anthology* staff was pleased that Mr. Cummings was interested, but that they "would rather not re-record if it can be avoided." Tucker sent Mr. Cummings three copies of the standard contract, of which the last two items were:

> Mr. Cummings agrees to provide the Project Supervisor with a list of poems which pertain to the series theme of freedom, with comment on each poem, the entire program capable of oral presentation by poet in approximately 30 minutes.
>
> Mr. Cummings further agrees to be available (at the University of Massachusetts, Amherst, Massachusetts, unless otherwise arranged) for 16 hours, if necessary, to insure the making of an acceptable tape.

Tucker's letter concluded: "If our usual procedure and agreement are not satisfactory to him, we'll be glad to consider other arrangements within the scope of our limitations and possibilities." To this letter he received the following reply from Miss Baumgarten on March 4.

> I sent Mr. Cummings your letter and the memorandum you enclosed, but I am sorry to tell you that it cannot be worked out exactly as you suggest.
>
> Cummings could only do it if you can arrange to have him make a recording in New York City at some quiet sound studio during the next sixty days. He would want the choice of what he reads left up to him, and the reading would have to be without any kind of comment, but simply those selections on freedom, as he understands it, taken from his three recent books—50 POEMS, 1 X 1, and XAIPE. If you can arrange this, let me know.
>
> He would, however, want the full $250 as soon as he has made the recordings.

Tucker replied to Miss Baumgarten on March 8, in part as follows:

> We can make a great part of the arrangement Mr. Cummings suggests. I expect to be in position March 13 to suggest a possible time to record in a quiet sound studio in New York City. And we shall be happy, for a series whose theme is freedom, if Mr. Cummings chooses the poems he will read. And, as he wishes, we shall make no comment nor expect any during the readings. . . .
>
> We are, alas, obliged by the terms of our grant to administer our funds as we have indicated on our agreement. Therefore, with reference to that agreement: although we gladly agree to waive the last 2 items, we are obliged to retain the first 4.[6]

If Mr. Cummings finds the agreement satisfactory in terms

of the arrangement I have described above and with the last two items understood to be waived in his case, would he please sign, date, and return 2 copies, retaining one for himself?

On March 13, Tucker wrote again to Miss Baumgarten to say that Mr. William Hodapp (Executive Director of a New York corporation producing public affairs television programs) had offered the courtesy of arranging for a quiet sound studio in New York City where Mr. Cummings could record his program. Mr. Cummings signed the contract, but with the understanding, relevant to the last two paragraphs, that he would plan his own program without editorial approval and that he would not need to come to Amherst.

Miss Baumgarten wrote to Tucker on March 25, 1954 enclosing a note from Mr. Cummings and the signed memorandum which Tucker was directed to initial in the margin beside the last two paragraphs and return to Miss Baumgarten. The note was our first from Mr. Cummings, who, after Miss Baumgarten's next letter, handled all correspondence.

4 Patchin Place

March 24 1954

Dear Mr Tucker—

   I sign this agreement with the understanding (1) that my reading will be preceeded,& if necessary followed,by a brief—one minute or less—announcement linking the recording with others made for Amherst;&(2) that all poems which I read shall be included As Is,in the order which I give them

      —sincerely

      E. E. Cummings

In reply to these letters, Tucker made a request to which other poets including Archibald MacLeish, Wallace Stevens, and Richard Wilbur, had acceded. Writing to Miss Baumgarten on March 29, 1954 Tucker said:

> Thank you and Mr. Cummings for your notes of March 25 and 24 respectively, and for 2 copies of our agreement. As directed, I return (enclosed) one copy which I've initialed in the margins beside the last two paragraphs.
>
> We would be honored if Mr. Cummings would become an Honorary Member of our Literary Society. We seek no further gift of those we honor than the privilege of using their names on our correspondence. Our correspondence will be used to procure books of poetry and equipment for our new Poetry Room in Goodell Library at the University. . . . In any event we are more pleased than we can say that Mr. Cummings is to participate in New England Anthology. We look forward to hearing the tape.

On April 7, Miss Baumgarten replied:

> I am returning the invoices covering the Cummings recordings. I have signed them as his agent.
>
> I hope you liked the tapes. As for using his name as an honorary member of your Literary Society, Cummings is very sorry, but he must decline. It is a matter of policy.

On March 20, Hodapp had written Tucker to say that the taping went well, and that Mr. Cummings was forwarding a chronological source list of the poems used on the broadcast. Mr. Cummings' list follows:

	name of book	number of poem	first line of poem
1	50 Poems	25	as freedom is a breakfastfood
2	One Times One	XXXV	except in your
3	" " "	IV	of all the blessings which to man
4	XAIPE	50	no time ago
5	"	49	this is a rubbish of human rind
6	One Times One	IX	a salesman is an it that stinks
			Excuse
7	" " "	X	a politician is an arse upon
8	Collected Poems	204	i sing of Olaf glad and big
9	" "	251	kumrads die because they're told)

name of book	number of poem	first line of poem
10 " "	142	a man who had fallen among thieves
11 " "	138	MEMORABILIA
12 50 Poems	50	what freedom's not some under's
13 " "		mere above
	34	my father moved through dooms of
		love

NB—I give the first lines of these poems in case their order as here listed should not coincide with the order of the poems *as recorded*, which is *the proper order.*[7]

When the Cummings recording, perhaps the most eloquent one he ever made, was heard, it electrified some—and shocked others. His reading of "i sing of Olaf" was particularly effective.

> i sing of Olaf glad and big
> whose warmest heart recoiled at war:
> a conscientious object-or
>
> his wellbelovéd colonel (trig
> westpointer most succinctly bred)
> took erring Olaf soon in hand;
> but—though an host of overjoyed
> noncoms (first knocking on the head
> him) do through icy waters roll
> that helplessness which others stroke
> with brushes recently employed
> anent this muddy toiletbowl,
> while kindred intellects evoke
> allegiance per blunt instruments—
> Olaf (being to all intents
> a corpse and wanting any rag
> upon what God unto him gave)
> responds, without getting annoyed
> "I will not kiss your f.ing flag"
>
> straightway the silver bird looked grave
> (departing hurriedly to shave)
>
> but—though all kinds of officers
> (a yearning nation's blueyed pride)

their passive prey did kick and curse
until for wear their clarion
voices and boots were much the worse,
and egged the firstclassprivates on
his rectum wickedly to tease
by means of skilfully applied
bayonets roasted hot with heat—
Olaf (upon what were once knees)
does almost ceaselessly repeat
"there is some s. I will not eat"
our president, being of which
assertions duly notified
threw the yellowsonofabitch
into a dungeon,where he died

Christ(of His mercy infinite)
i pray to see;and Olaf,too

preponderatingly because
unless statistics lie he was
more brave than me:more blond than you.[8]

The inclusion of "i sing of Olaf" and "a politician is an arse upon" raised the question as to whether FCC regulations would permit the educational radio stations to broadcast the tape, and, consequently, raised the further question whether it was right to submit this tape to NAEB as part of our series. To put it mildly (and to skip a great deal of what Mr. Cummings called "academic *Sturm und Drang*") there was a considerable difference of opinion. However, a compromise was reached. Tucker's personal position had been stated in his March 8 letter to Miss Baumgarten: "We shall be happy, for a series whose theme is freedom, if Mr. Cummings chooses the poems he will read." As Project Supervisor, however, he acted to carry out the Committee's compromise decision, which was as follows: It was decided that it should be made clear to Mr. Cummings that probably his tape would not be heard in its present form. Mr. Cummings was to be asked first, if he would agree to read a somewhat different group of poems. If Mr. Cummings rejected this proposal, he was to be asked if he would agree to cutting out "i sing of Olaf" and "a politician is an arse upon." If Mr. Cummings rejected this proposal also, the unchanged Cummings tape and copies of the complete correspondence about it were to be sent to NAEB.

William Hodapp had offered to negotiate with Mr. Cummings. Tucker wrote him on April 17, 1954 thanking him, and adding, ". . . we are selecting a new batch of poems, keeping what we can . . ." noting that Hodapp would "arrange with Mr. Cummings to make a new tape of those poems which we (quite honestly) admire and which are unquestionably related to the rest of the series of programs. . . ." Hodapp wrote to Mr. Cummings as follows (April 30):

> Your excellent tape of your poems has been reviewed by the University of Massachusetts, and they are delighted with your readings and your narrative style.
>
> However, the Committee met and asked me if you would be willing to record poems indicated in the attached list since, in subject matter, they approach more closely the central theme of the series. Would you have any objection, therefore, at your earliest opportunity next week to have another session, selecting from the attached list materials which might total the same time? They would be most grateful for your understanding of their problem and this additional inconvenience.
>
> Would you give me a call on Monday if you are willing, and I will see what the earliest recording date might be that we could arrange.

Mr. Cummings' reply to this letter is a masterpiece of design as well as of brevity. On a piece of 8½ x 11 white stationary, printed neatly with his address at the top, he typed, in quite formal fashion (though first on the red ribbon and then, over again, on the black) a date, a salutation, and a complimentary close. The signature is in dark blue ink. Challenging the gentility of this format, in the center of the page, and in red, stands the two-letter message: "no."

4 Patchin Place
New York City
11

May 1 1954

Dear Mr Hodapp--

no

--sincerely

ſ. ſ. ℂ

This seemed clear enough, but now Tucker, in his role as Project Supervisor carrying out the correspondence decision of the Committee, proceeded to the second plan, writing as follows to Mr. Cummings on May 18, 1954.

We want to thank you for your participation in New England Anthology; we think that yours is an exceptionally good tape. But we are informed that it won't be played over many stations because of certain words in "A politician is an arse upon" and "i sing of Olaf." It seems too bad that the tape won't be heard because of the inclusion of these 2 poems. Does it seem too bad to you?

If so, we would be glad to cut it at your direction and to fill in the remaining time with introductory and concluding material. Or, if you prefer, we could splice in place of these poems another poem or two which you could tape there.

If you are unwilling to change the tape, we shall send it AS IS to NAEB, but we think you should know that there is almost no chance of its being broadcast publicly.

May 23 1954

Dear Mr Tucker—
    concerning your letter of May 18th:
    let me say,as one individual to another,
    that I'm more than glad my recording
    pleases you as well as me;& that I
    shouldn't dream of sanctioning any change
    whatsoever,on behalf of any number of
    nonindividuals
                      —sincerely
                      E. E. Cummings

Mr. Cummings' rejection of the second plan left Tucker the responsibility of following the Committee's third choice, sending NAEB the unchanged tape and copies of the complete correspondence. The series was to be completed by July 1. When towards the end of June, Tucker arranged to have all the tapes shipped to NAEB, the Cummings tape (*and* a duplicate in the files of the recording studio in New York) had disappeared. Tucker was not then and is not now happy with the flimsy fabrication which appears below; nevertheless he retains it to indicate his despair at the unaccountable disappearance and for the sake of Mr. Cummings' reply which follows it. Tucker and David Clark took immediate steps to try to get the tape rerecorded in its original form so that the contract with Mr. Cummings could be fulfilled in both letter and spirit. Tucker wrote to Mr. Cummings on June 26:

One final letter on the tape and then I'm sure you hope, as I do, that that's an end to the matter—except for the good it will do in the broadcasting of it.

I came in to New York today to try to reach you to explain our dilemma—namely, that after all difficulties, the crowning blow came at school's end—when we were preparing to send it off with the other New England poets, yours had been erased by a careless student. What can I say? Except to hope that you'll understand—and help us complete the series by coming in to NBC for one LAST

session and doing the group exactly as before. Bill Hodapp
says he can set it all up quickly (wherever you are) and
your understanding of this crisis and helpfulness in sur-
mounting it will be appreciated beyond measure.

Please know that we're enormously grateful for your
patience—and hope fervently that you can help us repair
this mischance.

Will you call Bill H. . . . and he will undertake to make
the repeat as painless as possible for you. We will then
(also) be in position to give you a dupe tape for your files.

On June 30 Mr. Cummings replied from Silver Lake, New
Hampshire:

> your special delivery letter of the 26th
> has just arrived
> what astonishes our nonhero is the fact
> that,between the day I made the tape & the
> day a "careless" (!) "student erased" same,
> there existed ample (speaking softly) time
> to fabricate a sacrosanct "dupe tape" for
> your private files;not to mention a regular
> record. Quite incidentally—Mr. Hodapp
> himself, at the conclusion of our original
> séance,graciously offered me a *record*
> (& of his own volition)
>
> as it happens, I see no possibility of making
> you or him a second tape until late autumn,
> if then;& can only offer the far from practical
> suggestion that you restore your peaceofmind
> by shooting the student

It was sometime between Mr. Cummings' letter of June 30th
and his next letter July 18th that Tucker and Clark journeyed
to Silver Lake, New Hampshire, with a carful of recording
equipment hoping to persuade Mr. Cummings to rerecord the
exact program (unexpurgated) which was on the vanished
tape. They explained to him that they did not know what had
happened to the tape. The joke was that even if Mr. Cummings

were willing to redo the program, there was no electricity in the Silver Lake cottage. The most they could get was Mr. Cummings' agreement that he might redo the tape in late October.

After they had returned from Silver Lake, Tucker entered into an individual-to-individual correspondence with Mr. Cummings.

Before the following letter from Mr. Cummings, Tucker wrote thanking him for his hospitality at Silver Lake and expressing admiration for his poems, especially "i sing of Olaf" since, to Tucker, it seemed based on values which he associated with *mercy* (of which men seemed capable) rather than on those associated with *justice* (of which men did not seem capable, and which therefore seemed better left to God); Tucker also said that he would keep Mr. Cummings posted regarding our search for the lost tapes.

July 18 1954

Dear Mr Tucker—
>your letter is welcome. I'm naturally
>glad that certain of my poems give you
>deep pleasure:& more than appreciate
>your courtesy in keeping me posted anent
>the recording

>as for "justice" versus "mercy":our nonhero
>would doubtless exclaim (with his dark
>taxidriving friend) Heartily Agreed, if
>showing "mercy" didn't strike me as significantly
>easier than doing "justice"; which suggests
>that true justice & true mercy— vide a
>sublime New Testament passage quoted on pages
>66–67 of *i (six nonlectures)*— are one

>Marion & this correspondent enjoyed meeting
>not only yourself but yourself's staunch
>friend Mr Clark. Here's wishing both of you
>good luck
>>—sincerely
>>E. E. Cummings

Tucker, having read the passage recommended—that concerning Jesus' defense of the adulterous woman: "Let him who
is without sin amongst you cast the first stone"—reported to
Mr. Cummings that the passage seemed to support Tucker's
attitude regarding *mercy,* that if there were *justice* in it, that was
done principally in showing *mercy* to the woman. Mr. Cummings replied:

July 30 1954

Dear Mr Tucker—

     am naturally delighted,not only that
     you agree with me about the passage
     from John,but that you enjoy our
     unhero's nonlectures. Since he&I've
     no more to say on the subject of
     justice-mercy,let us give you a pair
     of(speaking mildly apropos) quotations

     (1) "Hate is a kind of 'passive suffering,'
     but indignation is a kind of joy. . .and joy
     is the salvation of the soul. You say we
     must love. Yes,but love is not pity. It
     does not desire to change its object. It
     is a form of the eternal contemplation of
     what is. . .Before all,I want to strengthen
     myself. It is not our business to reply to
     this and that,but to set up our love and
     indignation against their pity and hate."
     (Yeats;via *The Unicorn* by Virginia Moore,
     Macmillan, '54: page 413)

     (2) "Only a just man is a free man." (Plutarch;
     re Cato)

     incidentally,would you be so very kind as
     to send me a complete list of the poems which
     constitute my original(& not expurgated)
     "freedom" recording?
          —thanks

               E. E. Cummings

Meanwhile Tucker and Clark had become disturbed enough about the disappearance of the Cummings tape to make a notarized statement of their position and to send copies to associates in the project. Their statement said, in part:

> We were surprised and sorry to discover that by the end of the school year the seventh tape had unaccountably disappeared, both the copy here at the University and the one . . . in New York, where the tape was made. The disappearance of the tape subsequent to the discussions aforementioned is likely to arouse suspicions in the literary world. Therefore we wish, without stating or implying any charge against any person or persons, to dissociate ourselves from any alleged attempt to change, delete from, or suppress the tape without Mr. Cummings' express wish.

Mentioning that Mr. Cummings had agreed to redo the tape in October, they continued, "If further obstacles should arise, we feel that in order to protect our names we must make this statement public to interested persons in the literary world." They concluded that their reason for making the statement was to avoid the suspicion "of having violated the principles which New England Anthology was created to support," and they invited other members of the Anthology staff "who feel as we do" to make similar statements. The date of this statement was August 11th. On August 12th another member, Leon O. Barron, wrote to Tucker to make a similar statement. By August 14th the duplicate Cummings tape in the recording studio in New York had reappeared and was being sent to Tucker. Tucker wrote to Mr. Cummings August 20:

> Arrived at my house today a copy of your NEANTHOLOGY tape. . . . Now to splice on brief introduction and conclusion as arranged and send to NAEB.
>
> The next blessed event will be the birth of my second child, due to appear the 23rd.

> August 22 1954

> Dear Mr Tucker—
>   please accept my heartiest congratulations

re your immediately expected blessing!
As for the recent discovery: will you be so
very much more than kind as to check it
most carefully with the enclosed list (a
copy of which you kindly sent me during the
late disappearance) & let our unAndHowhero
know whether or not his labours are intact?
—thanks!

E. E. Cummings

P.S. supposing they *are* (by some miracle) intact, I'd naturally enjoy having a record of the tape-as-a-whole
for my strictly personal use; & would gladly pay for
the making of it

On September 2, Tucker wrote again.

Today I have mailed to NAEB—at long last and AS IS
—a copy our New England Anthology "freedom" tape.
I would like to say how pleased I am with it, and with the
fact that it's going to NAEB intact. But I know you will
be pleased and can say it better. Anyhow:

> We favor Grace who treats a guest
> As having passed examination
> And, bless her indiscrimination,
> Need never give a Loyalty Test.
> No one thinks of domination
> In her house. There she puts at rest
> Hearts whose first imagination
> Thought she'd love the others best.

When [a colleague returns for the fall semester] he
will make you a record of the tape-as-a-whole for your personal use. And without charge, for heaven's sake.

Timothy weighed in Sunday at 10 A.M.: 9 lb. 1 oz. He
and his good mother are fine. Jonathan who 2½ years ago
weighed in at 8 lb. 5 oz. is at the moment dubious; but I
have high hopes for amity sooner or later.

September 8 1954

Dear Mr Tucker—

      I rejoice to learn that naeb will,
at last,receive an AS IS tape of
my "freedom" recording;&(be it
needlessly added)shall treasure
my personal disk

      here's wishing your heavy- & middle-
weights health & happiness

                    —sincerely
                  E. E. Cummings

After Tucker had sent Mr. Cummings a personal recording of his program, along with a letter dated September 20th, the following postcard in Mr. Cummings' hand (postmarked October 5, 1954) arrived from Silver Lake, N.H.:

      the largesse (with directions
for enjoying it) has arrived
safely—Marion & I are most
grateful

      let me unnecessarily add that
am greatly cheerly by your
enthusiasm

                EEC

Mr. Cummings, with other poets of New England Anthology, was notified of a program featuring excerpts from the series at a fall meeting of the New England College English Association held at Babson Institute on October 30, 1954. He typed his reply on a postcard (postmarked November 4).

            4 Patchin Place
            New York City
                11

here's hoping the "Fall Meeting" was a
success—also that la grippe is less popular
in Amherst than on Manhattan

                Cummings

Then came the bad news that the NAEB would not release the Cummings program. On November 5, 1954 John Holt, Network Manager, wrote to Tucker:

> I have the pleasure of informing you for the Network Acceptance Committee that the *New England Anthology* series has been approved for distribution. We shall begin releasing the programs on March 20.
>
> As I believe you expected, we are not going to release the Cummings program. It is a fine piece of work, but would probably cause trouble, possibly with the FCC.
>
> We will not have a list of all accepting stations until the latter part of January. At that time Miss Rosaline Biason, our traffic manager, will send you a copy of the list.

To this letter Tucker replied as follows November 8.

> I'm not writing especially as Project Supervisor of New England Anthology who is, of course, grateful that the series is approved for distribution. I speak rather for myself as private citizen and with regard to the E. E. Cummings tape.
>
> First, I wonder how freedom (the series' theme, in fact) is to be achieved or maintained if all citizens are not given opportunities to speak or to choose, to discriminate among available material what they approve from what they don't. I should hate to lose the opportunity to make choices. Doesn't this suppression of Cummings' tape limit my range and yours, as well as his?
>
> Second, if (and I happen heartily to agree with you) "It is a fine piece of work," why are not others permitted to judge for themselves?
>
> Third, so trouble may arise? Trouble for whom? If freedom is dependent on opportunities to choose and if Cummings' is "a fine piece of work," it can be no trouble to defend or express what one values highly. I prefer liberty above many things. And it seems to me no trouble at all to express my judgments. We still have courts of law that

will permit me to defend them. But how long will that be so if I or you or anyone begins to suppress expression, "fine" or not?

On the same day Tucker wrote the news to Mr. Cummings and enclosed a copy of his letter to Mr. Holt.

[Tucker explained which poems of Cummings were used with others of the NEA series at the fall meeting of the College English Association.]

In a letter dated Nov. 5, John Holt, Network Manager of NAEB, 119 Gregory Hall, U. of Illinois, Urbana, Illinois, informs me that their committee approves the series for distribution; they begin releasing on March 20. Yet they are not going to release your program, which though "It is a fine piece of work . . . would probably cause trouble, possibly with the FCC."

This sounds familiar. However, if as a wiser private soul than as a project supervisor, I can further the hearing of your program, please call on me.

Mr. Cummings replied to Tucker as follows:

November 14 '54

Dear Mr Tucker—
        thanks most kindly for a good letter!

I appreciate your generosity in explaining
how my tape was constructed; & am glad the
excerpts were enjoyed. As for your Epistle
To The Philistines, sir,I consider it a chef-
d'oeuvre:& hereby proffer heartiest congratulations
let our nonhero only add that your offer to do
anything you can to render his efforts audible
touches me deeply
                —Vive La Liberté!
                E. E. Cummings

On November 11 Holt replied to Tucker as follows:

I am too much in sympathy with your general point of

view to "answer" any defense of freedom with anything but discomfort. Nevertheless, a few points do occur to me.

First of all, every station has the right—and the obligation —to select programs as it sees fit for its particular audience. This might not be true if a station could possibly broadcast every program available, but there are more programs and more program material available than there is broadcast time. Hence, selectivity is unavoidable. And this selection must be an exercise of practical judgment, because arbitrary or random selection is the forfeiture of freedom, not its exercise.

Sooner or later, the power, the right, the obligation, even the freedom, to select programs must be delegated to specific persons. It happens that, for the programs distributed on the NAEB Network, this function has been given to certain committees plus Association and Network Headquarters. When I personally enjoy a program as much as I did the Cummings opus, I am tempted to have it sent to every member station together with a note suggesting that each local program director listen to it and decide for himself whether or not to put it on the air. But I already know what the answer would be: "Bless you, John Holt, but each of us has his own job, and we have appointed and hired several other people for the task of reviewing that program. Thou shalt not pass the buck—especially a buck which is not yours to pass . . . Besides you know that most of us subscribe to the NARTB code."

Now concerning the specific program in question: I wrote to you that it "would probably cause trouble, possibly with the FCC." I think that the feeling that the program did not comply with FCC regulations and/or the general NARTB code provisions regarding decency of language was the heaviest point against it.

The National Association of Educational Broadcasters is just that—an association. The NAEB Network is a project of seventy-six broadcasters within the framework of that association. Neither the NAEB nor the NAEB Network has an "independent" existence. Each is an expression of the will of the membership. Therefore neither Association nor Network Headquarters has the moral right to challenge, or to imply a challenge of, FCC regulations unless it has been authorized to do so. Thus far, it has not been so authorized.

The NAEB Network has without qualm or hesitation distributed a number of programs which would be considered "too daring" by any commercial broadcaster. But in all cases, it has remained within legal bounds. If at any time we should see a revision of the FCC regulations—which is *most* improbable—we would have to be duly authorized by the NAEB membership through its accredited representatives, and we must do it through an effectively planned campaign—not through the random implied-challenge of the distribution of any single program which chanced to be included in any given series.

I have sent your letter to Dr. Harry J. Skornia and have received the following comment from him:

> We would defend the right to freedom to express ideas and viewpoints any time, but don't think the freedom to use profane or vulgar language over the radio which one hears in one's home (not in a lecture hall, university or otherwise, where one can be relatively sure there are not—sometimes unattended—children present, for instance). There are more important things to "go to the mat" or "stir up storms" over than the right to use a given word to describe a physical function. We don't believe that this is necessarily education in its best sense or that this really is a test of courage. It seems more like a test of good taste or tact. Not only *what* is said, but *how* it must be said, for a given medium—is involved.

Other arguments for the deletion of the Cummings program from the *New England Anthology* series might be elaborated, but I believe the above will suffice to indicate the nature of our position. I repeat that I personally like the program and that I sympathize with your attitude. Being psychologically and intellectually anti-authoritarian and anti-puritan, I find the very concepts of censorship or suppression repugnant, but I wonder if perhaps it is not less true that Mr. Cummings has been suppressed than that he has failed to take full advantage of an opportunity to promote the beliefs which he professes.

And I wonder what disposition *might* have been made of the program had Mr. Cummings condescended at least to preface his reading with some such remark as: "Ladies and gentlemen, the reading which follows will be in the language which you and I use, but—some of it—not often before our children. Perhaps you will wish to tuck in bed 'such as have need of milk, and not strong meat . . . Strong meat belongeth to them that are of full age, even those who by reason of use have their senses exercised to discern both good and evil.' "

In 1963 Holt and Skornia both commented further on the matter in giving permission for the publication of their letters. Skornia summarized the situation thus:

1) We were trying to get more NAEB stations to carry Mr. Cummings' poetry, & that of others. Each time an "incident" of the sort illustrated here took place, we had setbacks. More stations, jumped on by their boards, trustees & narrow minded constituencies, would drop out of the NAEB network, because it made them trouble. We tried to explain this to Mr. Cummings . . . the need to make haste slowly & to cooperate to that end. He wasn't very patient about it. Today, many years later, I think we could do it. We've gradually educated people who hear educational stations up to it.

2) We had comparable problems in other areas. Actually we were trying to *break* taboos, not create them. Schweitzer's appeal to cease atomic testing was not touched by the National networks because it came during Eisenhower-Stevenson campaign. NAEB carried it.

But (like segregation, I suppose) I felt we couldn't rush it too much, or we'd have no network.

. . . I always regretted that Mr. Cummings did not quite understand that we *did* believe in what he was doing—but were in a position where, to do him & poetry good in the *long* run we had to be careful at first.

Holt felt that:

The important thing is that the artist's mission is to expand and deepen human consciousness and sensibility by any and all means of communication but those who provide the means—the most potent means—operate within a certain conventional framework which, to do his job, the artist must challenge and even attempt to demolish. And those controllers of the various media—the publisher, the broadcaster—enjoy the same freedom of action and selection that the artist does. This inevitably leads to certain conflicts, even more so in the commercial arena than in the educational arena.

I don't find the NAEB'S stand at all unreasonable—but has there ever been an artist worth his salt who didn't directly or indirectly challenge mere "reasonableness"—even if he did it in the name of reason?

Answering Holt's 1954 statement, Tucker wrote on November 14 of that year:

I'm writing personally, glad that we sympathize, especially in our finding the concepts of censorship and suppression repugnant. Presumably you and I are people "who by reason of use have their sense exercised to discern both good and evil." And I suppose that in releasing programs "too daring" for commercial broadcasters one specific person—or each specific person—exercised his power, right, obligation, and freedom to use his senses. I'm grateful that in so doing he also showed more respect for my judgment as audience than the "commercial broadcaster" does. And, as citizen, I'm also very grateful for comparable decisions made by one or more specific persons when they amended the country's fundamental law the first 10 times especially. Somehow specific persons' decisions of these sorts result in a higher general opinion of my and your and everyone's power to use our senses. Yet, decisions of Censors and Suppressors and those who make laws which tend to lower the general opinion of anyone's capabilities, seem to me to do more harm than good. Except by opportunities to exercise sense, I fail to see how anyone (unattended child or grandmother) can get in position to discern both good and evil. Life and education are risks, of course, but why risk tyranny rather than responsibility and freedom?

I think the view with which we sympathize can easily be defended. The Censor's mind, I've noticed, fails to consider the context in which the "daring" items appear; its concern is with the item, rather than with how it's used or seen. Yet audiences (excepting the Censor), I've also noticed, are capable of taking the item as the artist shows it. The Censor wrests from context items which the artist has used with other items to support some definite human meaning or attitude. The Censor thus makes abstract ugliness out of what the artist makes human, especially in his basic assumption that his audience is composed of human beings, not beasts.

You and I seem to consider E. E. Cummings an artist. At least we enjoy his program very much. I hope you will yield to your temptation, passing it along to each member station not as a buck so much as something like a torch. It may help you to know that one who sympathizes favors your own instinct in this matter.

On the same day Tucker wrote to Mr. Cummings:

Enclose Tucker-Holt correspondence and hope la grippe has gone.

Would you consider coming up here before long for a

day to meet especially individuals of the *Anthology* staff
at a party or informally anyway? Personal meeting might
make all the difference in getting the tape broadcast.
We're playing the series privately at the Literary Society
meetings. Yours, the 7th, will be played on Dec. 7th.
David Clark and I agree that your presence here sometime soon would be of great educational value to us all.
What do you think?

Thursday [Nov. 18, 1954]

Dear Mr Tucker—

encore congratulations & a bravissimo!
I wouldn't have missed your November 14
riposte(not to mention the Holt-Skornia
hyperwhatnot) for anythingtotheNth
regarding an Amherst visit·la grippe now
isn't;but(strictly entre nous) a kind of
socalled arthritis,with which I've long
wrestled & which occasionally makes its
entertainer feel as if he could fall into
17 pieces,has just wallopped this correspondent
—who's due to read at NYU dayaftertomorrow
as well as at the Hebrew Y next week—
consequently shall,like Br'er Rabbit,"lay
low". Please keep your fighting fingers
crossed on my feeble be-half or rather - whole

should said Y-rendezvous materialize,I
plan to begin with Act II Scene 5 of *Him*
(starring John Rutter)& then say something
like the enclosed;& finally read those 13
poems. If you object,please let me know
by airmail. Under the shallwesay circumstances
I feel infinitely more than justified in letting
a lively-if-small "public" partake of
corruptio ad absurdum inc

—greetings to David Clark!
E. E. Cummings

This was Mr. Cummings' enclosure:

Y M & Y W H A
(introducing 2nd half of reading)

some months ago,a number of writers(including our non-hero)were cordially urged to make socalled tape-recordings on the subject of Freedom,with special reference to New England;& were assured that these recordings—collectively entitled "New England Anthology"—would be broadcast over the socalled NAEB national network . . . whatever that is

now (as it happens) I love Freedom even more than I loathe radio;so I decided to make a Freedom recording. My Freedom recording consisted of 13 already-published poems;each of them expressing,in his or her particular way,how Freedom feels to one alive human being:namely, myself

I tell you this for two reasons. The first reason is,that I have indirectly learned that my Freedom recording will NOT be broadcast. Why? Because, although it's (quote) *a fine piece of work*(unquote) it would (quote)*probably cause trouble, possibly with the FFC* (unquote). So much for (quote)Freedom (unquote). My second reason is, that I shall now try to read you precisely those 13 poems which constitute the not-to-be-broadcast recording itself— letting you draw your own conclusions,if any

Tucker replied on November 19:

May the Socalled Arthritis get walloped in return.

My only objection to your remarks for the Y-rendezvous is that FFC should be FCC (Federal Communications Commission).

I've not heard from Holt again. My hope is that he'll yield to his temptation to pass the tape along to the stations.

Clark and I have in mind a broadcast and possibly a

test-case, if it can be managed. . . . So far as we can see, only your coming will change or sufficiently reinforce their attitudes. If you can possibly manage a visit for overnight say the word.

I will be delighted to transport you hither and back in my '53 Ford, which rides easy. And we will put you up in comfortable quarters, making all things as pleasant for you as we can.

Then arrived the second draft of Mr. Cummings' YM and YWHA Poetry Center talk (printed at the beginning of this article) with a note at the bottom in his hand and signed by him; the note read, "am still 'doctoring'; but shall let you know if & when there's any chance of a visit—meanwhile, cordial thanks for the transportation offer!" In the bottom left hand corner was Mr. Cummings' phone number and the words doubly-underlined: "sub rosa."

On December 4 Tucker wrote again:

Are you feeling better? I hope your program at the Y made 'em indignant. . . . The impulse to Repression gets malignant, causing Clark (now Chairman) to project a Literary Society meeting re Censorship on December 14th. We'll begin by playing your tape AS IS. Could you come for it?

May I, if so, offer transportation?

Mr. Cummings replied by a postcard, in his own hand, unself-addressed (postmarked December 15):

> don't see even the slightest
> chance of leaving NYC; but
> have the honour to report
> that when I quoted Mr Holt's
> immortal dictum—"it
> would probably cause trouble"
> —a roar rent the YM &
> YWHA welkin
>
>   Cummings

Tucker wrote Mr. Cummings the following in return on December 16.

> Delighted that you could keep the Y appointment to make 'em roar.

> After we played your tape AS IS the other night, we discussed the matter of Good Taste and Freedom of Literary Expression. Most of em made as if to take charge of everyone's soul, as expected. And they—afraid to love— are hardest of all to love, I think. The stiffened necks— unlike stiffened puke—betray no need for love. Yet, plainly, they need it most. How to love the respectable?

> Clark and I will be in NYC Dec. 27 and 28 for the MLA meeting. I have your sub rosa phone number, thanks. May we see you again one of those evenings? We can report at length on our mutual topic: freedom as a breakfastfood in "Education." We'd love the pleasure and honor again, if you're willing and able.

> And an Xmas poem for you and Mrs. Cummings.

Tucker and Clark visited with Mr. and Mrs. Cummings, and remember the cordial hospitality with pleasure. Some years later Tucker wrote to Mr. Cummings in New York congratulating him on a well-produced musical version of *Santa Claus* which he had seen in Iowa City. Mr. Cummings replied on a postcard in red, white and blue crayon!

THANK YOU

And that is the end of the correspondence with E. E. Cummings except that in 1959 he responded kindly to a request by Clark with a poem for *The Massachusetts Review*.[9]

Tucker and Clark had been careful (after the event) to have personal copies of the Cummings tape made. These they preserved with a veneration and caution such as one might give to the lost egg of Leda. After Mr. Cummings' death it seemed right to try to get the tape broadcast on a memorial program. In consequence, *"The Massachusetts Review's* Tribute to E. E. Cummings"* was produced by WFCR (the Four-College—Amherst, Mount Holyoke, Smith, and the University of Massachusetts—radio station) and featured Mr. Cummings' freedom recording. Introducing the program, Tucker said

> E. E. Cummings was a staunch advocate of the ideals of liberty. . . . Protesting against individual failures to act freely and to grant freedom to others, Cummings took (and granted) liberties. He took, most memorably, the freedom of speech, liberty of expression—and will be long remembered for doing so. His example may at first have surprised, even shocked, his contemporaries; but serious afterthought has inevitably found the intention—to awaken us to possibilities beyond the conventional, to set us thinking and feeling about our own valuation of freedom for ourselves and freedom for others—praiseworthy. Cummings took liberties as Walt Whitman took liberties, and we and poetry are the richer for it. As free men, we should be grateful to the Educational Radio Network for making available to its listeners the voice of an American who took his liberties responsibly and whose point of view culminates in his own phrase, "love is the whole and more than all"—the poet, E. E. Cummings.

The first poem on the tape was:[10]

> as freedom is a breakfastfood
> or truth can live with right and wrong
> or molehills are from mountains made
> —long enough and just so long
> will being pay the rent of seem
> and genius please the talentgang
> and water most encourage flame
>
> as hatracks into peachtrees grow
> or hopes dance best on bald men's hair
> and every finger is a toe
> and any courage is a fear
> —long enough and just so long
> will the impure think all things pure
> and hornets wail by children stung

or as the seeing are the blind
and robins never welcome spring
nor flatfolk prove their world is round
nor dingsters die at break of dong
and common's rare and millstones float
—long enough and just so long
tomorrow will not be too late

worms are the words but joy's the voice
down shall go which and up come who
breasts will be breasts thighs will be thighs
deeds cannot dream what dreams can do
—time is a tree (this life one leaf)
but love is the sky and i am for you
just so long and long enough

Notes
List of Works Cited
Acknowledgments

NOTES

Introduction

1. I. A. Richards, Willliam Empson, Robert Penn Warren, and R. P. Blackmur I have known through their books. John Crowe Ransom, Allen Tate, and Cleanth Brooks I knew also as my teachers. I suppose that Cleanth Brooks has most influenced my approach to a poem, although John Crowe Ransom's classes always consisted of intensive analysis of the text from the point of view of technique. Allen Tate's *Reactionary Essays* were my first introduction to the intellectual excitement of literary study. I discovered them even before I discovered Eliot's essays. Maynard Mack and Louis Martz taught me in class and in their work how careful scholarship may suddenly take fire in critical revelations, and Martz's *Poetry as Meditation* enabled me to relate my religious and poetic interests. René Wellek and W. K. Wimsatt provided the map of all critical approaches. The most influential teacher of all is usually an undergraduate teacher, and in my case Fred B. Millett was pre-eminent, although Newton Arvin appeared for a memorable summer and Lloyd Reynolds for a memorable year.

The sensitivity, control, and breadth of mind of these antecedents is not to be emulated, although a superficial methodology could be. The criticism of Brooks and Warren, for example, always holds on to the whole poem, and such analyses as those in *The Well Wrought Urn* go beyond that to support a general theory of poetry. Brooks's concern with paradox, whether valid or not as a description of the nature of poetry, certainly is a useful tool for keeping the whole poem, the relation of each element to the whole, before the reader's and the critic's minds. It is, of course, much more than a tool, and Brooks's grasp of the total poem in his criticism antedates his interest in paradox.

Out of a People to a People

1. Held in the Antient Concert Rooms in Brunswick Street, later to be named Pearse Street after the leader of the 1916 Rising. Vice-Provost J. P. Mahaffy had forbidden holding the meeting at Trinity

College because "a man called Pearse," an agitator against recruiting for the British army, was to share the platform with Yeats (Yeats, *Tribute,* pp. 5–11).

2. O'Neill was a seventeenth-century general who fought for Catholic Ireland and administered sound defeats to the Parliamentary forces in the 1640's, but who died before being able to meet Cromwell effectively in 1649.

3. A less certain echo of *Gulliver's Travels* may be heard in "He that's mounting up must on his neighbour mount," which may recall Book I, Chapter I, where Gulliver contentedly reports that the Emperor's "great officers would by no means suffer his Majesty to endanger his person by mounting on my body" and that "there could not be fewer than ten thousand, at several times, who mounted upon my body by the help of ladders." Yeats's poem seethes with Swiftean anger at insult to human dignity.

4. In a "Revised Edition," Yeats "added a few pages of new verses towards the end, and softened some phrases in the introduction which seemed a little petulant in form" and wrote in "a few more to describe writers who have appeared during the last four years" (*A Book of Irish Verse,* 1900, p. xiii). There Yeats has the grace to give Mangan a saving passion "for books" as well as "for drink and opium" (*A Book of Irish Verse,* 1900, p. xxi).

5. It is remarkable to see Yeats distinguishing so clearly at this date between what he will later call the primary and the antithetical man.

6. Yeats once took the older poem seriously enough to use a sentence from it—"The sorrowful are dumb for thee"—as an epigraph to the first edition of *The Countess Kathleen* (1892). In quoting this expression of dumb helplessness Yeats may have mourned not only the death of his Countess but also what seemed the determined self-martyrdom of his beloved, Maud Gonne, after whom the Countess was modeled: "I thought my dear must her own soul destroy,/So did fanaticism and hate enslave it. . . ." ("The Circus Animals' Desertion," Yeats, *Variorum Poems,* p. 630). I give the name "Mary Rourke" as it appears in *A Book of Irish Verse,* p. 242, although the "Contents," p. x, give "Bourke," as do Yeats's other references to this poem.

Poussin & 'News for the Delphic Oracle'

1. From an address given at the opening of "W. B. Yeats, A Centenary Exhibition" in the National Gallery of Ireland, November 1965.

Oliver Gogarty's 'The Crab Tree'

1. Vivian Mercier feels that, because of his own weakness in Latin and Greek, Yeats's inordinate respect for Classical learning made him overestimate Gogarty (Mercier, "Gogarty," p. 35).

2. Mercier unaccountably finds that in "Ringsend" Gogarty half-redeems "a mediocre poem with a haunting final cadence" (Mercier, "Gogarty," p. 37). Brendan Kennelly, on the other hand, picks "Ringsend" alone of Gogarty's poems to anthologize (Kennelly, *Penguin Book of Irish Verse*, p. 315). Jeffares, disappointingly, seems to think of "Ringsend" as one of those few examples in print of Gogarty's many "wildly boisterous fits of comic invention," in other words bawdy rhymes (Jeffares, "Gogarty, Irishman," p. 153). "Ringsend" is neither boisterous, in final effect, nor bawdy, although Jeffares quotes other masterpieces of the genre—including what Horace Reynolds in his preface to the *Collected Poems* (p. xx) perhaps rightly calls "the cleverest parody in English Literature," a Keatsian sonnet "On First Looking through Kraft Ebbing's [sic] *Psychopathia Sexualis*," which ends: "Potent behind a cart with Mary Ann" (Jeffares, "Gogarty, Irishman," p. 151).

Some Poems by Seumas O'Sullivan

1. *To a Poet, who would have me Praise certain Bad Poets, Imitators of His and Mine*

> You say, as I have often given tongue
> In praise of what another's said or sung,
> 'Twere politic to do the like by these;
> But was there ever dog that praised his fleas?
> (Yeats, *Variorum Poems*, p. 263)

This poem is addressed to Æ, rejecting a request to praise the poets of Æ's circle, perhaps including Sullivan. This gentle man could be devastating. When the epigram appeared in *The Green Helmet and Other Poems* (Dundrum: The Cuala Press, 1910) the line read "But where's the wild dog that has praised his fleas?" It "should have annihilated the lesser poets of Dublin," Padraic Colum remarks, had not Sullivan quietly asked: "When did the wild dog ever know his sires?"

and followed this up by describing the "living speech" Yeats was recommending as "words with a spit upon them." "That wild dog never ran again as a poetic symbol," Colum reports (O'Sullivan, *Poems,* pp. 13–14), and it is true that Yeats tamed the animal for its appearance in *Responsibilities and Other Poems* (London: Macmillan and Co., 1916; New York: The Macmillan Company, 1916) where the rather lame line "But have you known a dog to praise his fleas?" occurs, and again in the version above, which first appeared in *Later Poems* (London: Macmillan and Company, 1922). O'Sullivan's *mots* may or may not have tamed the dog.

Thomas Kinsella's 'Downstream'

1. *Downstream* was first published by the Dolmen Press, Dublin, in 1962. The much altered and shortened version printed here first appeared, under the title "Downstream (II)" in *The Massachusetts Review,* V, 2 (Winter 1964), pp. 323–25. The version entitled "Downstream" in Kinsella's *Nightwalker and Other Poems* (New York: Alfred A. Knopf, 1968, pp. 98–101), is again slightly revised from "Downstream II," but my analysis pertains to the version in *The Massachusetts Review.*

Robert Frost's 'The Thatch' and 'Directive'

1. Randall Jarrell wrote of "Directive" that "it shows the coalescence of three of Frost's obsessive themes, those of isolation, of extinction, and of the final limitations of man—is Frost's last word about all three" (Jarrell, "To the Laodiceans," p. 46).

2. An exception is Nitchie, *Human Values,* though I find his reading of "The Thatch" (pp. 100–01, 103, 106–07, 214) a bit cold-blooded, as is his reading of "Directive."

3. "Directive" was first published in *The Virginia Quarterly Review,* Winter 1946, pp. 1–4. First book publication was in *Steeple Bush* (New York: Henry Holt and Company, 1947).

4. I could find almost nothing on the genesis or locale of "Directive." According to Elizabeth Shepley Sergeant, the poem "seems to have been born out of" the region of Concord Corners, Vermont, where Frost bought a summer home, settling in in 1937, the summer before Mrs. Frost's death in March 1938. Sergeant describes the place as "a new height of country" where there were "Two village cultures fading into

each other" (Sergeant, *Frost,* pp. 350–51). Concord Corners is across the border from Franconia, New Hampshire, where Frost had often lived during the hay-fever season. Lawrance Thompson speaks of Frost's "interest in the forlorn and nearly abandoned village" of Concord Corners (Frost, *Letters,* pp. 446, 449). However, if this really is the region described in "Directive," the name "Panther Mountain" must be fictitious.

I am grateful to Professor John R. Donnelly, Department of Forestry, University of Vermont, to State Librarian James Igoe, Montpelier, to someone in the Forestry Department at the University of New Hampshire whose name I have lost, and to William B. Overstreet, United States Board on Geographic Names, Washington, for assuring me that the appropriate reference works list no "Panther Mountain" in either New Hampshire nor Vermont. John W. Dunn, Assistant Reference Librarian, New Hampshire State Library, Concord, put me onto New York State as a possibility, as did also Mr. Overstreet. There are two "Panther Mountains" in New York state, one in Hamilton County and one in Ulster County, and a "Panther Peak" in Essex County. Mr. Overstreet has given the following reference: in 1940, six years before the first printing of "Directive," the WPA compilers of a guide to New York state recommended a foot trail starting in Piseco (Hamilton County, New York State Route 8) on the Northern tip of Piseco Lake: "Left on his foot trail 1.2m to Panther Mountain (2,713 alt.), a half-hour climb to a panoramic view of Adirondack peaks in the distance and Piseco lake spread out below" (*New York,* pp. 493–94). Eighty years earlier French's *Gazetteer* described Piseco as "once a busy village of some 250 inhabitants" but "now nearly deserted" (French, *Gazetter,* p. 337). In 1940 the WPA found a population of 20, a general store and gas station (*Loc. cit.*). But so much for idle speculation. Frost was a great hiker as well as stroller, and may well have investigated some of the places mentioned above, but I have no evidence that he knew any of the New York State Panther Mountains. There is also a Panther Mountain in Texas!

5. John Robert Doyle is suitably impressed by this remarkable bit of New England lingo. However he very strangely makes "Back" a verb in the imperative mood meaning "to go back to, return to an earlier, a former time" which "placed beside 'out of' becomes a visual image, 'to back out of a garage, a gate a door' " (Doyle, *Frost,* p. 19). Elizabeth Drew also allows this reading as one half of a "double meaning; both 'behind all this confusion' and *get* back, back out from this overwhelming 'now' " (Drew, *Poetry,* p. 231). But clearly "Back" is an adverb telling *where* "There is a house that is no more a house." Doyle's other comments on the passage are illuminating.

6. Reuben A. Brower, in his superbly sensitive and controlled chapter "The Height of the Adventure," finds that the journey metaphor

"embraces in fact several kinds of journey . . . a journey through geological time . . . a journey into the pre-world of myth . . . [a journey] traveling back through other lives . . . a journey into the reader's private history . . . [and finally a journey] beyond history geological and human, family and personal, and beyond our adult selves to an 'original source' " (Brower, *Constellations,* pp. 234–38).

7. Sergeant points out that "The Times Table" (Frost, *Poetry,* p. 263), is in its opening lines about "a spring with a broken drinking glass," "a humble forerunner" of "Directive" (Sergeant, *Frost,* p. 302). Like "The Thatch," too, it is full of feelings of guilt and fear about actions calculated "To close a road, abandon a farm."

8. Frost was humorously bitter about the kind of interest in "Directive" of which my analysis is a late example. "The boys [followers of T. S. Eliot] call it great. They have re-estimated me" (Sergeant, *Frost,* p. 394). Several critics have connected the "serial ordeal" with the Grail legend and have drawn parallels with Eliot.

9. Doyle (*Frost,* p. 14) studies the subtle way in which Frost avoids forcing the personification.

10. S. P. C. Duvall is, I believe, the first to note the "veiled allusion" to the story of Ali Baba. He relates it to Thoreau's paradox that avoiding delusion turns life into a fairy tale (Duvall, p. 486n).

11. In this reading of "Directive" I have not taken account of and, except for what the notes indicate, I am not indebted to the numerous critiques of the poem. I have read through the critiques after writing my analysis and am satisfied to let it stand as it is. Some of these critiques are very fine indeed. Cf. my "Excursus on the Criticism of Robert Frost's 'Directive,' " to appear soon in *Costerus: Essays in English and American Language and Literature.*

12. First published in *West-Running Brook* (New York: Henry Holt and Company, 1928).

13. Letter to Richard Thornton, September 17, 1937, quoted in Sergeant, p. 352.

14. It is also the cottage in which Frost wrote the famous "The Road Not Taken," suggested by the life of Edward Thomas (Sergeant, p. 143).

15. A more detailed description is given by Lawrance Thompson (Thompson, *Early Years,* pp. 456–58), who also quotes a poem about the cottage by Wilfrid Gibson—strangely enough in the same meter as "The Thatch," but with a much more cheerful and conventionally poetic attitude than Frost's. (Thompson, *Early Years,* p. 457, quotes from the Reverend J. E. Getyn-Jones, *Dymock Down the Ages* (Dymock 1951, pp. 132–33).

16. John W. Haines, a Gloucester solicitor who knew Frost as a walking companion during the Dymock interval.

17. Frost could have known both "Lady Lost" and "Two in August"

before approving a contract with Holt for *West Running Brook* in late May, 1928 (Thompson, *Triumph*, p. 314). "Lady Lost" was first published in *The Fugitive* IV, 4 (December 1925), 119. "Two in August" was first published in the volume *Two Gentlemen in Bonds*, but this was accepted by Knopf in the Spring of 1926 to issue in 1927, and, although I do not have the publication date, the reviews began at least as early as one by Donald Davidson in the *Nashville Tennessean*, January 23, 1927, so that the book was probably out in January, 1927. *West-Running Brook* was published on November 19, 1928 (*Frost, Letters*, p. lvii). Frost had had a high admiration for Ransom's poetry since Christopher Morley had handed him the manuscript of *Poems about God* (1919) to read and Frost had recommended the publication of the book to Henry Holt and Company (Cowan, p. 26, cf. also Cleanth Brooks *et al., Conversations on the Craft of Poetry,* New York: Holt, Rinehart and Winston, 1961, pp. 11–12). Many critics have found this first volume Frostean, and Vivienne Koch even suggests that Ransom may have made a close study of Frost (Koch, p. 16). Robert Graves, found an affinity between Frost and Ransom (Ransom, *Grace after Meat,* pp. 8–9).

It may be that the influence was not in one direction only and that Frost found a suggestion for subject matter in Ransom's poems about domestic conflict, one of which, "The Overture," appeared in Ransom's first book. Frost's interest in Ransom's work was no doubt heightened by Ransom's invitation to Frost to lecture in the South in the winter of 1922–23 and to confer there with the Fugitives (Gould, p. 233). By 1952 Frost so much admired Ransom's technical skill as to call him his favorite living American poet (Stewart, p. 250). Therefore there is reason to think that Frost would have read eagerly a new volume by Ransom. In "Two in August" situation and imagery are somewhat like those in "The Thatch," the woman remaining in the house "circuiting the dark rooms like a string of amber," and the man walking "the long ditch of darkness" outside, while the birds are disturbed by the human conflict.

> High in the trees the night-mastered birds were crying
> With fear upon their tongues, no singing or flying
> Which are their lovely attitudes by dawn.
>
> (Ransom, *Selected Poems,* pp. 46–47)

18. According to a letter to Charles A. Monroe, the Frosts came over to England from France on September 4, 1928 (Thompson, *Triumph*, pp. 332, 635 note 9). Mertins gives the date as late August (Mertins, *Frost,* p. 176).

19. The house was not, however, permanently abandoned or a total ruin. It was inhabited in 1953, the Mertins found, by "a clergyman's daughter" who had to be careful whom she let in. She excluded the Mertins! (Mertins, *Frost,* p. 347).

Hart Crane's Technique

1. I have made a few corrections in Weber's transcriptions on the basis of photocopies of the original worksheets.

2. "As a poet I may very possibly be more interested in the so-called illogical impingements of the connotations of words on the consciousness (and their combinations and interplay in metaphor on this basis) than I am interested in the preservation of their logically rigid significations at the cost of limiting my subject matter and perceptions involved in the poems" (Crane and Monroe, "Discussion," p. 417).

Hart Crane's 'Repose of Rivers'

1. "Monody" appeared in Melville's *Timoleon* (New York: The Caxton Press, 1891) and in Melville's *Poems* (London: Constable, 1924), volume 16 of *The Works of Herman Melville: Standard Edition*.

Hart Crane's 'The Dance'

1. The "glacier woman" too is an image of an encroachment of white on red. I know no Indian myth of a white female goddess, but Crane may have invented her to parallel the white male god Quetzelcoatl. The glacier would be a geological parallel to a European (and puritan) invasion. The thaw and fruition in which she "rose in maize to die" would suggest potentialities for regeneration. In these opening images white invades red, but then itself becomes the "swift red flesh," a hopeful example for us of successful assimilation into the natural life of the continent. Aztec mythology looms behind "The Dance." "The serpent with the eagle in the boughs" may be seen on the Mexican flag. Quetzelcoatl, the "plumed serpent," was also the evening and morning star, and Crane probably derived his star symbol for the Indian from this fact: "He holds the twilight's dim perpetual throne."

2. Crane got the name from a cab driver drinking companion who had Indian blood and whose middle name it was. Cf. "The Dance," typed manuscript, 1 p., circa June 1927, in the University of Pennsylvania Library. Kenneth Lohf, *The Literary Manuscripts of Hart Crane*

(Ohio State University Press, 1967), p. 40, lists this as manuscript B19.

3. I owe this thought to Mr. Larry Weller, although I suspect I have not accurately reported it. I owe some of the other ideas at the beginning and end of this essay to members of a student and faculty seminar at Sir George Williams University, Montreal, Summer 1972.

4. The swarm of meanings stirred up by "In cobalt desert closures made our vows" is mind-boggling. The principal relevant meaning of "closure" is "an enclosed place." The following additional definitions, arranged to be increasingly esoteric, show how resonant the word is: "making an end" (The Indian's folding his arms, or their being folded for him, suggests death. The "vows," "closures," treaties were the end of the Indian.); "fort, entrenchment" (This meaning is not irrelevant to the making of treaties in Indian wars.); "a method of ending debate" (The suppression of the Indian was certainly the end of the argument about who should control the western lands.); "the method of closing the breech in a breech-loading gun" (Making "vows" in "closures" could be like sending "Greeting . . . on the arrow's oath." A treaty concluded by rifle fire is concluded indeed.); in surveying, the "act of closing" (This meaning may relate to the setting of precise legal limits in space, measured by surveyors, as the bases of treaties or the formation of reservations.).

The *Dry Tree* When Green: A Record of Writing Some Poems

1. "Robin" first appeared under the title "Cycle," in *Folio* (Indiana University), XX, 2 (Spring, 1955); "Mountain Ash" in *The Dublin Magazine*, XXXIII, 1 (January–March, 1958); "Tree" in *Voices*, 166 (May–August, 1958); "Pinnacle" in *Poetry*, XCII, 3 (June, 1958); "The Bee Space" in *The Transatlantic Review*, 2 (Winter, 1959–1960). All these poems are in my volume *Dry Tree*. All but "Tree" and "Pinnacle" are in *A Curious Quire*, poems by colleagues on the University of Massachusetts English Faculty (cf. List of Works cited).

Freedom, Joy & Indignation: Letters from E. E. Cummings

1. Broadcast over stations in Boston, Albany, New York City, Philadelphia, Hartford, Washington, and Syracuse.

2. The complete series consisted of Archibald MacLeish, Frank

Prentice Rand and David Morton, Wallace Stevens, Robert Hillyer and John Holmes, Emily Dickinson (by Stephen Whicher), Richard Wilbur and John Ciardi, E. E. Cummings, Richard Eberhart and Peter Viereck, Robert Francis and Arnold Kenseth, Robert Frost.

3. From a typescript marked "2nd draft of opening speech of latter half of YM&YWHA reading—Nov 26, '54." This is the second of two drafts which Mr. Cummings sent to Robert Tucker prior to the reading. Another version of the talk appears in Norman's, *The Magic Maker E. E. Cummings* (New York: 1958), pp. 356–357. Norman reports that this talk and reading were given before the English club of the University of North Carolina in November of 1955. All letters and documents by E. E. Cummings Copyright © 1963 Mrs. E. E. Cummings.

4. According to our records, although the reply mentions February 4th.

5. cummings, *i, SIX NONLECTURES*. Pages 8–13 are a description of Mr. Cummings' father and mother, seen as heroic personalities. Pages 23–24 declare for individuality versus collectivity, while telling of Mr. Cummings' childhood and youth in Cambridge.

6. The poets were to receive 85% of honorarium when they recorded and 15% upon completion of the series.

7. The numerals 1–13 are in red, as is the note.

8. Copyright 1931, © 1959 by E. E. Cummings. Reprinted from POEMS, 1923–1954 by permission of Harcourt, Brace, Jovanovich, Inc.

9. e. e. cummings, "Poem," *The Massachusetts Review,* I, i (Fall, 1959), 154–55. Cf. pp. ooo–oo of this book.

10. Copyright, 1940, by E. E. Cummings. Reprinted from POEMS, 1923–1954 by permission of Harcourt, Brace, Jovanovich, Inc.

LIST OF WORKS CITED

A Book of Irish Verse
    A Book of Irish Verse, selected from modern writers with an introduction and notes by W. B. Yeats (London: Methuen and Co., 1895).
A Book of Irish Verse, 1900
    A Book of Irish Verse, selected from modern writers with an introduction and notes by W. B. Yeats (London: Methuen and Co., 1900).
Arnold, *Selected Poetry*
    Matthew Arnold, *Selected Poetry and Prose,* introd. Frederick L. Mulhauser (New York, Toronto: Rinehart & Co., 1953).
Beach
    Joseph Warren Beach, "Hart Crane and Moby Dick," *Western Review,* 20 (Spring 1956), 183–96.
Blackmur
    R. P. Blackmur, *The Double Agent* (New York: Arrow Editions 1935).
Boyd, *Ireland's Literary Renaissance*
    Ernest Boyd, *Ireland's Literary Renaissance* (New York: Alfred A. Knopf, 1922).
Brower, *Constellations*
    Reuben A. Brower, *The Poetry of Robert Frost: Constellations of Intention* (New York: Oxford University Press, 1963).
Byron, *Selected Poetry*
    George Gordon, Lord Byron, *Selected Poetry and Letters,* ed. Edward E. Bostetter (New York, Toronto: Rinehart & Co., 1951).
Campbell, *Irishry*
    Joseph Campbell, *Irishry* (Dublin and London: Maunsel & Co., n.d. [1913]).
Clarke, "A Centenary Celebration"
    Austin Clarke, "A Centenary Celebration," *Irish Renaissance: A Gathering of Essays, Memoirs and Letters from The Massachusetts Review,* ed. Robin Skelton and David R. Clark (Dublin: The Dolmen Press, 1965), pp. 90–93.
Clarke, *Nineties*
    Austin Clarke, *The Celtic Twilight and the Nineties,* introd. Roger McHugh, The Tower Series of Anglo-Irish Studies 1 (Dublin: The Dolmen Press, 1969).

Cowan
   Louise Cowan, *The Fugitive Group: A Literary History* (Baton
   Rouge: Louisiana State University Press, 1959).
Crane and Monroe, "Discussion"
   Harriet Monroe and Hart Crane, "A Discussion with Hart Crane,"
   Poetry, 29 (October 1926), pp. 35–41, reprinted in Weber, p. 3.
Crane, *Complete Poems*
   The Complete Poems and Selected Letters and Prose of Hart Crane,
   ed. Brom Weber (New York: Liveright Publishing Corporation,
   1966).
Crane, *Letters*
   The Letters of Hart Crane, 1916–1932, ed. Brom Weber (Berkeley
   and Los Angeles: University of California Press, 1965).
cummings, *i, Six Nonlectures*
   e. e. cummings, *i, Six Nonlectures* (Cambridge: Harvard University
   Press, 1953).
cummings, *Poems*
   e. e. cummings, *Poems 1923–54* (New York: Hartcourt, Brace &
   Co., 1954).
Curious Quire
   A Curious Quire, Poems by Stanley Koehler, Leon O. Barron, David
   R. Clark, and Robert G. Tucker, with Lithographs by Donald R.
   Matheson (Amherst: The University of Massachusetts Press, 1962;
   second printing 1967).
Doyle, *Frost*
   John Robert Doyle, *The Poetry of Robert Frost* (Johannesburg:
   Witwatersrand University Press; New York: Hafner Publishing Co.,
   1962).
Drew, *Poetry*
   Elizabeth Drew, *Poetry: A Modern Guide to Its Understanding and
   Enjoyment* (New York: W. W. Norton and Co., 1959).
Dry Tree
   David R. Clark, *Dry Tree* (Dublin: The Dolmen Press, 1966).
Duvall
   S. P. C. Duvall, "Robert Frost's 'Directive' Out of *Walden,*" *Amer-
   ican Literature,* 31, 4 (January 1960), 482–88.
Eliot, *Complete Poems*
   T. S. Eliot, *The Complete Poems and Plays, 1909–1950* (New York:
   Harcourt, Brace & World, 1962).
Elizabethan Verse
   Elizabethan Verse and Prose, ed. George Reuben Potter (New York:
   Henry Holt and Co., 1928).
Ellmann, *Identity*
   Richard Ellmann, *The Identity of Yeats* (New York: Oxford Uni-
   versity Press, 1954).

French, *Gazetteer*
  J. H. French, *Gazetteer of the State of New York* (Port Washington, L. I., N. Y.: Ira J. Friedman, 1969; first published 1860).
Frost, "Burroughs"
  Robert Frost, "Stephen Burroughs," *Cupid and Lion* (New York, n.d. [ca. 1924]).
Frost, *Letters*
  Selected Letters of Robert Frost, ed. Lawrance Thompson (New York, Chicago, San Francisco: Holt, Rinehart & Winston, 1964).
Frost, *Poetry*
  The Poetry of Robert Frost, ed. Edward Connery Lathem (New York, Chicago, San Francisco: Holt, Rinehart and Winston, 1964, 1967).
Gogarty, *Collected Poems*
  The Collected Poems of Oliver St. John Gogarty ([New York]: The Devin-Adair Company, [1954]).
Gould
  Jean Gould, *Robert Frost: The Aim Was Song* (New York: Dodd, Mead, & Co., 1964).
Hazo
  Samuel John Hazo, *Hart Crane: An Introduction and Interpretation* (New York: Barnes & Noble, [1963]).
Henn, *Lonely Tower*
  T. R. Henn, *The Lonely Tower: Studies in the Poetry of W. B. Yeats* (London: Methuen, 1965).
Hood, *Works*
  The Works of Thomas Hood, ed. His Son and Daughter (London: Ward, Lock & Co.; New York: Ward, Lock & Co., 1869–73).
Irish Literature
  Irish Literature, ed. Justin McCarthy *et al.,* 10 vols. (Philadelphia: John D. Morris & Co., 1904), 3:1224.
Jarrell, "To the Laodiceans"
  Randall Jarrell, "To the Laodiceans," *Poetry and the Age* (New York: Vintage Books, 1955; first published 1953), pp. 34–62.
Jeffares, "Gogarty, Irishman"
  A. Norman Jeffares, "Oliver St. John Gogarty, Irishman," *The Circus Animals: Essays on W. B. Yeats* ([London]: Macmillan [and Co.], 1970).
Kinsella, "Downstream"
  Thomas Kinsella, "Downstream II," *The Massachusetts Review,* 5, 2 (Winter 1964), 323–25.
Kinsella, *Nightwalker*
  Thomas Kinsella, *Nightwalker and Other Poems* (Dublin: The Dolmen Press, 1968).

Koch
> Vivienne Koch, "The Achievement of John Crowe Ransom," *John Crowe Ransom: Critical Essays and a Bibliography,* ed. Thomas Daniel Young (Baton Rouge: Louisiana State University Press, 1968).

Lewis
> R. W. B. Lewis, *The Poetry of Hart Crane: A Critical Study* (Princeton: Princeton University Press, 1967).

Loveman
> *"Hart Crane," A Conversation with Samuel Loveman,* ed. Jay Socin and Kirby Congdon (New York: Interim Books, 1964).

MacGreevy, *Nicolas Poussin*
> Thomas MacGreevy, *Nicolas Poussin* (Dublin: The Dolmen Press, n.d.).

Melville, *Moby Dick*
> Herman Melville, *Moby Dick, or The Whale,* introd. Newton Arvin (New York, Toronto: Rinehart & Co., 1950).

Mercier, "Gogarty"
> Vivian Mercier, "Oliver St. John Gogarty," *Poetry,* 93, 1 (October 1958), 35–39.

Meredith, *Poetical Works*
> *The Poetical Works of George Meredith,* ed. G. M. Trevelyan (New York: Charles Scribners Sons, 1912).

Mertins, *Frost*
> Louis Mertins, *Robert Frost: Life and Talks Walking* (Norman: University of Oklahoma Press, 1965).

Mertins, *Intervals*
> Louis and Esther Mertins, *The Intervals of Robert Frost* (Berkeley and Los Angeles: University of California Press, 1947).

Milton, *Poetical Works*
> *The Complete Poetical Works of John Milton,* ed. Douglas Bush (Boston: Houghton Mifflin Company, 1965).

New York
> *New York: A Guide to the Empire State,* compiled by the workers of the Writers Program of the Works Projects Administration in the State of New York. American Guide Series (New York: Oxford University Press, 1940, 8th printing 1962), pp. 493–94.

Nitchie, *Human Values*
> George W. Nitchie, *Human Values in the Poetry of Robert Frost* (Durham, N.C.: Duke University Press, 1960).

Norman
> Charles Norman, *The Magic Maker, E. E. Cummings* (New York: The Macmillan Company, 1958).

O'Donnell, "Frost and New England"
    William G. O'Donnell, "Robert Frost and New England: A Reval-
    uation," *The Yale Review*, 37, 4 (June 1948), 698–712.
O'Donnell, "Frost at Eighty-Eight"
    W. G. O'Donnell, "Robert Frost at Eighty-Eight," *The Massachu-
    setts Review*, 4, 1 (Autumn 1962), pp. 213–18.
O'Sullivan, *Collected Poems*
    Seumas O'Sullivan, *Collected Poems* (Dublin: The Orwell Press,
    1940).
O'Sullivan, *Poems*
    The Poems of Seumas O'Sullivan, introd. Padraic Colum (Boston:
    B. J. Brimmer Company, 1923).
Oxford Book of Irish Verse
    The Oxford Book of Irish Verse, ed. Donagh MacDonagh and Len-
    nox Robinson (Oxford: At the Clarendon Press, 1959).
Oxford Book of Modern Verse
    The Oxford Book of Modern Verse, 1892–1935 (Oxford: At the
    Clarendon Press, 1960; first published 1936).
Plotinus
    The Essence of Plotinus, based on the trans. by Stephen MacKenna,
    comp. by Grace H. Turnbull (New York: Oxford University Press,
    1934).
Pound, *Cantos*
    The Cantos of Ezra Pound ([New York]: A New Directions Book,
    1948).
Quinn
    Vincent Quinn, *Hart Crane* (New York: Twayne Publishers,
    [1963]).
Ransom, *Grace after Meat*
    John Crowe Ransom, *Grace after Meat*, introd. Robert Graves
    (London: Leonard and Virginia Woolf, 1924).
Ransom, *Selected Poems*
    John Crowe Ransom, *Selected Poems* (New York: Alfred A. Knopf,
    1945).
Sergeant, *Frost*
    Elizabeth Shepley Sergeant, *Robert Frost: The Trial by Existence*
    (New York: Holt, Rinehart and Winston, 1960).
Stevens, *Collected Poems*
    The Collected Poems of Wallace Stevens (New York: Alfred A.
    Knopf, 1955).
Stewart
    John L. Stewart, *The Burden of Time: The Fugitives and Agrarians*
    (Princeton: Princeton University Press, 1965).

Thompson, *Early Years*
Lawrance Thompson, *Robert Frost: The Early Years, 1874–1915* (New York, Chicago, San Francisco: Holt, Rinehart and Winston, 1966).

Thompson, *Triumph*
Lawrance Thompson, *Robert Frost: The Years of Triumph, 1915–1938* (New York, Chicago, San Francisco: Holt, Rinehart and Winston, 1970).

Weber
Brom Weber, *Hart Crane* (New York: 1948).

Whitaker, *Swan and Shadow*
Thomas R. Whitaker, *Swan and Shadow: Yeats's Dialogue with History* (Chapel Hill: The University of North Carolina Press, 1964).

Wilde, *Artist*
The Artist as Critic: Critical Writings of Oscar Wilde, ed. Richard Ellmann (New York: Random House, 1968, 1969).

Wilde, *Poems*
The Poems of Oscar Wilde (London: Methuen and Co., 1908). Reprinted in the *First Collected Edition of the Works of Oscar Wilde, 1908–1922,* ed. Robert Ross (London Dawsons of Pall Mall, 1969).

Wilson, *Tradition*
F. A. C. Wilson, *W. B. Yeats and Tradition* (London: Victor Gollancz, 1958).

Wordsworth, *Selected Poems*
William Wordsworth, *Selected Poems,* ed. George W. Meyer (New York: Appleton-Century Crofts, 1950).

Yeats, *Autobiography*
The Autobiography of William Butler Yeats (New York: The Macmillan Company, 1953).

Yeats, *Broadsides*
W. B. Yeats, *Broadsides, A Collection of Old and New Songs, 1935* (Dublin: The Cuala Press, 1935).

Yeats, *Essays and Introductions*
W. B. Yeats, *Essays and Introductions* (New York: The Macmillan Company, 1961).

Yeats, *Fairy and Folk Tales*
Irish Fairy and Folk Tales, ed. W. B. Yeats (New York: The Modern Library, n.d.).

Yeats, *Letters on Poetry*
Letters on Poetry from W. B. Yeats to Dorothy Wellesley (London: New York, Toronto: Oxford University Press, 1940).

Yeats, *Tribute*
W. B. Yeats, *Tribute to Thomas Davis* (Cork: Cork University Press; Oxford: B. H. Blackwell, 1947).

Yeats, *Uncollected Prose*
Uncollected Prose by W. B. Yeats, ed. John P. Frayne (London: Macmillan & Co., 1970).

Yeats, *Variorum Plays*
The Variorum Edition of the Plays of W. B. Yeats, ed. Russell K. Alspach assisted by Catharine C. Alspach (New York: The Macmillan Company, 1966).

Yeats, *Variorum Poems*
The Variorum Edition of the Poems of W. B. Yeats, ed. Peter Allt and Russell K. Alspach (New York: The Macmillan Company, 1957).

Acknowledgments

My first acknowledgment must be to the staff of the University of Massachusetts Press for unfailing consideration, encouragement, and expert help. Of others, Miss Elizabeth Case encouraged me to complete the book in an earlier form, and I am grateful. I thank Mrs. Karen Wright, not only for typing the first, now much revised, versions of many of these essays, but also for her keen critical appreciation. I thank my son Ridgley for checking the permissions and writing for them.

Various persons are thanked in the notes for specific aids to my research. Mr. Kenneth Lohf and Mr. Brom Weber have responded cheerfully to my inquiries about Hart Crane manuscripts.

Some of these essays have appeared elsewhere, and I thank their publishers for permission to reprint. "Cummings' 'anyone' and 'noone'" first appeared in *The Arizona Quarterly*. The essay on Robert Frost's "The Thatch" and "Directive" first appeared in *Costerus Essays in English and American Language and Literature*. "Joseph Campbell's 'The Dancer'" first appeared in *Eire-Ireland*. My analysis of Cummings' "Poem" first appeared in *The Explicator* under the title "Cummings' POEM (it's/so damn sweet when Anybody—)." "Thomas Kinsella's 'Downstream'" first appeared in *Reading Poetry: Second Edition*, ed. Fred B. Millett, Arthur W. Hoffman, and David R. Clark (New York: Harper & Row, 1968). "Yeats: 'Out of a People to a People'" first appeared in *The Malahat Review*. "Freedom, Joy & Indignation: Letters from E. E. Cummings" is reprinted from *The Massachusetts Review*, © 1963 The Massachusetts Review, Inc. It is a pleasure to thank my co-editor, the principal editor of this piece, Mr. Robert Tucker, for permission to reprint. "Hart Crane's Technique" originally appeared in the University of Texas *Studies in Literature and Language*, V, 3 (Autumn, 1963) 389–97. Copyright by the University of Texas Press. "Poussin and 'News for the Delphic Oracle'" first appeared in *Wascana Review*.

Thanks are due for permission to quote material copyrighted by the following or in some other sense belonging to them:

To Mr. Simon Campbell for "The Dancer" by Joseph Campbell.

To Jonathan Cape Ltd., the Estate of Robert Frost, and Edward Connery Lathem for quotations from *The Poetry of Robert Frost*, ed. Edward Connery Lathem.

To the Clarendon Press, Oxford, for quotations from *The Oxford Book of Modern Verse*.

To the Columbia University Libraries, owners of the original manuscripts of Hart Crane's "Atlantis," for permission to quote from these manuscripts.

To Constable and Company, Ltd., and the Devin-Adair Company, Publishers, for quotations from *The Collected Poems of Oliver St. John Gogarty.* C/R 1954 by Oliver St. John Gogarty.

To the Dolmen Press and Thomas Kinsella for "Downstream II," reprinted from *The Massachusetts Review,* © 1964, *The Massachusetts Review,* Inc. "Downstream II" is much shortened and changed from the poem in *Downstream* (Dublin: The Dolmen Press, 1962), © Thomas Kinsella, 1962.

To Faber and Faber Ltd. for quotations from *Collected Poems, 1909–1962,* by T. S. Eliot, reprinted by permission of Faber and Faber Ltd.

To Granada Publishing Ltd. for quotations from *Complete Poems* by E. E. Cummings, MacGibbon and Kee Ltd., publisher.

To Harcourt, Brace, Jovanovich, Inc., for "anyone lived in a pretty how town" by E. E. Cummings: Copyright, 1940, by E. E. Cummings; copyright, 1968, by Marion Morehouse Cummings. Reprinted from *Poems 1923–1954* by E. E. Cummings by permission of Harcourt, Brace, Jovanovich, Inc.

To Harcourt, Brace, Jovanovich, Inc., for poetry of T. S. Eliot: Excerpts from the poetry of T. S. Eliot are reprinted from his volume *Collected Poems 1909–1962* by permission of Harcourt Brace Jovanovich, Inc.; copyright © 1963, 1964, by T. S. Eliot.

To Harcourt, Brace, Jovanovich, Inc., for "i sing of Olaf" by E. E. Cummings: Copyright, 1931, 1959, by E. E. Cummings. Reprinted from his volume *Poems 1923–1954* by permission of Harcourt, Brace, Jovanovich, Inc.

To Harcourt, Brace, Jovanovich, Inc., for "as freedom is a breakfast-food": Copyright, 1940, by E. E. Cummings; copyright, 1968, by Marion Morehouse Cummings. Reprinted from *Poems 1923–1954* by E. E. Cummings by permission of Harcourt, Brace, Jovanovich, Inc.

To Harcourt, Brace, Jovanovich, Inc., for "it's/so damn sweet" by E. E. Cummings: © 1959 by E. E. Cummings. Reprinted from his volume *73 Poems* by permission of Harcourt, Brace, Jovanovich, Inc.

To Holt, Rinehart, and Winston, Inc. for quotations from *The Poetry of Robert Frost,* edited by Edward Connery Lathem. Copyright 1923, 1928, 1934, 1939, 1947, © 1947, 1969 by Holt, Rinehart and Winston, Inc. Copyright 1951, © 1956, 1962 by Robert Frost. Reprinted by permission of Holt, Rinehart, and Winston, Inc. Also for quotations from *Selected Letters of Robert Frost* edited by Lawrance Thompson. Copyright © 1964 by Holt, Rinehart, and Winston, Inc. Reprinted by permission of Holt, Rinehart, and Winston, Inc. Also for quotations from *Robert Frost: The Trial by Existence* by Elizabeth Shepley Sergeant. Copyright © 1960 by Elizabeth Shepley Sergeant. Reprinted by permission of Holt, Rinehart, and Winston, Inc. Also for a brief quotation from *Robert Frost: The Early Years 1874–1915* by Lawrance Thompson. Reprinted by permission of Holt, Rinehart, and Winston, Inc.

To Alfred A. Knopf, Inc., and to Thomas Kinsella, for "Downstream II," reprinted from *The Massachusetts Review*, V, 2 (Winter 1964). © 1964, *The Massachusetts Review, Inc.* "Downstream II" is much shortened and changed from the poem in *Downstream* (Dublin: The Dolmen Press, 1962). © Thomas Kinsella, 1962. A final revision appears in *Nightwalker and Other Poems* (Dublin: The Dolmen Press, 1968), © 1968 Thomas Kinsella, and in *Nightwalker and Other Poems* (New York: Alfred A. Knopf, 1968), © 1962, 1964, 1965, 1966, 1967, 1968 by Thomas Kinsella. Reprinted by permission of Thomas Kinsella, the Dolmen Press, *The Massachusetts Review,* and Alfred A. Knopf, Inc. Also for quotations from "Two in August," from *Selected Poems,* by John Crowe Ransom, copyright 1924, 1927, 1934, 1939, 1945 by Alfred A. Knopf, Inc. Reprinted by permission of Alfred A. Knopf, Inc.

To Liveright Publishing Corporation for quotations from *The Complete Poems and Selected Letters and Prose of Hart Crane* by Hart Crane. Permission of Liveright, Publishers, N. Y. Copyright © 1933, 1958, 1966 by Liveright Publishing Corp.

To the Macmillan Company, New York, for passages reprinted with permission of The Macmillan Company from *The Variorum Edition of the Poems of W. B. Yeats,* edited by Peter Allt and Russell K. Alspach. Copyright 1903, 1906, 1912, 1916, 1919, 1924, 1928, 1933, 1934, 1957 by The Macmillan Company. Copyright renewed 1931, 1934 by William Butler Yeats. Copyright renewed 1940, 1944, 1947, 1952, 1961, 1962 by Bertha Georgie Yeats. Copyright renewed 1956 by Georgie Yeats. Copyright 1940 by Georgie Yeats. Copyright renewed 1968 by Bertha Georgie Yeats, Michael Butler Yeats and Anne Yeats. Copyright © by Bertha Georgie Yeats, Michael Yeats and Anne Yeats, 1968.

To the Macmillan Company, New York, for passages reprinted with permission of The Macmillan Company from *The Variorum Edition of the Plays of W. B. Yeats,* edited by Russell K. Alspach. Copyright © by Russell K. Alspach and Bertha Georgie Yeats, 1966.

To the Macmillan Company, New York, for passages reprinted with permission of The Macmillan Company from *Autobiography* by William Butler Yeats. Copyright 1916, 1936 by The Macmillan Company, renewed 1944 by Bertha Georgie Yeats.

To the Macmillan Company for passages reprinted with permission of The Macmillan Company from *Essays and Introductions* by William Butler Yeats. © Mrs. W. B. Yeats, 1961.

To *The Massachusetts Review,* Inc., for quotations from Austin Clarke's "A Centenary Celebration" copyright 1965 by *The Massachusetts Review,* Inc., and from Thomas Kinsella's "Downstream II" reprinted from *The Massachusetts Review,* copyright 1964 by *The Massachusetts Review,* Inc. "Downstream II" is much shortened from the poem in *Downstream* (Dublin: The Dolmen Press, 1962), copyright Thomas Kinsella, 1962. Reprinted by permission of Thomas Kinsella, *The Massachusetts Review,* and the Dolmen Press.

To the National Gallery of Ireland, Dublin, Ireland, for permission to reproduce a photograph of "The Marriage of Peleus and Thetis" by Nicolas Poussin, No. 814 in the collection (Lane bequest, 1918).

To Mr. Alfred Rice, Trustee for the Estate of Marion Morehouse Cummings, for permission to reprint the earlier version of the poem "its/so damn sweet when Anybody" © 1964 by Marion Cummings and letters and documents of E. E. Cummings Copyright © 1963 Mrs. E. E. Cummings.

To Dr. Michael Solomons for permission to quote from the poems of Seumas O'Sullivan.

To Miss Anne Yeats and Senator Michael Yeats, and to the Macmillan Company of Canada and Macmillan & Company, London, for permission to quote from the work of W. B. Yeats.

To Mr. Brom Weber for permission to quote from *The Letters of Hart Crane,* 1916–1932, ed. Brom Weber, copyright 1952 by Brom Weber.

To the Literary Executors of the Late Duchess of Wellington, and to Withers, their Solicitors, for permission to quote from *Letters on Poetry from W. B. Yeats to Dorothy Wellesley.*